BUDDHIST SUTRAS

KŌGEN MIZUNO

BUDDHIST SUTRAS

Origin, Development, Transmission

KŌSEI PUBLISHING CO. • *Tokyo*

This book was first published serially in the monthly magazine *Kōsei* and later in book form under the title *Kyōden: Sono Seiritsu to Tenkai*. Translation by Morio Takanashi, Koichiro Yoshida, Takahiro Matsumura, and Kazumasa Osaka adapted by Rebecca M. Davis.

Shown on the cover are early nineteenth-century palm-leaf manuscripts of portions of the section Saḷāyatana-vagga (Book on the Six Sense Organs) in the Saṁyutta-nikāya (Kindred Sayings), one of the Five Nikayas of the Pali canon. The manuscripts, in the collection of the National Library of Thailand, are reproduced by permission of the Fine Arts Department of the Ministry of Education, Bangkok. Photographs by Sone Simatrang.

Cover design by Nobu Miyazaki. Editing, book design, and typography by Rebecca M. Davis. The text of this book is set in Monotype Baskerville with hand-set Optima for display.

First English edition, 1982
Sixth printing, 1995

Published by Kōsei Publishing Co., Kōsei Building, 2-7-1 Wada, Suginami-ku, Tokyo 166.
Printed in Japan.

ISBN 4-333-01028-4   LCC Card No. 82-175400

Contents

Map follows page 63

Preface

THE HISTORY of the transmission of Buddhism from India, the land of its origin, to those countries where it took root and flourished is in essence the story of the transmission of its teachings as recorded in its sutras, or scriptures. In an age of almost instantaneous communications via satellite and when enormous numbers of people are qualified to translate materials into one or another of the world's languages, it is easy for us to lose sight of the magnitude of the difficulties encountered by the priests and monks who began carrying the message of an Indian sage to other countries some two and a half millennia ago.

When Shakyamuni, the historical Buddha and founder of Buddhism, first preached his message, India was already a country of many mutually unintelligible languages, few of which had written forms. Though the task of disseminating the teachings of Buddhism was thus difficult even in the land of that religion's birth, still greater obstacles had to be overcome in taking Buddhism to China, where its practice, study, and development burgeoned and whence its influence extended to Korea and Japan.

A trickle of Indian and Central Asian Buddhist monks and priests made their way to China in the early centuries of the Christian Era. After perilous journeys, most often on foot, across forbidding mountain ranges and deserts, they had to cope not only with unfamiliar languages but also with a vastly different culture and philosophical

7

system. As the teachings these monks took with them gained adherents, the Chinese in their thirst for greater knowledge began to
seek the original scriptures of their new religion.

In order to learn more about the religion and take that knowledge
back to China, a number of earnest, intrepid Chinese pilgrims made
their way to India, following many of the same desert and mountain
routes their preceptors had taken. The depth of their belief can be
judged by such pilgrims as Fa-hsien (340?–420?), who undertook
the arduous journey to India when he was already in his sixties—in
a time when few people reached the age of sixty. For more than a
thousand years, beginning around the second century A.D., Buddhist
scriptures were transmitted to China and rendered into Chinese by
many translators, both Central Asian and Chinese; the Chinese
pilgrim and eminent translator Hsüan-tsang (ca. 596–644) translated the largest quantity of scriptures. Today the Chinese canon
contains by far the largest body of Buddhist scripture, including a
great many important works for which the Indic originals are no
longer extant.

Because China was the one country in which Buddhist scriptures
were always translated into the local language and studied ex-
haustively, and because China gave birth to most of the extant sects
of Mahayana Buddhism, the story of the transmission of Buddhist
scriptures to China is a particularly important and fascinating one.
And because Buddhism became and has remained a source of solace
and spiritual support for a large portion of the world's population,
I decided to recount some of that story for general readers some
years ago in a series of articles that appeared in twenty-eight con-
secutive issues of the magazine *Kōsei*. In 1980 those articles were
gathered together and published as a book in Japanese, appearing
in the book in the same order in which I had written them for the
magazine. For this English-language version of that book, I have
completely reorganized the material.

Because I intended this book for the general reader, I have used
simplified transliterations of Pali and Sanskrit words throughout
the text, but the orthodox spellings are included in the appendix
and the index. Since I refer to documents and teachings belonging
to both the Northern and the Southern Buddhist traditions, I have

used both Sanskrit and Pali in the text, depending on which is appropriate, Northern Buddhist texts having been written in Sanskrit and Southern Buddhist texts in Pali. Thus I have used both Tipitaka (Pali) and Tripitaka (Sanskrit) in referring to the same kind of scriptural collection. The Wade-Giles system of romanization has been used throughout for Chinese words, partly because it is more familiar and perhaps more readable than the new Pin-yin system, but principally because it is the established system in Western works on Chinese Buddhism. Hence readers interested in doing further reading can easily find in other books the people, places, and works mentioned here. Some Chinese place names, such as Nanking, are given consistently in their modern form because they have had numerous names throughout the long history of China. With the names of those few Japanese who figure in this story of the transmission of the sutras, I have followed the Japanese practice of giving the surname followed by the personal name.

Finally, although in recent years it has become a common practice in general works on Buddhism to use the terms Mahayana and Theravada to designate the two major streams of Buddhism—that is, Northern and Southern Buddhism—in this book I use the terms Mahayana and Hinayana for specific reasons. Though Hinayana (literally, "Small Vehicle") was a derogatory term coined by Mahayana (or "Great Vehicle") Buddhists, it designates the entire stream of Abhidharma Buddhism, of which Theravada (Way of the Elders) was only one among many sects.

During the age of primitive Buddhism, the religion's earliest period, there was but one body of Buddhism. Not long after 300 B.C., however, that age came to an end with the division of the religion into two sects that later subdivided into eighteen or twenty sects, ushering in the period of Abhidharma, or sectarian Hinayana, Buddhism, which lasted until the beginning of the first century A.D. From that time until about A.D. 300, which is the period of early Mahayana Buddhism, Mahayana and Hinayana Buddhism existed side by side. The middle period of Mahayana Buddhism, from about 300 to about 700, was dominated by Mahayana and Hinayana scholastic Buddhism. Following the age of primitive Buddhism, a number of Mahayana and Hinayana sects were born and flourished. Today Theravada Buddhism is the only survivor of all the Hinayana sects, and in that sense it is not incorrect to equate modern Theravada and modern Southern Buddhism; but for the periods of which I speak in this book such usage is unacceptable.

BUDDHIST SUTRAS

ONE

Introduction

PROBLEMS OF DEFINITION   The word *sūtra* in Sanskrit, or *sutta*
in Pali, refers primarily to Buddhist
scripture. Although it is easy enough to recognize a sutra, or scripture, it is not easy to say exactly what constitutes a sutra.

To use an analogy, we have vague ideas about many things we
could not explain fully or clearly if asked to do so because the things
we can see or hear are easier for us to describe than are abstract
concepts. Religion, for instance, is a difficult concept to define, since
it encompasses such a variety of beliefs, from the very primitive to
the most mature. Major religions, such as Buddhism, Christianity,
and Islam, would all be defined differently, and even within each
of these religions we find diverse interpretations. The many sects
and schools of Buddhism, for instance, do not always agree completely in their thinking on religion or Buddhism. Moreover, not all
people have the same depth of faith and degree of understanding
of religion. This is why scholars still cannot agree on one incontro-
vertible definition of religion.

The following parable from the Pali sutra Udana (Solemn Utterances of the Buddha) is a classic illustration of the pitfalls of
defining something.

A king invited a group of blind men to his palace and brought
an elephant before them. He then asked each man to say what he
thought the elephant looked like. The first man touched the

13

elephant's head and said it was like a jar; the second man felt its ear and was certain it resembled a winnower; the third touched the elephant's tusk and declared that it was like a pointed spear; the fourth man patted the elephant's leg and stated it was like a pillar; and so they continued.

Each man, on touching the elephant with his own hands, had a definite opinion of what it was like and, thinking himself right and the others wrong, flatly denied the others' reports. None would admit that another explanation could possibly be right because each allowed for only a partial description.

With this parable the historical Buddha, Shakyamuni, demonstrated to his disciples that, by disputing one another's beliefs and insisting on their own theories of life and the world, the non-Buddhist philosophers and people of religion prevented themselves from attaining enlightenment. Their insistence on the correctness of their own theories and views, which were based on an incomplete examination of the whole question, resembles the blind men groping at the elephant. Through this parable the Buddha taught his disciples that they must have an all-embracing view of the world and of life.

We, too, must have a correct view of both religion and Buddhism as a whole, yet an abstract concept is difficult to understand and define correctly. We can more easily understand and correctly define something that can be comprehended directly through our senses.

Even when we are dealing with something concrete, however, our understanding of it may be different from someone else's because of our personal relationship to it. For example, in Buddhism water is understood in four ways, depending upon the audience. Hungry spirits, who thirst for water, see it as purulent because their evil karma from the past causes the water to look like pus and blood to them. To fish, water is an abode. Heavenly beings are said to regard water as land ornamented with lapis lazuli and jewels, since, viewed from high above, lakes are seen as beautiful and brilliant crystals or jewels. And then there is water as we human beings understand it.

But even human beings see water in many ways. Chemists know it as H_2O; to physicists it is liquid, vapor, clouds, ice, or snow; and to a thirsty person it is relief. On the one hand, we need water for drinking, washing, extinguishing fires, irrigation, and electric power. On the other hand, water causes floods, tidal waves, and landslides. Obviously even water must be considered from many points of view and can be defined and explained in many ways.

THE MEANING OF THE WORD SUTRA   The word sutra had been used in Brahmanism before the advent of Buddhism; it was used in Jainism at the time that Buddhism was first propounded; and it was used in various schools of Indian philosophy in later periods. The Sanskrit word *sūtra* originally meant a string or thread. Important words or brief phrases strung together were thus called sutras by analogy with the string or thread with which a garland of flowers is made. Sutra, therefore, once referred to a prose collection of short, important sayings and did not include verse.

This form of sutra, used in Brahmanism, was handed down over the centuries, and some of the Brahmanic sutras are still extant. The Shrauta-sutra, for instance, presents the official prayer rituals conducted by a Brahman using three fires; the Grihya-sutra explains the private prayer ritual performed by the head of a family using one fire; and the Dharma-sutra contains civil laws and regulations, including those pertaining to the caste system on which Indian society was based. These three classics are composed in short, simple prose designed to be committed to memory and handed down orally.

The form and style of the Brahmanic sutras were adopted by Buddhism, and for this reason in Buddhism, too, "sutra" once meant only teachings recorded in simple prose. The Buddha's sermons, said to number eighty-four thousand, were grouped in several categories according to form and content. Originally the word sutra referred to only one of those categories, and teachings that did not fall into that category were not called sutras. Here sutra is used in its original, narrower sense and means simply a collection of essential teachings cast in straightforward prose.

Today, the word sutra is rarely used in the above sense: it refers instead to all the sermons of the Buddha. The oldest compilations of his sermons, the Five Nikayas of the Pali canon and the Four Agamas of the Chinese canon, are known collectively as the Agama sutras and are also called the Sutra-pitaka, or Sutra Basket, meaning a collection of scriptures.* Each sermon included in the Sutra-pitaka is called a sutra. Although the Mahayana sutras were compiled well after the Agama sutras, they too are called sutras, since they are composed in the same form as the Agama sutras and are regarded as true accounts of the Buddha's teachings.

Apart from the sermons collected in the Sutra-pitaka, numerous precepts, or monastic rules (*vinaya*), were recorded to form the Vinaya-pitaka, or Ordinance Basket, and became part of the Buddhist canon along with the Sutra-pitaka. Some time after the death of the Buddha, leading disciples who began to study the sutras organized and arranged the Buddha's teachings theologically and philosophically and composed the doctrinal commentaries called Abhidharma that are found in the Abhidharma-pitaka, or Treatise Basket.

The period of primitive Buddhism was followed by the age of Abhidhamma (or Hinayana) Buddhism, in which the Pali Sutta-pitaka, Vinaya-pitaka, and Abhidhamma-pitaka were regarded as the Law Treasure of Buddhism. Together these three works are known as the Tipitaka, or the Three Baskets, but only the scriptures in the Sutta-pitaka are usually called sutras.

When Buddhist scriptures were first translated into Chinese, the organization of the Tipitaka was not known in China; hence the Chinese regarded as sutras not only the sermons in the Sutta-pitaka but also the precepts and commentaries in the Vinaya- and Abhidhamma-pitakas. Eventually, as more scriptures were translated into

* The Agama sutras of the Pali canon consist of the complete Pali Sutta-pitaka, containing the Five Nikayas: Digha-nikaya (Long Sayings), Majjhima-nikaya (Middle-Length Sayings), Samyutta-nikaya (Kindred Sayings), Anguttara-nikaya (Gradual Sayings), and Khuddaka-nikaya (Minor Sayings). The Agama sutras of the Chinese canon consist of a Sutra-pitaka, translated from Sanskrit, comprising the Four Agamas—Dirgha-agama, Madhyama-agama, Samyukta-agama, and Ekottara-agama, the Sanskrit equivalents of the first four of the Five Nikayas. (The Chinese Agama sutras also contain some fragments and independent sutras not found in the Pali Agama sutras.)

Chinese and the customs of Indian Buddhism became better known, only the scriptures in the Sutta-pitaka were called sutras. Other works were given clearly different titles, such as the Four-Category Vinaya and the Treatise on the Completion of Truth.

Some original Indic sutra texts are not called sutras even when they are in fact sutras. In the Chinese versions, however, the Chinese word for sutra is used in their titles. For example, the Dhammapada (or Dharmapada), which does not contain the word sutra in its title, is included in the Sutta-pitaka; and since it is regarded as the teaching of the Buddha, it can be called a sutra.

With the appearance of more Chinese translations of the Sutta-, Vinaya-, and Abhidhamma-pitakas drawn from both Hinayana and Mahayana sources, the translations were recorded in catalogues or stored in temple libraries. The translations were referred to collectively by the Sanskrit title Tripitaka, translated as "Great Storehouse Scripture," meaning a complete collection of the sutras.

The Chinese Tripitaka includes not only the Sutta-, Vinaya-, and Abhidhamma-pitakas but also works by high-ranking Indian monks and by non-Buddhist teachers of the Vaisheshika and Sankhya schools. Moreover, other famous works, commentaries, histories, and catalogues of Buddhist scriptures composed in China also came to be included in the Chinese Tripitaka, and all those works can also be regarded as sutras.

In a larger perspective it becomes easy to see just how indistinct the concept of a sutra is. In addition to the various kinds of sutras already mentioned, in Japan certain works written by the Japanese founders of Buddhist sects are recited, and those works too are called sutras, in the broader sense.

THE ORIGIN OF
THE SUTRAS

There is a certain uniformity in the styles of the works that are generally called Buddhist sutras. For instance, sutras commonly begin with the phrase "Thus have I heard" and end with the words "Hearing the Buddha's sermon, the entire audience rejoiced greatly and believed and accepted the teachings" or "The entire audience rejoiced greatly, accepted and kept the words of the Buddha, to whom they paid their respects, and then departed." Immediately following the words "Thus have I heard," sutras present a description of the site where the Buddha was preaching.

Not only are sutras used to make a teaching clear so believers can understand and practice it, but also they are used for recitation, since in Mahayana Buddhism, for example, reciting a sutra is believed to bring merit to the reciter. Thus it was necessary that written sutras be both easy to read and pleasant to the ear. At the beginning of the fifth century A.D., Kumarajiva, the great translator of such important scriptures as the Lotus Sutra, paid considerable attention to the fact that they would be spoken aloud and took great care to fashion sentences that would both convey the original meaning correctly and be euphonious. Kumarajiva's excellent style of translation became the model for all subsequent translations into Chinese.

The oldest sutras handed down to the present were assembled at the First Buddhist Council, which the Buddha's foremost disciples convened shortly after his death (around 480 B.C.) in order to compile his sermons. At that council one of the Buddha's ten great disciples, Ananda, who was famous for his memory and is said to have memorized all the Buddha's sermons, recited for those present everything that he had heard from the Buddha. According to tradition, Ananda began his accounts of the sermons with the words "Thus have I heard," and when his fellow disciples had heard and approved his recitations, they were regarded as sutras, true teachings of the Buddha.

Both Shariputra and Maudgalyayana, the Buddha's two greatest disciples, had died about a year before the council; and the Buddha, feeling discouraged, knew his own death was approaching. While on a teaching mission in Magadha, Maha-Kashyapa, who was now considered the Buddha's chief disciple, sensed that the death of the eighty-year-old Shakyamuni was near, and so with his five hundred companions he set out to return to the north.

When Maha-Kashyapa's group reached the village of Pava, they encountered a believer of another religious sect. Their questions as to the whereabouts of Shakyamuni were answered with the news that the Buddha had died about a week before in nearby Kushinagara and that the flower the believer held in his hand had been part of the funeral decorations.

That news was a great shock. The monks who were enlightened endured their sadness, believing that living beings were born to die, in accordance with the truth "All things are impermanent." The monks who had not yet reached enlightenment wept and prostrated themselves.

But Maha-Kashyapa overheard one man who had become a monk in his old age saying that the death of Shakyamuni was a cause for rejoicing, not sorrow, since, with him gone, they would all be free to do precisely what they wanted without being advised and reprimanded by him at every turn. Maha-Kashyapa thought that if monks of this kind, willing to break the moral precepts, were to increase in the Buddhist Order, the Buddha's true teachings would not be preached and thus would not be followed. He saw at once that to prevent this it was essential to compile the Buddha's true teachings and decided to produce a collection of the sutras.

When Maha-Kashyapa reached Kushinagara, the funeral ceremonies were over. He called together the monks gathered there and suggested a council to compile all the teachings of the Buddha. This was essential if the true Law was to survive and if false laws and precepts were to be prevented from springing up. The assembly agreed and chose five hundred *arhats,* or enlightened disciples, to participate in the task. The ensuing council, held three months after Shakyamuni's death during the three-month rainy season, met in the Cave of the Seven Leaves at the foot of Mount Vibhara near Rajagriha, the original capital of Magadha.

I have said that five hundred *arhats* were delegated to collect the teachings, but in fact only four hundred and ninety-nine were *arhats,* since Ananda had not yet reached the final stage of enlightenment when the council was convened. Nevertheless, Maha-Kashyapa and many other monks agreed it would be impossible to exclude him, because during the last twenty-five years of Shakyamuni's life Ananda had been in constant attendance on their master. He had heard more of Shakyamuni's sermons than anyone else and had remembered all of them perfectly. Moreover, he had heard and learned from Shakyamuni and fellow monks all the sermons delivered before he himself had entered the religious life.

Ananda wanted desperately to achieve total enlightenment before the great work began, yet on the night before the council was to meet he still had not attained his goal. He stayed up until late but without success. According to tradition, when he finally went to bed his feet refused to stay down and his head rose from the pillow. Suddenly, in that instant, he was enlightened and was at last fully qualified to participate in the council.

During the meeting, led by Maha-Kashyapa, Ananda recited all the sermons and Upali, known for his thorough knowledge of the precepts, recited all the ordinances. Seated before the assembly, Ananda recited the Buddha's teachings one by one from memory, starting each sermon with the words "Thus have I heard." Deeply moved, the assembly listened thoughtfully, made oral corrections when necessary, and finally approved Ananda's recitation, completing the first compilation of sermons.

The majority of the primitive Agama sutras consist of the Buddha's own teachings, but many recorded sermons were either preached by his chief disciples at his request or preached by disciples and later approved by him.

On one occasion, for example, the Buddha taught his many disciples the Law of the Four Noble Truths* and then complimented his two greatest disciples, Shariputra and Maudgalyayana, who were present. The Buddha said that since Shariputra was like a biological mother and Maudgalyayana was like a foster mother, all his disciples should be close to both of them. He went on to say that Shariputra would explain the Law of the Four Noble Truths in detail and then left. Shariputra did explain the Law of the Four Noble Truths and the teaching of the Eightfold Path,† and his

---

* The Four Noble Truths are: (1) the Truth of Suffering, that is, all existence entails suffering; (2) the Truth of Cause, that is, suffering is caused by ignorance, which gives rise to craving and illusion; (3) the Truth of Extinction, that is, there is an end to suffering, and this state of no suffering is called nirvana; and (4) the Truth of the Path, that is, nirvana is attained through the practice of the Eightfold Path.

† The Eightfold Path consists of right view, right thinking, right speech, right action, right living, right effort, right memory, and right meditation.

sermon is recorded in the sutra known as the Discourse on the Analysis of the Truths (Sacchavibhanga-sutta). And at another time, when the Buddha was indisposed because of back pain, Shariputra preached to the assembly in his stead.

The nun Dhammadinna had been the wife of Visakha, a rich man in Rajagriha. Visakha, a devoted Buddhist who listened intently to the Buddha's sermons, had attained the level of enlightenment called *sakadagamin,* meaning he would have to experience only one more rebirth into this world. Though he always remained kind to his wife, after he attained this level of enlightenment his sexual desire gradually decreased. Dhammadinna asked him the reason, and he replied that having faith in the Buddha's teaching lessened his physical desire. Understanding then for the first time that he was indeed a devout Buddhist, she obtained his permission to enter the order of nuns. Through wholehearted religious discipline Dhammadinna attained the highest level of enlightenment earlier than her husband, becoming an *arhat.* Wishing to share this faith with her husband, she went to visit him and expounded many teachings, which are recorded in the sutra known as the Lesser Discourse of the Miscellany (Chulavedalla-sutta). Dhammadinna eventually came to be the greatest preacher of all the nuns.

Chitta, the wisest of all the lay Buddhists, was as well versed in the Buddha's teachings as the monks. Though he remained a lay believer, he disseminated the teaching, led friends and relatives to the Buddha's way, and converted people of other religions to Buddhism. He also engaged in doctrinal discussions with monks, sometimes preaching to them, and his words too were recorded.

There are other sutras that are said to record theological discussions between the Buddha and the Hindu deities Brahma and Indra and between the Buddha and various kinds of demons.

Such sutras as these, composed by authors both human and nonhuman, were still regarded as the teaching of the Buddha because the preachings of others were reported to the Buddha, who verified their accuracy. In this sense, even though the sermons were not actually preached by the Buddha, if they correctly conveyed his teachings, they were, with his approval, regarded as equivalent to his preaching and were accepted as sutras.

There are also many sermons that were preached by the Buddha's disciples after his death. Not all of the extant sutras were recited at the First Buddhist Council: some were not recited until the second council, or even later, but they were still regarded as containing the correct teaching and as being consistent with the Buddha's truth. Since the later sutras also begin with the phrase "Thus have I heard," we can infer that these words were uttered not only by Ananda at the First Buddhist Council but also by the reciters at following councils.

The extant sutras do not necessarily contain the Buddha's exact words because they were not recorded as he spoke. Furthermore, the intelligence and mental capacities of the people who heard him differed, so the way in which they understood the content of the preaching differed. This is another reason that the exact words of the Buddha could not have been handed down to us. Moreover, no sutra has been handed down in a language the Buddha himself used. The sutras were transmitted in other Indic languages of later periods, and without doubt conscious and unconscious changes in the Buddha's words were made during several centuries of oral transmission. In spite of all this, however, both the primitive sutras regarded as the oldest extant sutras and the Mahayana sutras of later periods are considered correct records of the Buddha's words.

It should be noted that the primitive sutras were not compiled as biography, since at the time that Shakyamuni was with his disciples, his preaching and his disciples' concerns centered on faith and its practice, not the recording of his acts. However, even though those sutras were not intended to describe the Buddha's acts, many of them do contain detailed accounts of his life at the beginning of his teaching ministry—after he attained enlightenment—and of the events surrounding his death.

Many of the Buddha's sermons recorded in the primitive sutras are actually biographical. Because the descriptions in the primitive sutras were not intended as biography, however, they were not embellished and the Buddha was not depicted as a superhuman being. In this respect the primitive sutras are more reliable than the conscious biographies of later ages.

Two or three centuries after the Buddha's death, when memory of Shakyamuni was diminishing, many Buddhists wanted a biography of the Buddha, and each sect of Buddhism compiled its own biography. More than ten biographies are extant in Chinese translation, two in a language close to pure Sanskrit, and one in Pali; and biographies were also transmitted to Sri Lanka, Burma, and other countries. Of the extant biographies, the *Mahavastu-avadana* (Great Story), in Buddhist Hybrid Sanskrit, is regarded as one of the oldest. (An English-language translation of this work, *The Mahavastu,* by John J. Jones, was published in London in 1949.) The biographies produced by various sects also mention Shakyamuni's religious disciplines in his previous lives, and some Buddhist practices still current today are based on those accounts.

TWO

The Sutras and Their Languages

LANGUAGES OF THE SUTRAS   It is most desirable for sutras to be transmitted in the language of the people using them so that their meanings can be well understood. Thus as Buddhism spreads to more societies, the sutras must be translated into more languages. Among the world's religious texts, the Bible has been translated into the most different languages—over sixteen hundred of the world's roughly five thousand languages and dialects—and has been distributed in about five hundred languages and dialects in nearly two hundred countries.

When Buddhism was transmitted from India to Central Asia more than two thousand years ago, the sutras were translated into the local languages. Of all Buddhist scriptures, the Pali Dhammapada has been translated into the most languages (including English, French, German, Italian, Japanese, and Russian) and is the most widely read; therefore, in the West it is considered representative of Buddhist sutras. Yet the Dhammapada, which is in the Hinayana tradition, is simply a presentation of introductory teachings for beginners.

Four Chinese translations of the Dharmapada are extant; but until the early nineteenth century, they were neither studied nor read in China and Japan, where principally Mahayana Buddhism was accepted. The Pali Dhammapada was held in high esteem by Westerners, however; and its influence finally spread to Japan,

25

where it was widely read and studied. Although many Mahayana sutras contain more profound teachings than the Dhammapada, the essence of Mahayana Buddhism is not well known in the West because its sutras have rarely been translated into Western languages.

The original language of the sutras seems to have been Magadhi, which Shakyamuni used in preaching. Of all the Indic-language versions of sutras used as Buddhist texts today, those written in Pali are the most numerous and are widely used in the Southern Buddhist countries Sri Lanka, Burma, and Thailand. According to Southern Buddhist tradition, Pali is regarded as the language that Shakyamuni spoke, and therefore it is called Magadhi or the fundamental language. However, recent studies show that although a little of the Magadhi influence is still evident in the Pali language, the basic characteristics of the two languages are different.

The two important language families of India are Indic and Dravidian. All Buddhist sutras were originally compiled in Indic languages, which developed in various parts of India over a period of three or four thousand years. In present-day India more than ten major languages—including Hindi, Urdu, Bengali, Bihari, Marathi, and Punjabi—belong to this family, and together they number several hundred dialects. Sanskrit and fourteen modern languages are now officially sanctioned by the Indian constitution, and in a large house it is possible for several of the recognized languages to be in use, since servants from different areas and family members would all speak in their own languages or dialects.

This rich linguistic heritage was noted in earlier times, when, for example, in plays one could identify a character's occupation and social status through the prescribed language he or she spoke. Kings, ministers, and Brahmans spoke Sanskrit, the most highly esteemed and inflected language; queens, princesses, nuns, and courtesans spoke a graceful language called Shauraseni; the general populace, such as merchants and artisans, spoke Magadhi; and the lower classes spoke Paishachi. Even lyrics had their own pleasant-to-the-ear language, Maharashtri.

The five languages just mentioned originated in the dialects of different areas, but the languages in Shakyamuni's time belonged to a period earlier than that of these five languages. However, even in Shakyamuni's time regional languages already differed, and each language had its own unique characteristics, as we can see from the edicts of Emperor Asoka, issued about two centuries after the death of Shakyamuni. Asoka had his edicts carved on large rocks and stone pillars, and one particular edict was written in a different language in each of the eight areas where it has been found. The languages of the edicts in India, which can be divided into four or five regional groups corresponding to the spoken languages of various areas, correspond to the five languages used in the drama of later periods. In time they became regional languages of the Apabhramsha family, and still later they developed into the modern Indic languages.

The language Shakyamuni spoke was the one in general use around the middle reaches of the Ganges, where he was active. Since the area was later called Magadha, its language was called Magadhi (or Old Magadhi), and because many of Emperor Asoka's edicts have been found in this area, we have an idea of what the Magadhi Shakyamuni spoke was like.

In the time of Shakyamuni, the Vedas, the holy scriptures of Brahmanism, were transmitted in Vedic Sanskrit, which was the forerunner of classical Sanskrit. (Both Vedic Sanskrit and classical Sanskrit are elegant, highly inflected, complex languages.) The Vedic scriptures were transmitted only to the educated upper classes, never to the lower classes. Shakyamuni, who wanted his teachings to reach all classes of society equally, thought that the lower classes should be the focus for his ministry and therefore preached his teaching in Magadhi, the everyday language of the common people, so that even the lower classes could understand him. The popularity of Buddhism can thus be understood, for on hearing his teaching, not only nobles, ministers, and Brahmans but also the untouchables, who had never before been offered religious instruction, took refuge in the Buddha.

Two Brahman brothers named Yameru and Tekula, impressed by Shakyamuni's preaching, became Buddhist monks. Believing that preaching the precious teaching in the coarse Magadhi marred the dignity of Buddhism, they asked Shakyamuni to preach in the inflected, sonorous Vedic Sanskrit of the Brahmanic scriptures. Shakyamuni, who cherished the hope of bringing his teaching to all classes, admonished them, saying that anyone who preached Buddhism in Vedic Sanskrit would be punished.

With the spread of Buddhism to various areas of India, Buddhist sutras seem to have been translated into the languages commonly used in those areas. As the Buddha's ministry became increasingly well known, disciples came to Shakyamuni from far away to become monks, and after attaining enlightenment they returned to their homes, where they most likely spread the Buddha's teaching in their native languages. For instance, Purna, distinguished among the disciples as a preacher, was very active in the seaside district of western India and won many believers there; and Maha-Kaccha-yana, foremost among the disciples in preaching widely, spread the teaching in the western areas centered on Ujjeni, the capital of Avanti. (Thanks to their efforts, centers of Buddhism prospered in western India after the death of Shakyamuni. Many great ancient Buddhist relics, such as the great stupas of Sanchi and Bharhut and the cave monasteries of Ajanta and Ellora, still survive in that area.)

After Shakyamuni passed away at the age of eighty, five hundred of his leading disciples convened the First Buddhist Council, on the outskirts of Rajagriha, in Magadha. Recitations at that time were in Magadhi. The teachings gradually diffused to more distant parts of India, and aided by Emperor Asoka's embracing Buddhism and propagating the Buddha's teaching, the religion became widespread in and around India. As Buddhism was disseminated abroad, the sutras seem to have been translated from Magadhi into other local languages.

Following the initial rupture of the Buddhist Order—around the time of Emperor Asoka, in the third century B.C.—some eighteen or twenty schools of Buddhism eventually emerged. The differences among the schools consisted partially in their understanding and interpretation of the sutras and precepts, and a number of those differences arose because of a lack of communication owing to geographical barriers and because of translating the sutras into many different languages.

PALI STUDIES   Pali is a dialect of Indic Prakrit, and of all extant documents written in Middle Indic languages, those written in Pali are by far the most numerous. Next come the Jain scriptures written in Ardha-magadhi (Half Magadhi), which is close to Pali.

Since Jainism was born at almost the same time and place as Buddhism, prospered in company with Buddhism, and held similar beliefs, Western scholars for a time regarded Jainism as a sect of Buddhism because the content and language of the scriptures of the two religions resemble each other. Although some of the differences are subtle, scholars eventually recognized that they were in fact different religions.

The Pali language of Buddhism, which developed earlier than the Ardha-magadhi language of Jainism, was more inflected than Ardha-magadhi. Among the Prakrit languages that are known today, Pali is the oldest, and except for the Buddhist Hybrid Sanskrit used in Mahayana sutras, for example, it is closest to orthodox Sanskrit (classical Sanskrit). Ancient word forms seen in Vedic Sanskrit still survive today in Pali.

Linguistically, Pali is a form of the ancient Paishachi tongue. Before and during Emperor Asoka's time, Paishachi was in common use in western India, and the sermons that Shakyamuni delivered in Magadhi were translated into Paishachi, which later developed into Pali. But when Buddhism was taken to Southeast Asia by Asoka's son Mahinda, the sermons were transmitted in Pali and thus were unintelligible to the people they were meant for, a situation far from the intention of Shakyamuni, who wished to let all people know Buddhism. (Interestingly, though the word Pali means "holy scripture," it does not appear in primitive sutras.)

Mahinda was born to the young prince Asoka's first wife, Devi—a devout Buddhist and the daughter of a powerful family—while Asoka was governor-general in western India. Eventually Asoka returned to the capital city of Pataliputra (present-day Patna) as emperor, leaving Mahinda behind to be raised by his mother, whose language was Paishachi. The Buddhism Mahinda transmitted to Sri Lanka in Paishachi, or Pali, was the Theravada (Way of the Elders) Buddhism that was widely accepted in western India.

Theravada Buddhism was transmitted from Sri Lanka to Burma, Thailand, and other countries after the first century A.D., and Pali was probably used for communication.

Sinhalese, a language of Indic extraction, was spoken in Sri Lanka; Burman, of Tibetan origin, in Burma; and Thai, of Chinese extraction, in Thailand. Pali, the language of the holy scriptures, was therefore a convenient language for communication among Buddhists from these countries. Pali was a practical language for communication and conversation, and even today monks in these countries speak Pali and communicate with monks in other countries in this language.

A great many ancient Pali sutras have been preserved in such Southern (or Theravada) Buddhist countries as Sri Lanka, Burma, and Thailand. In addition to the eighteen or twenty schools of Hinayana Buddhism in India, there were also various schools of Mahayana Buddhism; but of all the sects and schools of Buddhism, Theravada Buddhism, one of the major Hinayana schools, is the only one that possesses a complete canon in a single language.

The beginning of Southern Buddhism dates from about the third century B.C., when Emperor Asoka sent his oldest son, Mahinda, a Buddhist monk, to Sri Lanka with his disciples as one of the emperor's missionary delegations to nine places inside and outside India. When Theravada Buddhism was later transmitted to Burma, Thailand, Cambodia, and Laos—where it is still practiced devoutly—its sutras were handed down in Pali. But Pali-language Buddhist texts were introduced into Japan only in the nineteenth century, with the influx of Western learning.

Westerners started traveling to the Orient in the fifteenth century, and in the early nineteenth century the English and French became interested in Theravada Buddhism, which was popular in India and Sri Lanka. At that time the Westerners who studied Buddhism were mostly Christian missionaries who attempted to prove Buddhism an inferior religion in order to propagate Christianity. The missionaries possessed a strong scholarly curiosity about Buddhism: some were interested in the Pali language, and others were concerned with the doctrines and history of Buddhism. Thus Westerners came to study Pali sutras seriously.

Copies of Pali sutras from India and Sri Lanka were collected in England, France, Germany, and Denmark. In 1815, while Sri Lanka was under English rule, the British studied Pali in order to control the country, and in 1824 a Christian missionary in Colombo published a voluminous Pali grammar with an extensive Pali vocabulary. In 1826, the young French scholar Eugène Burnouf (1801–52) and Christian Lassen (1800–1876), a Norwegian-born German who was studying in France at the time, presented their "Essay on Pali." Although the Pali language was then little known in Europe, their essay elicited a favorable response in the academic world. From that time on, the study of Pali and Pali-language Buddhist texts gradually advanced in both Sri Lanka and Europe. A real achievement was the publication, in 1855, of the Pali Dhammapada by a young Danish scholar named Michael Viggo Fausbøll.

Before becoming a professor there in 1878, Fausbøll (1821–1908) was a librarian at the University of Copenhagen library, which housed a large collection of works in Pali, including *jatakas,* stories of the previous incarnations of Shakyamuni. Although Fausbøll initially took up Pali in order to study the *jatakas,* his first publication was the Pali Dhammapada, which was published in romanized Pali with a Latin translation and careful revisions. After twenty years of immense labor, he finally published a six-volume translation of the original texts of the *jatakas.*

In the late 1870s, original Pali texts also began to be published in other countries, including Germany and England, and after 1882 all Pali texts were published by the Pali Text Society in London through the cooperation of scholars throughout the world. The books published by that society number over one hundred and fifty, and comprehensive Pali dictionaries and translations of the sutras are also available.

Influenced by the work of Western scholars, Japanese scholars of Buddhism began to study the Pali language and Pali texts late in the nineteenth century. They undertook a comparative study of sutras in Pali and in Chinese, and today each of the thousands of sutras that comprise the Pali canon has been investigated in comparison with Chinese versions. Such study has helped give Japanese Buddhologists a clearer understanding of the meaning of the sutras.

The Agama sutras, which were regarded as an inferior teaching before the nineteenth century, came to the fore. Since the Pali Agama sutras belong to the ancient school of Buddhism, their true teaching could have been lost or distorted over such a long period of time; however, they record the words and deeds of the Buddha and contain almost all the sources of Mahayana teachings. Thus, in Japan it is commonly held that, for a correct understanding, a thorough study of Mahayana Buddhism must include both primitive and fundamental Buddhism.

The study of Pali sutras has served three important purposes. It has helped to provide a correct understanding of both primitive and fundamental Buddhism as the basis of Buddhism; to advance unity and cooperation among Japanese Buddhists of different sects, since the Mahayana Buddhist sects all originate in the same sources—primitive and fundamental Buddhism; and to provide agreement that Shakyamuni was the founder of Buddhism.

Romanized Pali sutras and their English translations were published in London, and sutras in Pali were published in Sri Lanka, Thailand, and Burma using the indigenous scripts. In honor of Takakusu Junjirō (1866–1945), who had made great contributions in introducing Pali Buddhism, Western Buddhology, and Indian philosophy to Japan, a Pali Tipitaka, a complete collection of Pali-language scriptures, was translated into Japanese. Over forty Japanese scholars of Buddhism translated the collection, which was compiled as sixty-five fascicles in seventy books and took almost six years to complete. The publication of that work, in 1941, contributed greatly to the study of Pali texts in Japan.

NON-PALI SUTRAS   In addition to Pali three other Indic languages are known in extant primitive sutras. One is a language close to classical Sanskrit; another is a Sanskrit derivative; and the third is Gandhari Prakrit, a member of the same language family as Pali.

The first of these languages was used in the sutras of the Sarvastivadin sect and in many of the Mahayana sutras. The Sarvastivadin sect prospered in northwestern India—in Kashmir and Gandhara (in present-day Pakistan). Sanskrit had been born in those regions, and there the sutras were transmitted in a corruption of classical Sanskrit that was in common use. Later, classical Sanskrit came into use in general studies, religion, and literature, and the Sarvastivadin sect and followers of Mahayana Buddhism made revisions in their sutras that brought the language of their scriptures closer to classical Sanskrit.

The doctrine of the Sarvastivadin sect, which produced a number of outstanding scholars, was regarded as representative of Hinayana Buddhism, and its theory influenced other Hinayana sects and Mahayana Buddhism as well. Most of the Hinayana Buddhist teachings transmitted to China were those of the Sarvastivadin sect. Many of this sect's original Sanskrit texts have been discovered in India, Nepal, and Central Asia, but most of them are incomplete.

The second language was a corrupt Sanskrit spoken in north-western India and seems to be the language first used for the written sutras of the Sarvastivadin sect. The oldest Mahayana sutras were also written in this language. After classical Sanskrit became an established scholarly language, this corrupt vernacular was also modified to more closely imitate classical Sanskrit.

Although it is easy to translate prose into Sanskrit, it is extremely difficult to translate verse because of differences in the number of syllables required to suit the meter. Since it was not possible to render the verse sections of the sutras into Sanskrit, they have come down to us in their original form. Thus the extant Sanskrit texts of early Mahayana sutras, such as the Lotus Sutra and the Sutra of Infinite Life, contain the corrupt vernacular in the verse sections and classical Sanskrit in the prose portions. The Sanskrit derivative used in Buddhist sutras is called Buddhist Hybrid Sanskrit, and some scholars call it the Gatha dialect because it is used in the *gatha* (or verse portions) of Mahayana sutras. Some Abhidhamma Buddhist sutras also were transmitted in Buddhist Hybrid Sanskrit.

The third language, Gandhari Prakrit, bears the least resemblance to Sanskrit. An extant fragmentary Dhammapada written in this language was originally known as the Prakrit Dhammapada. Today called the Gandhari Dharmapada, this scripture is discussed below.

The Dhammapada, or Dharmapada, is a collection of the Buddha's most noteworthy sayings taken from the Agama sutras. The preface to the Chinese Dharmapada states that its verses record the essence of a number of sutras and that each verse has a unique reason for being preached and can be found in various sutras. The preface further says that after the Buddha's death believers from different sects excerpted four- or six-line verses from the Agama sutras, organizing and editing them into their own Dharmapada. Each Hinayana Buddhist sect, in fact, does seem to have handed down its own distinctive Dharmapada.

When the Chinese Dharmapada was compiled, almost eighteen hundred years ago, its thirty-nine chapters (totaling 752 verses) were translated from three versions of the Dharmapada that existed then: the Dharmapada in five hundred verses, seven hundred verses, and nine hundred verses. The twenty-six principal chapters of the Chinese Dharmapada were translated from the five-hundred-verse Pali Dhammapada. Additional selections from the nine-hundred-verse Dharmapada of the Sarvastivadin sect and from the seven-hundred-verse Dhammapada were added to those twenty-six chapters to form the present Chinese Dharmapada.

Similar sutras were translated into Chinese somewhat later, and three Tibetan versions of the Dharmapada survive. Both the Chinese and the Tibetan translations contain only verse or verse with commentary. Most of the translations are from the Dharmapada of the Sarvastivadin sect, which is called the Udana-varga and consists of thirty-three chapters, totaling more than nine hundred verses. Fragments of the Udana-varga in Sanskrit—discovered in Central Asia by Western explorers early in the twentieth century— were taken to England, France, and Germany, where they were published; but the complete sutra was already known through extant Chinese and Tibetan translations.

Fragments of the Gandhari Dharmapada, which has also been called the Prakrit Dhammapada, were discovered independently in Central Asia in the 1890s by a Frenchman and a Russian. Each man obtained roughly one-third of the whole scripture, and the remaining third was lost.

This scripture is said to have been unearthed at the remains of a monastery in Khotan, where Buddhism prospered in the second or third century A.D. The scripture was written in Kharoshti, a script then in use in the Gandhara region of northwestern India. The total length of the birch bark on which it is written is estimated to have been about five meters, with the Dharmapada written on both sides. The discoverer of the bark tore it into fragments, which were then sold individually. In 1892 a French explorer named Dutreuil de Rhins bought some of the fragments and sent them to France. Although they arrived safely, Dutreuil de Rhins lost his life in Tibet without learning the value of his purchase.

With its territorial expansion in Central Asia and Tibet in the late nineteenth century, Russia established a consulate in Kashgar. The consul general, Nikolai Petrovsky (1837–1908), saw the Dharmapada fragments that were being sold and bought all that remained in order to prevent their being lost. Petrovsky's fragments were sent to St. Petersburg (present-day Leningrad), but we do not know the fate of the final one-third of the manuscript: whether those fragments were sold to a third party or were lost or destroyed.

The Dutreuil de Rhins manuscript fragments were studied in France by Émile C. M. Senart (1847–1928), and the Petrovsky fragments were studied in Russia by Serge Oldenburg (1863–1934). By coincidence both Senart and Oldenburg presented papers at the Eleventh International Congress of Orientalists, held in Paris in September 1897, and at that time it became apparent that their separate manuscripts were parts of the same scripture.

Oldenburg placed his material at Senart's disposal, and the following year Senart published in the *Journal Asiatique* a much longer paper incorporating some information from the Russian manuscript. However, the thirty lines from the Dharmapada that Oldenburg presented at the Congress of Orientalists were only a fraction of the manuscript the Russians possessed. The remainder had not been published because the language had not been identified. Through comparative study of the manuscript fragments and inscriptions and documents that were discovered later, the language was identified as Gandhari, a Prakrit language in use in Gandhara, in northwestern India.

In 1962, after long study, John Brough, professor of Sanskrit at the University of London, published *The Gandhari Dharmapada* (Oxford University Press), comprising both the French and the Russian manuscripts, with the missing portions reconstructed on the basis of comparison with other extant Dharmapada. Professor Brough's text consists of twenty-six chapters, the same number as in the Pali Dhammapada, but there are about one hundred and twenty more verses than in the Pali text.

SCRIPTS AND SUTRAS   The two ancient Indic scripts that were used in both Buddhist scriptures and the edicts of Emperor Asoka are Brahmi and Kharoshti. Neither of these scripts was indigenous to India: both developed from Semitic writing forms.

In the beginning a spoken language has no direct relationship to its written form because they are not born at the same time. Spoken languages developed with the emergence of humankind, but the invention and use of written characters came much later. In Japan, for example, where a spoken language has existed for several thousand years, a writing system was not introduced until around the fourth or fifth century A.D., after Japan had had contact with the Chinese. But the ideograms borrowed from China were not widely used by the Japanese until some were greatly simplified to create the two syllabaries still in use today.

Although Indic, or Indo-Aryan, languages existed several thousand years ago, their written scripts do not appear to have evolved until some three or four hundred years before the founding of Buddhism. Thus there is little immediate relationship between the spoken languages and the written scripts of India.

One of the two writing systems in ancient India, Kharoshti, was used only in northwestern India and in the neighboring area of Central Asia during a limited period of roughly seven hundred years, between the fifth century B.C. and the third century A.D. This system seems to have been based originally on the Old Persian and Brahmi scripts used in northwestern India after the Persian king Darius the Great conquered the area at the end of the sixth century B.C. Like the Arabic or Iranian system today, it was written horizontally from right to left.

So far, edicts of Emperor Asoka have been found in some thirty-odd sites throughout the area of ancient India, but only the edicts discovered in two places in the northwest, in modern Pakistan, are written in Kharoshti. The Gandhari Dharmapada was also written in Kharoshti, but since this script was used for a limited period in a limited area, the number of Kharoshti texts and fragments is extremely small in comparison with those in Brahmi. As Brahmi came into common use in northwestern India after the third or fourth century A.D., Kharoshti was displaced.

According to ancient Indian tradition, the Brahmi characters were devised by Brahma, the Hindu deity of world creation, who taught them to mortals. Various studies, however, have revealed a close relation between India's ancient Brahmi and the old scripts of Mesopotamia and Asia Minor. Many hypotheses have been offered as to the origin of the Brahmi script, but it is now thought to have been developed from Phoenician around 800 B.C.

Indian Brahmi was at first written horizontally from right to left, like Phoenician script. Later, but only in northwestern India, this method of writing was adopted for the edicts of Emperor Asoka. All other edicts were written horizontally from left to right, like Western languages. Buddhist scriptures in Brahmi and its derivatives were all written horizontally from left to right.

The Phoenician script, which figures in the origins of Brahmi, is believed to have developed from Egyptian glyphs. In fact, the majority of the world's written languages in use today derive from the lineage of Egyptian and Phoenician characters. In the Middle and Near East the modern characters are derived directly from Phoenician script, either through cuneiform characters or through the characters used in the scriptures of Judaism, Christianity, and Islam; in the East, there are Brahmi and Kharoshti; in Southeast Asia there are writing systems that developed from Brahmi; and modern alphabets in the West are based on Greek and Roman characters, which in turn derive from Phoenician. In essence, all the world's written languages except Chinese and languages that use its writing system descend from Egyptian and Phoenician scripts.

The Brahmi script used by Emperor Asoka around the third century B.C. continued to evolve gradually. By the beginning of the Christian Era, the Brahmi characters in the north of India began to become a little different from those used in the south, and the difference became more marked as time passed. The northern characters became very angular, while those used in the south became noticeably rounded.

The language of the Mahayana sutras and of northern Hinayana Buddhist sutras was Sanskrit or Buddhist Hybrid Sanskrit. Those sutras are all written in northern-Brahmi characters, and Buddhist sutra manuscripts discovered in Nepal are also written in various northern-Brahmi scripts. In fact most of the Nepalese characters that have been in use since the tenth century A.D. are derived directly from northern Brahmi. The oldest are probably the Siddhan characters, which were used in northern India from the sixth to the twelfth century A.D.

Since most of the scriptural manuscripts conveyed to China during the T'ang dynasty (618–907) were written in Siddhan characters, in China and Japan the name Brahmi actually refers to the Siddhan script.

The latest of the scriptural manuscripts discovered in Nepal are written in Devanagari characters. This northern script, descended from Brahmi, appeared in its mature form after the twelfth or thirteenth century and was the most systematized of all the Brahmi scripts.

Today, in addition to a number of modern Indian languages, sacred and philosophical writings of orthodox Brahmanism, Indian literary and scientific works, and Buddhist sutras in Sanskrit and Buddhist Hybrid Sanskrit are all written and printed chiefly in the Devanagari script. Such works are also sometimes transcribed in the Latin alphabet for the sake of non-Indians. Sanskrit Mahayana sutras published in the West and in Japan are written in either the Devanagari script or the Latin alphabet.

Another of the northern-Brahmi–derived scripts was Tibetan, which was first devised for writing translations of the sutras when

Mahayana Buddhism was introduced to Tibet from India around the seventh century A.D. These characters were adopted from the northern-Brahmi script used in the neighboring area of India around that time, and thus it could be said that the Tibetan script originated wholly in India. Later, when Tibetan Buddhism (Lamaism) was introduced to Mongolia and Manchuria, the Tibetan characters influenced the development of both Mongolian and Manchurian scripts devised for translated sutras. In addition, the *han'gul* writing system of Korea is thought to have also been created under the influence of the Tibetan script.

Although Pali-language sutras are used in such Southern Buddhist countries as Sri Lanka, Burma, Thailand, and Cambodia, they are written in the local scripts: Sinhalese in Sri Lanka, Burmese in Burma, Thai in Thailand, and Khmer in Cambodia. Those scripts are all derived from the southern Indian, rounded form of Brahmi. In Sri Lanka, the angular script of Emperor Asoka was used at first, but under the influence of the southern-Indian characters it eventually became more rounded.

Since the Pali canon in use in those southern countries has now been transcribed in their national scripts, it is impossible to read the Pali canon if one is not familiar with one of those writing systems. For convenience, even Western scholars of Buddhism learning the Pali language or publishing the Pali canon have transcribed the various scripts in one form only, the Latin alphabet.

THREE

Translating the Scriptures

THE EARLIEST   As I mentioned earlier, Shakyamuni
CHINESE TRANSLATIONS   ordered his disciples to transmit his
teachings in the local languages of the
districts in which they would be preaching. Therefore, in India
Buddhist scriptures were communicated in the vernacular. When
Emperor Asoka dispatched Buddhist monks on teaching missions in
various places within and outside India, Buddhist scriptures were
translated into both Indic and non-Indic languages as a matter of
course.

In the case of the conservative Southern school of Buddhism,
however, this practice was not followed, and the scriptures were
transmitted in Pali when Theravada Buddhism was taken to Sri
Lanka. Although the sutras were sometimes translated into Sinhalese, Pali remained the orthodox liturgical language. This was
also the case in Burma, Thailand, Cambodia, and Laos. In one
sense, this practice contradicted Shakyamuni's desires, since Pali-
language transmission was not based on local knowledge and conditions. But the Theravada Buddhists believed the Buddha's Law
should be communicated without any of the misunderstandings
that can result from translation. In Southern Buddhist countries
the Pali language and Buddhism were familiar not only to monks
but also to the general populace, and both were accustomed to
studying and understanding the meaning of the scriptures in the

41

Pali original. Hence Theravada Buddhists thought the Pali original was appropriate for others to accept, believe, and practice in the traditional manner as the traditional teaching.

In contrast, when Buddhism was taken to the area that is present-day Afghanistan and to other Central Asian districts, it was translated into the local languages. This was especially true in the case of Mahayana Buddhism, since the Mahayana Buddhists felt that the purpose of communicating Buddhism was to impart its true spirit without the hindrance of considerations for the subtleties of its literature.

Modern exploration and excavation in Central Asia have brought to light numerous ancient Buddhist texts. Among them are scriptures written in Sanskrit and other Indic languages, as well as Chinese, Tibetan, and such unfamiliar or now dead languages as Uighur, of the Turkic group; Sogdian and Saka (or Khotanese), both of the Iranian group; and Agnean (or Tokharian A) and Kuchean (or Tokharian B), both from western China. Thus we know that the scriptures were translated into indigenous languages when Buddhism was transmitted to Central Asia. Many of the scriptures in these languages, as well as scriptures in various Indic languages, are thought to have been taken to China and translated into Chinese.

The majority of the scriptures that were translated into Chinese arrived in China via the Silk Road, although some were transmitted from India and Sri Lanka by sea. Despite its various hazards, such as deserts, canyons, and steep mountains, the overland route was shorter and less dangerous than the sea route; hence most Buddhist scriptures were imported over the Silk Road rather than by sea. Among the extant Chinese translations of scriptures imported overland, renderings from the middle of the second century A.D. seem to be the oldest, and translations made some seventy years later, around the beginning of the third century A.D., appear to be the oldest Chinese versions of texts that arrived by sea.

At the same time, however, one tradition holds that the transmission of Buddhism to China and the first translation of Buddhist scriptures into Chinese occurred during the reign of the "First Emperor" (Shih Huang-ti; r. 246–210 B.C.), of the short-lived Ch'in dynasty. According to this story, eighteen wise men brought the Buddhist scriptures from India to China, where Buddhism was accepted. Later, however, under an extreme policy designed to eliminate all books and teachings deemed inimical to the First Emperor's rule, vast numbers of philosophical works and Chinese classics were burned and scholars were silenced through either banishment or execution. But the tradition maintains that because they had been hidden, the Buddhist scriptures were able to escape the fate of the other unacceptable works.

This story ignores historical fact, however. It certainly would have been possible for the First Emperor to receive one of Emperor Asoka's missions, since they lived at roughly the same time, but there was little interchange between China and India in those days. Nomadic "barbarians" living on the northwestern frontier of China effectively disrupted communication between Central Asia and China.

In order to discourage the nomads' frequent, damaging raids, the northern Chinese states built defensive walls along the border. Under the First Emperor those walls were strengthened and united in a single barrier well over twenty-two hundred kilometers in length. We know that structure as the Great Wall of China. It was not until the reign of the Former Han emperor Wu Ti (r. 141–87 B.C.), about one hundred years after the First Emperor, that open commerce between China and Central Asia was established, following a decline in the strength of the nomadic Hsiung-nu, whose descendants would much later be known to us as the Huns.

In 139 B.C. Wu Ti dispatched an army led by Chang Ch'ien to enlist the aid of the powerful Yüeh-chih nation, far to the west, in a joint campaign against the Hsiung-nu. Defeated and taken prisoner by the Hsiung-nu, Chang Ch'ien was forced to marry a Hsiung-nu woman, who bore him a child. Remembering his mission during his long years of captivity, Chang Ch'ien eventually escaped and reached Yüeh-chih. There Wu Ti's proposal fell on deaf ears, so Chang Ch'ien made his way back to China, finally returning in 126 B.C., more than ten years after he had set out. Although Chang Ch'ien failed in his mission, his journey increased Chinese knowledge of Central Asia. Through subsequent negotiations, China eventually established alliances with countries in Central Asia, and communications between east and west were opened.

On his first expedition, Chang Ch'ien had heard in Bactria that the teachings of the Buddha were practiced in India, so Buddhism must have been known in Central Asia by that time. Hence it is likely that the Chinese first learned of Buddhism late in the second century B.C. Therefore, we know that Buddhism and the Buddhist scriptures were not transmitted one hundred years earlier, during the reign of the First Emperor.

Tradition aside, it is said that Buddhism was introduced into China in A.D. 67, although it may have been earlier, around the beginning of the Christian Era. At the outset, however, not many Chinese believed in Buddhism, and those who did were chiefly the immigrants and merchants who had come from Central Asia. At that time it was not necessary to translate into Chinese the Buddhist scriptures that were written in the languages of Central Asia, but by the second or third generation, the mother tongues of the immigrants were forgotten, and it became necessary to translate the Buddhist scriptures into Chinese. By that time too the indigenous Chinese had gradually come to believe in Buddhism, and Chinese translations of the scriptures were much more necessary.

The first Chinese translation of Buddhist scriptures is thought to have been made during the reign of the Later Han emperor Ming Ti (r. A.D. 57–75). It was said that a dream Ming Ti had in A.D. 64 caused him to dispatch the mission to the west that brought Kashyapamatanga, Mdian Dharmaraksha, and other monks to China from India or Central Asia and that together these monks translated a number of works, including the Sutra of Forty-two Chapters, at a temple in Loyang—the Later Han capital—in A.D. 67. This is regarded as the first Chinese translation of Buddhist scriptures. According to tradition, the extant Sutra of Forty-two Chapters (Ssu-shih-erh-chang-ching) is the translation made jointly by Kashyapamatanga and Mdian Dharmaraksha. They may have translated the Sutra of Forty-two Chapters, as tradition insists; however, the extant translation of that sutra does not appear to be a translation from the period of the Later Han dynasty (A.D. 25–220), although it is fairly old. It may be a translation from the period of the Three Kingdoms (220–80). (The terms used and the style of translation indicate the age of a translation.)

The oldest extant Chinese translations of Buddhist scriptures were made by An Shih-kao (d. ca. A.D. 170) and Lokakshema (A.D. 147–85), of Kushan, who crossed into China around the middle of the second century. An Shih-kao was a prince of Parthia. An is an abbreviation of An-hsi, or Parthia, and his name meant simply Shih-kao who comes from An-hsi. (It was the custom among Buddhists of ancient China to take the name of one's birthplace as a surname.) Having no desire to succeed to the throne after his father's death, An Shih-kao abdicated in favor of an uncle and retired into religion. In those days Parthia was being harassed by the powerful forces of Kushan, which bordered Parthia on the east, and it is suggested that An Shih-kao retreated into religion because he sensed the impermanence of worldly things. After he mastered Buddhist doctrine, his teaching ministry took him to China, where he became proficient in the language and translated some thirty-five Buddhist scriptures in forty-one fascicles. Twenty works, totaling more than twenty of those fascicles, are still extant, most of them Hinayana Buddhist texts.

The terminology and the literary style of those sutras are the oldest among extant translations. The verse portions of the texts were translated as prose, and because they were early translations and Buddhist terminology had not yet been firmly established, they use many terms that are not familiar to us. For example, the Eightfold Path was translated as the Eightfold Right Practice.

Lokakshema, who went to China at about the same time as An Shih-kao, was born in Kushan, a large country that spread from Central Asia to northwestern India and was the most powerful nation in the area. Kanishka, a devout Buddhist, was its king. In order to transmit Buddhism, which was then flourishing in Central Asia, Lokakshema went to China and at Loyang translated into Chinese twelve scriptures in twenty-seven fascicles.

Of Lokakshema's translations, nine works in twenty fascicles are still extant. Many of the scriptures he translated were Mahayana sutras, and included among them is the oldest extant translation of the Perfection of Wisdom Sutra in Eight Thousand Lines (Ashtasahasrika-prajnaparamita-sutra). Although the wording of his translations is fairly close to that of later versions, his translation of the five aggregates* is the same as that of An Shih-kao. Lokakshema's translations also include many unique transliterated words, some of which do not correspond to the correct Sanskrit words. It is therefore assumed that the original versions of Lokakshema's translations were not in Sanskrit but in some Indic vernacular or Central Asian language. His translations, however, are fairly sound and reliable.

In contrast to An Shih-kao's translations, which were chiefly of Hinayana sutras, Lokakshema's translations were mainly of Mahayana sutras; hence we suppose that Hinayana Buddhism was practiced in Parthia, An Shih-kao's homeland, and that Mahayana Buddhism was popular in Kushan.

OTHER EARLY
CHINESE TRANSLATIONS

We have noted that Buddhist scriptures were initially translated into Chinese— in the second and third centuries A.D.— for the benefit of the descendants of Central Asian immigrants to China who could no longer understand the mother tongues of their ancestors. Since Buddhism was an Indian religion, reflecting the Indian philosophical and cultural background, the indigenous Chinese had difficulty understanding the Buddhist doctrines and terminology. Although many Chinese were curious about Buddhism and were interested enough in the sutras to want to study them, they could not really comprehend the alien Buddhist doctrines or philosophy; thus they read primarily the general moral teachings and stories that neither contain technical terms nor expound doctrine. Those simple teachings and stories, presented in ordinary language, were comprehensible, interesting, and useful.

Representative among the numerous sutras that are collections of moral teachings is the Sutra of Forty-two Chapters, said to be the

---

* The five aggregates are the elements or attributes of which every human being is composed: (1) form, or the body; (2) receptivity, sensation, feeling; (3) mental conceptions and ideas; (4) volition, or various mental activities; and (5) consciousness. The union of these five aggregates dates from the moment of birth and constitutes the individual.

first sutra translated into Chinese. In order to introduce Buddhism to the Chinese, basic Buddhist teachings were excerpted from various sutras and compiled as the forty-two entries in this sutra, which imparts easily assimilated knowledge of Buddhism and its moral teachings. The following excerpts from the Sutra of Forty-two Chapters indicate the nature of the material it presents.

"The Buddha said, 'One who has left his parents for ordination to practice the Way is called a monk. He always keeps the two hundred and fifty precepts. . . .'

"The Buddha said, 'For human beings, ten things are good, while ten other things are evil. Three are of the body; four are of the mouth; the other three are of the mind. The three [evils] of the body are needless killing, stealing, and sexual misconduct. The four [evils] of the mouth are a double tongue, slander, lying, and improper language. The three [evils] of the mind are covetousness, anger, and foolishness. . . .'

"The Buddha said, 'If the evil man would criticize the wise man, that is as a man who spits looking up at heaven. His spit does not defile heaven, but his own body instead. That is [also] as a man who throws rubbish at the windward man. The rubbish does not defile him, but the thrower himself instead. You should not criticize the wise man. Your own faults are certainly enough to ruin yourself.' "

Chief among the sutras that tell stories are the many, such as the Lalitavistara (Detailed Narration of the Sport of the Buddha), that relate the biography of Shakyamuni. In simple language, those story sutras detail Shakyamuni's life, beginning with his disciplines in previous incarnations, then going on to his birth at Kapilavastu, his life as the son of a king, his renunciation of the secular life, his period of ascetic practices, his attainment of enlightenment, and his forty-five-year teaching ministry as the Buddha. Through such stories, which were interesting and entertaining in themselves, people came naturally and effortlessly to an understanding of the Buddhist way of thinking.

Another kind of story sutra that was popular is the *jataka,* or birth story, which tells of Shakyamuni's lives in previous incarnations. There are numerous *jatakas,* differing in both length and content. The Sutra of the Collection of the Practices of the Six Perfections

(Shatparamita-samgraha-sutra) is representative of those that were translated into Chinese. A third type of story sutra, exemplified by the sutra Avadana (Stories), teaches the law of cause and effect, that is, that a good cause produces a good effect and an evil cause, an evil effect. The Dharmapada, a collection of ethical teachings, constitutes yet another type of sutra that was translated.

By the end of the third century A.D., examples of each of these sutra types had been translated into Chinese, and they were very helpful in transmitting a general knowledge of Buddhism. Yet the fundamental, systematic doctrines of Buddhism were hard for the average Chinese to understand, and the difficulties were greater in the case of doctrines that expounded a higher spiritual state. Despite their difficulty, the Chinese made great efforts to understand the Buddhist doctrines; and some Chinese Buddhists attempted to interpret Buddhism through the more familiar and somewhat similar Taoist terminology of Lao-tzu in order to make Buddhist thought more comprehensible to their countrymen. The Buddhism explained in the Taoist vocabulary is known as *ko-i* Buddhism.

At the same time, in order to establish the primacy of Taoism, some Taoists claimed that after his disappearance Lao-tzu went to India, converted the people there, and became the Buddha (or, in another version, that Shakyamuni was merely one of the eighty-one incarnations of Lao-tzu). At the beginning of the fourth century this claim was put forth in the spurious Sutra on the Conversion of the Barbarians (Lao-tzu Hua-hu-ching), by Wang Fu. Later, as Buddhism prospered and became recognized as superior to the Taoist philosophy, Taoism and Buddhism came into open conflict. Taoists took advantage of the Sutra on the Conversion of the Barbarians to press their attack on Buddhism, declaring that Taoism was an ancient, indigenous teaching and that Buddhism was merely a new offshoot, since Shakyamuni was a reincarnation of Lao-tzu. Because distortion is inevitable if Buddhist thought and teachings are explained in the vocabulary of Lao-tzu's Taoist philosophy, when Buddhism eventually came to be understood correctly by the Chinese, Buddhist adherents began to denounce *ko-i* Buddhism.

In the meantime, however, Chinese Buddhist scholars worked diligently to increase their understanding of Buddhism. In A.D. 179

Lokakshema made his translation of the Mahayana Perfection of Wisdom Sutra in Eight Thousand Lines, but the Chinese found it extremely difficult to understand. In the mid-third century, the religious scholar Chu Shih-hsing, eager to have a more easily understood version of that sutra, left for the west, seeking another copy of it. He went to Khotan, where he had heard there was a complete manuscript of the Perfection of Wisdom Sutra, and asked the king for the scripture.

Hinayana Buddhism, rather than Mahayana Buddhism, was flourishing in Khotan at that time, and the Hinayana Buddhists believed Mahayana Buddhism was evil. To prevent having what they considered an evil theory transmitted abroad, Hinayana Buddhists advised the king not to give the manuscript to Chu Shih-hsing. The king wavered in making a decision, but Chu Shih-hsing told the king that if the Buddhists in Khotan considered the sutra heretical, it would surely be burned. He pleaded with the king to give him the sutra so it would not suffer that fate. Just as the manuscript was to be burned in the plaza before the palace, the king consented to give it to Chu Shih-hsing.

Although it was somewhat scorched, the sutra was saved. Chu Shih-hsing sent it to China to be translated, and today we know that translation, made in 291 by Wu-ch'a-lo, as the Perfection of Wisdom Sutra in Twenty-five Thousand Lines (Panchavimshati-saha-srika-prajnaparamita-sutra). Incidentally, in China it is said that sutras came to be copied on yellow paper in commemoration of the scorched, yellowed original of that sutra.

It was Tao-an (A.D. 312–85) who rendered the greatest service to Chinese Buddhism, ensuring the correctness of its teachings and eliminating the Taoist terminology of *ko-i* Buddhism. He had a lifelong desire to know the correct teachings of Buddhism, and since in those days many monks and priests came to China from India and Central Asia to translate sutras, Tao-an was able to learn from them about Indian Buddhism. But they could not satisfactorily answer his questions about Buddhist doctrine.

From such monks Tao-an heard of the distinguished scholar Kumarajiva, who was active in Central Asia at that time, and he pleaded with his ruler, Fu Chien (338–85) of the Earlier Ch'in state, to invite Kumarajiva to China. Northern China at that time was the scene of much strife, with sixteen Chinese kingdoms and five "barbarian" tribes vying with one another for supremacy in the region, yet Fu Chien commanded one of his generals, Lü Kuang, to bring Kumarajiva to his capital, Ch'ang-an. While on that mission, Lü Kuang learned that Fu Chien had been killed and the country taken over by another ruler, and he decided to remain in Central Asia. Eventually he met Kumarajiva, but because of many difficulties, Kumarajiva did not arrive in Ch'ang-an until sixteen years after Tao-an's death.

The effects of Tao-an's activities extended to many areas of Chinese Buddhism. For example, although monks until that time had retained their own surnames, Tao-an insisted they take the surname Sha (Shih in Chinese)—the first syllable of the name of the Buddha's clan, Shakya—because he maintained that all Buddhist monks were disciples of Shakyamuni. Tao-an called himself Shih Tao-an, and in time Shih became the surname of all monks. Tao-an's was not a capricious decision but reflected the Buddha's teaching in the Agama sutras, where it is said that any monk from any caste in India becomes an equal disciple of Shakyamuni by forsaking the surname and caste of his birth, just as the waters of great rivers become nameless when they empty into the ocean.

Though the way of life and the clothing of ordained monks had not previously been different from those of laymen, Tao-an introduced prescribed garments for monks and established precepts and regulations in order to make the way of life of Chinese monks the same as that of monks in India. He gained many disciples under those new disciplines and taught them true Buddhism.

Another of Tao-an's great achievements was the compilation in 374 of a catalogue of all the sutras that had been translated into Chinese. He and his disciples collected five or six hundred copies of sutras from throughout China, and friends also sent him sutras, all of which he examined personally in compiling his catalogue, the first of its kind. Although the catalogue no longer exists, it is possible to know what sutras he included in it because later catalogues list and comment on the sutras in Tao-an's catalogue.

A great many of the sutras Tao-an gathered did not have titles.

Originally, in India the titles of scriptural manuscripts were written on not the first but the last page. If the last page was lost, as not infrequently happened, the title of the sutra would also be lost. To the untitled sutras, Tao-an gave new titles that reflected their content. It should also be noted that the original sutras in India were not divided into fascicles, as were the Chinese translations. For example, today the Chinese translation of the Lotus Sutra is divided into twenty-eight chapters in eight fascicles, while the Indic original was divided only by chapters. Since sutras in China were written on long sheets of paper intended to be bound as hand scrolls, or individual fascicles, the paper was cut to the proper length for a scroll that people could conveniently open and read. Today, even though the number of fascicles is no longer significant when book form is used, the fascicle divisions are usually indicated in printed books, and sutras are still divided according to the traditional fascicles when they are copied as scrolls.

At about the time of Tao-an a considerable number of new sutras were being translated. When the Agama sutras Madhyama-agama (Middle-Length Sayings) and Ekottara-agama (Gradual Sayings) were translated into Chinese, Tao-an was so delighted that he wrote prefaces for them. Philosophical treatises, including the Vibhasha-shastra (a partial translation of the Abhidharma-mahavibhasha-shastra, or Great Commentary), were translated, and much of the Vinaya-pitaka, or Ordinance Basket, a collection of monastic rules, was also translated. Thus, light was gradually shed on a sphere of sutras then unknown in China. Although not a translator himself, Tao-an was instrumental in getting such translations made and wrote prefaces for them.

Tao-an also wrote commentaries on sutras, some of which still survive, but he died without gaining a full understanding of the difficult doctrines, even though he always strove for a better comprehension of Buddhism. Tao-an regretted not meeting Kumarajiva because he had wanted to learn from Kumarajiva. Tao-an's last wish was to see and hear directly from the future Buddha, Maitreya, those teachings that he had not been able to understand. For that reason he wished to be reborn in Tushita, the heaven of Maitreya.

Because of the numerous disciples fostered by Tao-an, when Ku-

marajiva later came to China he was able to translate many important sutras. Although Kumarajiva was a great scholar, he could not
have achieved so much in the short space of about a dozen years
without the cooperation and assistance of those excellent disciples.

PROBLEMS IN RENDERING   Some of the many difficulties en-
SANSKRIT INTO CHINESE   countered in translating Buddhist
                         scriptures from Indic languages into
Chinese arose from the fact that the languages belong to completely
different language stocks. Another source of difficulties was the vast
difference between Chinese and Indian philosophy and culture:
not only did translators discover it was nearly impossible to find
equivalent words or concepts for the scriptures in the Chinese language, but also they found a very basic difference between the ways
of thinking and of expressing thoughts in the two languages. With
regard to the difficulties inherent in translating the sutras into
Chinese, Tao-an, who actively furthered translation before Kumarajiva came to China, conceived the concept of "five losses and three
difficulties"; and later, during the T'ang dynasty (618–907), the
great translator Hsüan-tsang explained the "five kinds of untranslatable words."

Tao-an's theory of "five losses and three difficulties" referred to
five points in which the meaning of the original was lost through
translation and to three things that were not easy to accomplish in
translating. The first of the five losses was caused by reversing the
word order in the Indic originals to conform to Chinese grammar.
For example, in Chinese the first sentence of "Taking Refuge in the
Three Treasures" (the Buddha, the Law, and the community of
believers) is "自歸依佛" ("I take refuge in the Buddha"), whereas
in the Indic original it is expressed in reverse word order as *"Bud-
dham saranam gacchami"* ("To the Buddha, to the refuge place, I go").

Second, the Indians preferred simple, unadorned writing, whereas the Chinese were fond of ornate, polished writing. Thus, to please
their readers, translators needed to consider literary style above all,
and hence lost the simplicity of the original. However, when Chih
Ch'ien of the brief Wu dynasty (222–80) attempted to translate the

Dharmapada in the stylish Chinese manner, the Indian monk Wei-chi-nan—who had brought the original to China—cautioned him against shrouding the Buddha's words in beautiful prose, since it was most important for their meaning to be conveyed accurately so that readers could grasp the Buddha's teachings and understand them correctly. Chih Ch'ien followed the monk's advice and translated the Dharmapada simply and accurately.

Third, when writers of Indic languages wished to emphasize a point, they repeated a sentence or sentences several times. This writing style did not appeal to the Chinese, who deleted all repetitions when making translations into Chinese. Furthermore, since the original sutras had been handed down orally, they abounded with the repetitions that make oral literature easier to memorize. These repetitions, too, were eliminated.

Fourth, Indic writing often contained sentences within sentences. For instance, it was not unusual to find a long explanatory passage of over a thousand characters introduced into the middle of a sentence so that the original point was obscured. To one who was accustomed to that style of writing, the explanatory material did not detract from the whole, but such interpolations were generally deleted in Chinese translations; hence the complex meaning of the Indic original was lost.

Fifth, in Indic writing even after a point had been fully explained, the explanation was often repeated in a subsequent passage. These repetitions, too, were all deleted in the Chinese translations.

To the "five losses" Tao-an added "three difficulties." The first was caused by the fact that the graceful and highly inflected ancient Sanskrit, for example, had to be translated into plain, comprehensible Chinese. The second difficulty was that although Sanskrit sentences expressed very subtle nuances, in keeping with Indian thought of the Buddha's time, the Chinese translations had to be clear to contemporary readers. Third, even at the First Buddhist Council, the five hundred *arhats* led by Maha-Kashyapa conferred with one another and scrupulously compiled the sutras by reconfirming the accuracy of each phrase. Yet these sutras were later translated quite carelessly. Tao-an believed the careless translations stemmed from the irresponsibility of translators who were ignorant of the Buddha's Law. Therefore, the third difficulty referred to the profound understanding translators must have to truly interpret sutras.

Hsüan-tsang's theory of "five kinds of untranslatable words" referred to five instances in which Indic-language words were not translatable into Chinese. The first kind of untranslatable words involved those words whose meanings were so profound they defied a single, simple definition. Those words, such as *dharani* (a kind of magical incantation), were simply transliterated, rather than being translated into Chinese.

The second kind of untranslatable words included those that have many meanings. As Hsüan-tsang pointed out, the word *bhagavat* has six meanings, and if only one meaning was translated into Chinese, the other meanings would be lost. Therefore, such words were not defined in translation but merely reproduced phonetically. For example, the word *bhagavat* has the following meanings: one who possesses auspicious signs; one who destroys illusions and evil; one who is provided with such auspicious virtues of freedom as the Law, fame, good signs, desire, and diligence; one who has completely understood the Four Noble Truths; one who receives and keeps various excellent practices; and one who has abandoned the wandering of transmigration. All six of these definitions must be understood to grasp the full meaning of *bhagavat*.

The third kind of untranslatable words referred to those things for which there were no Chinese equivalents, such as the names of plants, animals, minerals, and places that were unknown to the Chinese.

The fourth kind of untranslatable words had traditionally been transliterated, that is, transcribed phonetically. For example, *anuttarasamyaksambodhi* could be translated as the "supreme way" or "supreme enlightenment," but by custom it has always been transliterated. Hsüan-tsang said, "Because [translators] follow established usage, words like *anuttarasamyaksambodhi*, although they are translatable, have been transliterated [according to the Sanskrit pronunciation] ever since [the translations made by] Kashyapamatanga [in the first century A.D.]."

The fifth kind of untranslatable words included those that would lose their special meanings if translated into Chinese. For instance, although *prajna* does mean wisdom, such a prosaic translation would rob it of its more profound meaning. Yet by transliterating the word, its fuller meaning of perfect wisdom is preserved.

Because the translation of sutras into Chinese, which first began around the second century A.D., continued for over a thousand years, some words have several different translations or transliterations, reflecting the changing influences of the time, associates, and collaborators of the translators. Depending on when they were made, Chinese translations are usually designated by one of three terms: "ancient translations," "old translations," or "new translations." "Ancient translations" are those made before the time of Kumarajiva, that is, prior to the latter part of the fourth century. The "old translations" are those made between the time of Kumarajiva and 645, when Hsüan-tsang began translating. The "new translations" include the works by Hsüan-tsang and all later translators, who generally followed his choices in the translation of specific terms.

Although some of the terms from the "new translations" by Hsüan-tsang are used today, the terms devised by Kumarajiva—in the period of the "old translations"—are still in common use. Apart from the inherent difficulties of the theories and doctrines of Buddhism, present-day study of Chinese sutras is hindered by the fact that there are a number of translations for a single term.

FOUR

Early Translators

KUMARAJIVA   During the hundreds of years that sutras transmitted from India and Central Asia were being
translated into Chinese, some six or seven thousand fascicles of
translations were completed. Of the nearly two hundred translators
who were prominent during those years, the four most eminent were
Kumarajiva, at the beginning of the fifth century; Paramartha, in
the middle of the sixth century; Hsüan-tsang, in the mid-seventh
century; and Amoghavajra, in the middle of the eighth century.
Although Hsüan-tsang and Amoghavajra each translated a large
number of sutras, the sutras translated by Kumarajiva have had the
greatest influence on Buddhism in China and Japan.

It could be said that the essential meaning of Buddhism was introduced to China through the sutra translations of Kumarajiva,
even though several hundred sutras had already been translated
into Chinese before he began his work. By the latter part of the
fourth century the true doctrines of Buddhism still had not been
conveyed fully to the Chinese, either because lack of knowledge
prevented their understanding completely those sutras that had
been translated or because the true concepts of Buddhism had not
been transmitted in the translations. The Chinese did not truly understand Buddhism until Kumarajiva had translated sutras, lectured, and written his commentaries. Thus Kumarajiva's work was
extraordinarily important to Buddhism in both China and Japan.

According to tradition, Kumarajiva (344–413) was born in Kucha, in Central Asia. His father, Kumarayana, was a Brahman from India whose family had been government ministers for generations. Kumarayana's father, Datta, was a distinguished minister, and Kumarayana was said to be as wise as Datta. But Kumarayana was wearied by the shallowness of his life, and when it came time for him to assume his ministerial post, he became a priest instead. His travels as an itinerant priest happened to take him to Kucha.

The king of Kucha had a twenty-year-old sister who was both beautiful and brilliant. She had been born with a red mole on her body, which was said to be a sign that she would bear an exceptional child. Yet even though she received many proposals from the kings and princes of neighboring countries, she refused them all. When she saw the young priest Kumarayana, however, she was attracted to him at once and begged her brother the king to permit her to marry this priest. The king was happy that she had at last found someone acceptable, and he compelled Kumarayana to accept the proposal. Their first son was named Kumara, after his father, and Jiva, after his mother.

Tradition also says that Kumarajiva's mother became unusually wise during her pregnancy. For example, when she went to a large temple in the country, she was able to understand the sutras being recited there in an Indic language. Upon discovering this, the high priest Dharmaghosha told her that a wonderful child would be born to her. (It is said that the mother of Shariputra, the foremost of the Buddha's disciples, also gained extraordinary wisdom in the same way during her pregnancy.)

Kumarajiva's mother very much wanted to become a nun after his birth, but her husband would not permit that until after the birth of a second son. She finally overcame her husband's opposition when Kumarajiva was seven and entered the Buddhist order, taking him with her, and soon attained the level of enlightenment called *sotapanna,* the stage of one who has entered the stream leading to nirvana. With his mother, Kumarajiva learned sutras, and it was said that he could recite a thousand sutra verses from memory.

When Kumarajiva was nine or ten he went with his mother to India to study under the noted priest Bandhudatta, who instructed them in the Dirgha-agama (Long Sayings) and Madhyama-agama (Middle-Length Sayings). Kumarajiva became so adept that he could refute non-Buddhist teachers in debate. Returning to Kucha when he was about twelve years old, Kumarajiva and his mother visited various countries in Central Asia. In Kushan, an *arhat* (an enlightened person) predicted to his mother: "If this child keeps the Buddhist precepts until he is thirty-five years old, he will disseminate the Buddha's teachings widely and save great numbers of people. However, if he breaks the precepts, he will become merely a clever priest."

Kumarajiva and his mother spent one year in Kashgar, where Kumarajiva studied Buddhist philosophy through the Abhidharma treatises and the Ekottara-agama (Gradual Sayings), one of the four Agama sutras of the Chinese canon. He then returned to Kucha and mastered the Vedas (the basic scriptures of Brahmanism) and studied the sciences. Later, under the high priest Buddhayashas, he read the Ten-Category Vinaya (Sarvastivadin-vinaya), containing the precepts of the Sarvastivadin school. Suryasoma, a prince of Yarkand, taught him the theories of Mahayana Buddhism through such works as the Treatise on the Middle (Madhyamaka-shastra), the Treatise in One Hundred Verses (Shatika-shastra), and the Treatise on the Twelve Gates (Dvadashamukha-shastra). Kumarajiva was also able to obtain copies of several Mahayana scriptures.

It is said that when Kumarajiva had assimilated the teachings of Mahayana Buddhism, he stated, "I thought Hinayana Buddhism was the best teaching before I encountered Mahayana Buddhism: I was like a man who does not know of gold and therefore thinks brass is best."

Kumarajiva became a fully ordained priest at the age of twenty, accepting the precepts that Buddhist monks and nuns follow. His mother, who had attained the level of enlightenment called *anagamin* (meaning that it was not necessary for her to experience another rebirth into this world), returned to India alone, but before leaving, she encouraged Kumarajiva to carry the true teachings of Buddhism to China.

Through his teaching activities and discussions, Kumarajiva became well known in Kucha and the surrounding area. Eventually

Kumarajiva invited his former teacher Bandhudatta, who had initi-ated him in Hinayana Buddhism, to come to Kucha. Kumarajiva instructed Bandhudatta in the teachings of Mahayana Buddhism, which Bandhudatta at last accepted. The rulers of neighboring states also received instruction from Kumarajiva at annual lec-tures, and his reputation spread to China. Even the famous Chinese priest Tao-an had heard of Kumarajiva.

King Fu Chien (338–85) of the Earlier Ch'in state thought highly of Tao-an and, at his request, planned to bring Kumarajiva to the capital, Ch'ang-an. Around 382 Fu Chien sent General Lü Kuang and an army of seventy thousand to subdue Kucha, but it was not until almost twenty years later that Kumarajiva finally reached Ch'ang-an. Although Kumarajiva had counseled the king of Kucha to surrender to the Ch'in army, the king ignored Kumarajiva and was captured and killed.

When Lü Kuang met Kumarajiva, he regarded the priest as a man of common ability because Kumarajiva, at only about forty years of age, was very young to have such an imposing reputation. Lü Kuang, who was not a Buddhist, enjoyed subjecting Kumara-jiva to various indignities. He tried to coerce Kumarajiva to marry a princess of Kucha, but Kumarajiva refused. Lü Kuang then forced Kumarajiva to drink strong wine and locked Kumarajiva and the princess in the same room. Under those circumstances, Kumarajiva eventually violated the precepts he had vowed to keep. Though intrigued by Kumarajiva, Lü Kuang continued to harass him with similar affronts. Kumarajiva weathered those humilia-tions, however, and Lü Kuang came to respect him.

Because Fu Chien was no longer alive, Lü Kuang did not return at once to China following his victory in Kucha; instead he remained in northwestern China, usurping the rulership of Liang-chou and keeping Kumarajiva with him. In Liang-chou Kumarajiva gained disciples and became fluent in the Chinese language, which achieve-ment was invaluable when he later translated scriptures.

In 384 the throne of Fu Chien had been usurped by Yao Ch'ang (d. 393), who established the Later Ch'in state, whose capital re-mained in Ch'ang-an. A Buddhist, Yao Ch'ang knew of Kumara-jiva's reputation and pleaded with Lü Kuang to send Kumarajiva to Ch'ang-an, but Lü Kuang would not release Kumarajiva. After Yao Ch'ang's death, his son Yao Hsing (r. 393–415) sent an army to Liang-chou to overthrow Lü Kuang, and Kumarajiva's long-cherished wish was fulfilled in 401, when he at last arrived in Ch'ang-an. He was already well over fifty at that time.

Yao Hsing honored Kumarajiva with the title National Preceptor (*Kuo-shih*) and asked him to take charge of translating sutras into Chinese. Kumarajiva not only knew many treatises and sutras by heart but also had a profound understanding of their meaning. Many of the scholars who had been educated by Tao-an gathered around Kumarajiva to learn the true meaning of the teachings, and they helped him with his translations. Kumarajiva pointed out errors and omissions in earlier translations, and because of his outstanding scholarship previously obscure points were made clear.

Yao Hsing had provided Kumarajiva and his colleagues with quarters where they could work on their translations; and when Kumarajiva translated the Perfection of Wisdom Sutra in Twenty-five Thousand Lines (Panchavimshati-sahasrika-prajnaparamita-sutra), Yao Hsing participated by holding the earlier translations, comparing all the translations, and correcting errors. Between 401 and his death, Kumarajiva translated thirty-five sutras and treatises (totaling 294 fascicles), including Perfection of Wisdom sutras, the Lotus Sutra (Saddharma-pundarika-sutra), the Amitabha Sutra (Sukhavati-vyuha), the Treatise on the Great Perfection of Wisdom Sutra (Mahaprajnaparamita-upadesha), the Treatise on the Middle, the Treatise in One Hundred Verses, the Treatise on the Twelve Gates, and the Ten-Category Vinaya.

Kumarajiva's scriptural translations contributed both to the development of true Buddhism in China and to the establishment of various Chinese Buddhist sects. For example, Kumarajiva's translations of the Treatise on the Middle, the Treatise in One Hundred Verses, and the Treatise on the Twelve Gates were the basis of the San-lun (Three Treatises) school, and the basic scriptures of the T'ien-t'ai sect are the Lotus Sutra and the Treatise on the Middle, which Kumarajiva had translated. Moreover, Kumarajiva's translations of Buddhist precepts, such as the Ten-Category Vinaya, met a need long felt by such Chinese priests as Tao-an.

Tradition holds that Yao Hsing, who deeply admired Kumarajiva, was afraid that with Kumarajiva's death his great talent would be lost, so with the intention of having Kumarajiva beget an heir, Yao Hsing commanded ten comely young women to wait upon Kumarajiva. Yao Hsing also built luxurious quarters for the young women and Kumarajiva, who was obliged to accede to the ruler's wishes. Kumarajiva appears to have been very aware of the unusual circumstances in which he lived, for at the beginning of his lectures he would tell his disciples: "You must take only the lotus flower that grows out of the mire and not touch the mire."

Some of the non-Chinese priests were outraged to see Kumarajiva living a life of ease in royal quarters instead of living humbly in a temple. For instance, the Central Asian monk Buddhabhadra (359–429), who translated the Flower Garland Sutra (Avatamsaka-sutra), faithfully observed the precepts and was critical of Kumarajiva's way of life. Thus he incurred the ill will of Kumarajiva's disciples, who compelled Buddhabhadra to leave Ch'ang-an. He went to Mount Lu, in southern China, where he was warmly welcomed at the monastery of Hui-yüan (334–416).

Hui-yüan, a disciple of Tao-an, moved to Mount Lu in about 384 and spent the remainder of his life in seclusion there. Hui-yüan practiced *nien-fo,* that is, invoking the name of Amitabha Buddha in order to be reborn in that buddha's Pure Land. In 402 he and one hundred and twenty-three followers formed a group called the Pai-lien-she (White Lotus Society) and vowed to be reborn in the Pure Land. Sometime after 404, Hui-yüan and Kumarajiva engaged in a lengthy correspondence on fine points of doctrine. In his daily life Hui-yüan, who revered Shakyamuni, strictly observed all the precepts for monks. When he became old and infirm, his disciples offered him broth and wine and even honey, but he refused it all, admonishing the disciples to recall the precepts.

FA-HSIEN   Most of the early translators of the sutras were Indian
             or Central Asian monks or priests, like Kumarajiva,
who had taken the original sutras into China and translated them
in order to transmit Buddhism to the Chinese. However, many

Chinese pilgrims seeking the Law made their way to Central Asia and India and brought sutras back to China to be translated into Chinese. Of the monks who sought the Law in this way, the most well known are Fa-hsien, Hsüan-tsang, and I-ching.

The *Record of Buddhist Kingdoms* is Fa-hsien's account of his journey to India at the beginning of the fifth century. Hsüan-tsang recorded his travels in Central Asia and India in his *Record of the Western Regions*, a valuable work giving us insight into the customs, habits, geography, history, and religions of various parts of India in the mid-seventh century. I-ching's four-fascicle *Record of the Buddhist Kingdoms in the Southern Archipelago* is a concrete introduction to the customs and daily life of the monks in Buddhist temples in India in the late seventh century, rather than a travel sketch.

Fa-hsien, the first important Chinese pilgrim, believed that many aspects of Buddhism were still unfamiliar to the Chinese, especially the precepts, or monastic rules for monks, even though Tao-an had already established the Buddhist teachings themselves. Thus in 399 Fa-hsien set out for India to seek a complete original text of the *vinaya*, or rules of discipline.

Just two years after Fa-hsien's departure Kumarajiva arrived at Ch'ang-an, and not long afterward such great masters of the precepts as Vimalaksha and Buddhayashas, with whom Kumarajiva had studied, also crossed into China. By 404 Kumarajiva and Punyatara had translated the sixty-one-fascicle Ten-Category Vinaya, and in 408 (or possibly between 410 and 412) Buddhayashas, along with others, translated the sixty-fascicle Four-Category Vinaya (Dharmaguptaka-vinaya). Had Fa-hsien waited but a few years, his journey to India would have been unnecessary. Yet, Fa-hsien's experience was immensely useful both to him and to Chinese Buddhism.

In the time of Fa-hsien many Indian and Central Asian monks had gone to China, and some Chinese had attempted to travel to India or Central Asia. According to the *Record of Buddhist Kingdoms,* Chih-yen, Hui-chien, Seng-shao, Pao-yün, and Seng-ching were among those few Chinese pilgrims who had set out seeking the Law before Fa-hsien made his journey, accompanied by Hui-ching, Tao-cheng, Hui-ying, and Hui-wei. Chih-yen and Pao-yün were very

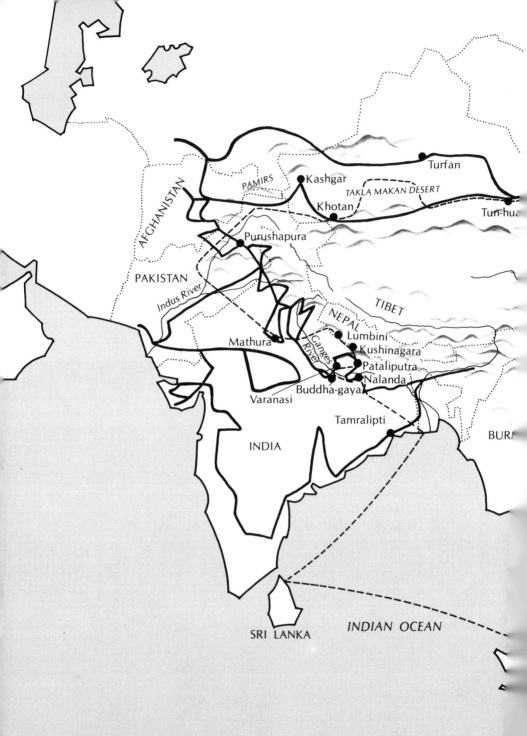

Turfan

PAMIRS Kashgar

TAKLA MAKAN DESERT

Khotan

Tun-hua

AFGHANISTAN

Purushapura

PAKISTAN

Indus River

TIBET

NEPAL

Mathura

Ganges River

Lumbini

Kushinagara

Pataliputra

Nalanda

Buddha-gaya

Varanasi

Tamralipti

BURMA

INDIA

SRI LANKA

INDIAN OCEAN

- - - - - Pilgrimage route of Fa-hsien
————— Pilgrimage route of Hsüan-tsang

SEA OF JAPAN

Tokyo

Peking

Kyoto

KOREA

JAPAN

YELLOW
SEA

Loyang

Nanking

EAST
CHINA SEA

Ch'ang-an
(Sian)

PACIFIC OCEAN

CHINA

Fu-chou

TAIWAN

VIETNAM

OS

SOUTH CHINA SEA

PHILIPPINE ISLANDS

LAND

CAMBODIA

VIJAYA
TRA)

active in translating Buddhist sutras following their return to China, and Chih-yen was considered the greatest native Chinese translator in China at that time.

Twenty-five other monks, including Fa-yung, Seng-meng, and T'an-lang, set out on a journey to seek the Law about twenty years after Fa-hsien did. Five of those monks, Fa-yung among them, succeeded in achieving their goal, and although we do not know if they made records of their travels, we do know that after their return to China they devoted themselves to translating the sutras. About one hundred years after Fa-hsien's journey, the monks Hui-sheng and Sung Yün also went to India. A brief diary by Hui-sheng still survives, and journals by both Hui-sheng and Sung Yün are listed in the fifth volume of the *Loyang chia-lan-chi* (Record of the Monasteries in Loyang).

Such extant journals and documents make it clear that a large number of Chinese traveled to India and Central Asia through the ages, but Fa-hsien, Hsüan-tsang, and I-ching were without doubt the most successful in their search for the Law.

We do not know how old Fa-hsien was when he set out for India with his companions, but he may already have been about sixty. In spite of his advanced age he spent fourteen years seeking the Law before returning to China.

Hsüan-tsang (ca. 596–664), who traveled during his thirties and forties, had a magnificent constitution and handsome features, and those physical blessings were advantages that people admired. Moreover, his memory was excellent, as were his intellect and linguistic ability, and he seems to have suffered no hardships wherever he went. In contrast, Fa-hsien became weak with old age, and his obstinacy prevented his being good at foreign languages. He stayed in Magadha for a few years to learn the local language and Sanskrit, but he could not manage to master them.

Fa-hsien's *Record of Buddhist Kingdoms* describes the difficulty of his journey. Fa-hsien made his way from Ch'ang-an westward to Tun-huang, gateway to Central Asia. The Takla Makan Desert, which lies to the west of Tun-huang, is mentioned in Fa-hsien's journal: "In the desert there exist a great many evil spirits, and a fiery wind blows. No one who meets them can survive. There is no bird that flies overhead and no beast that runs on the ground. There is nothing around us, and we cannot even find our direction. We can go on only by using the scattered skeletons as our guides."

Fa-hsien and his companions were able to lodge in Buddhist temples along the way, and they finally reached the Pamirs, which they had to cross to get into India. Fa-hsien spoke colorfully of the mountains: "On the Pamirs there is snow in both summer and winter. A poisonous dragon also lives there. If men anger him, he vomits a poisonous wind, makes snow fall, and throws gravel and rocks. None who meet this calamity survive." Even after entering India, Fa-hsien's party still had the steep mountain path ahead of it. Fa-hsien's description is vivid: "For fifteen days, as we move to the southwest along the mountain ridges, the path is steep, the precipice towering steeply, the mountains an impassable rock wall. One feels dizzy when one looks down, and even if one wishes to proceed, there is no place to put one's foot. Below is the Sindhu [Indus] River. People of the past chiseled a path out of the rock and drilled about seven hundred holes across the face of the cliff for handholds. After traversing the path, one crosses the river by means of ropes that are strung across it. The river is about eighty paces wide."

Since the cliff along which the path had been cut was several thousand meters high, just standing on the steep path made people feel dizzy and weak: nowhere was the ground level. Small holes had been drilled at intervals of about thirty centimeters, and by means of two short sticks, which they thrust into alternate holes, travelers pulled themselves along the path across the face of the cliff. If one missed but a single handhold, one could fall to one's death. After that dangerous crossing one still had to negotiate a swift river some sixty meters wide. Only one person at a time could cross the precarious ropes stretched across the river. Once safely on the other side, that person signaled so the next person could make the crossing.

Some people who had joined up with Fa-hsien's party turned back at Purushapura (present-day Peshawar). Fa-hsien, Hui-ching, and Tao-cheng continued the difficult journey, but Hui-ching became ill along the way and died. Fa-hsien and Tao-cheng continued on to the Buddhist center Mathura, in central India; the Jetavana

Monastery, at Shravasti; Kapilavastu, where Shakyamuni grew up; Lumbini Garden, the birthplace of Shakyamuni; Kushinagara, where Shakyamuni died; and the Vajji city Vaishali. Some six years after leaving China, they finally crossed the Ganges and arrived in Pataliputra (modern Patna), then the capital of Magadha. The two monks visited various places in Magadha, including Rajagriha, the original capital of Magadha; Gridhrakuta, or Vulture Peak, where Shakyamuni had often preached; and Bodh Gaya, where Shakyamuni attained enlightenment. After returning to Pataliputra they went up the Ganges to Mrigadava, or Deer Park, on the outskirts of Varanasi (also called Benares), where Shakyamuni had preached his first sermon after enlightenment, and then on to Kaushambi, the capital of Vatsa, as well as south to the Vindhya Range in order to visit Buddhist pilgrimage sites in that area.

At that time both Mahayana and Hinayana Buddhism were flourishing in India. The four great Buddhist holy places—Lumbini, Bodh Gaya, Mrigadava, and Kushinagara—were popular pilgrimage sites. Indian Buddhism gradually declined, however, and by the time of Hsüan-tsang, about two hundred years later, both Mahayana and Hinayana Buddhist temples had been abandoned in some regions.

After his journey to the Vindhya Range, Fa-hsien returned again to Pataliputra, where he stayed for three years (406–8) in order to learn Sanskrit and the Brahmi script and to transcribe sutras. There were no sutra manuscripts in northwestern India, and Fa-hsien obtained a few manuscripts only when he visited central India. It was not until he went to Magadha that he was able to acquire a number of sutras, *vinaya* texts, and treatises. Tao-cheng decided to remain in Magadha rather than return to China because he felt that the true teachings of the Buddha could not be learned in the Chinese countryside and that Magadha was the best place to study Buddhism. Fa-hsien parted company with Tao-cheng and continued his travels in the belief it was his mission to communicate true Buddhism to the people of China. He went down the Ganges River and stayed two years in the port city Tamralipti (present-day Tamluk, near Calcutta), where he transcribed sutras and sketched Buddhist images.

Learning of the prosperity of Buddhism there, Fa-hsien went to Sri Lanka for two years (411–12) and was able to obtain such scriptures as the Five-Category Vinaya (Mahishasaka-vinaya), Dirgha-agama (Long Sayings), and Samyukta-agama (Kindred Sayings). From the *Record of Buddhist Kingdoms* we can get a fairly accurate picture of the state of Buddhism in Sri Lanka at the beginning of the fifth century. In Anuradhapura, the capital of Sri Lanka, there was the magnificent Buddhist temple Abhayagiri-vihara, where five thousand monks lived, studying both Mahayana and Hinayana Buddhism. Fa-hsien also stayed there. A nine-meter-tall emerald image encrusted with gold and jewels stood in the temple, and one day Fa-hsien saw a merchant offering before this statue a white silk fan made in China.

Twelve or thirteen years had passed since Fa-hsien had left his homeland. He had parted with or lost his traveling companions, and it was more than two years since he had last seen Tao-cheng. All that he saw and heard was strange to him; everything from the languages to the scenery was different from things in China. In his journal he described his feelings upon seeing the Chinese-made fan: "I could not help being filled with deep emotion and could not keep tears from filling my eyes."

Fa-hsien at last set out for his native land, having learned what should be learned and having obtained as many scriptures and other liturgical implements as he could. For this journey he determined to take the southern sea route.

He took the sutras and Buddhist images and implements aboard a large ship, which sailed to the east on a favorable wind. Very soon, however, the ship encountered a violent wind and sprang a leak. The passengers threw their baggage overboard, and Fa-hsien abandoned all his belongings except the sutras and statues, praying to the Bodhisattva Avalokiteshvara for safety. The ship managed to reach Shrivijaya (present-day Sumatra) three months later. Brahmanism prospered in Shrivijaya; Buddhism had not yet become popular, although roughly two and a half centuries later (when I-ching studied Sanskrit and Buddhism there) Palembang, the capital of Shrivijaya, was a great Buddhist center.

Fa-hsien stayed in Shrivijaya five months, finally boarding a ship for China sometime in 414. That ship also ran into a severe storm, and it reached Shantung Province over eighty days later, having been swept far to the north of its original destination, Kwang-tung Province. Fa-hsien then went south to Nanking, where he met Buddhabhadra. With Buddhabhadra's assistance Fa-hsien was able to translate a portion of the sutras and the Vinaya-pitaka, or Or-dinance Basket, that he had brought back from India. Among them were six fascicles of the Sutra of the Great Decease (Mahaparinir-vana-sutra) and forty fascicles of the *vinaya*, or precepts, of the Ma-hasanghika school (Mahasanghika-vinaya).

OTHER EARLY TRANSLATORS   A number of important Mahayana and Hinayana sutras were
not translated until around the middle of the fifth century A.D., some thirty or forty years after the death of Kumarajiva. With the work of the Buddhist translator Hsüan-tsang in the seventh cen-tury, the Chinese canon as we know it was mostly complete, and about one hundred years later, near the middle of the T'ang dy-nasty, translation of the Tantric Buddhist sutras was completed.

In addition to the Madhyama-agama (Middle-Length Sayings) and Ekottara-agama (Gradual Sayings) sutras, which were trans-lated before Kumarajiva's journey to China, the Dirgha-agama and Samyukta-agama sutras were translated after the death of Kumarajiva, completing the four Agamas of the Chinese canon. Kumarajiva translated the Ten-Category Vinaya (Sarvastivadin-vinaya), and later translators translated the Four-Category Vinaya (Dharmaguptaka-vinaya), Five-Category Vinaya (Mahishasaka-vinaya), and Mahasanghika-vinaya, which completed the Chinese Vinaya-pitaka.

Although a considerable number of Mahayana sutras had already been translated before Kumarajiva arrived in China, he translated the significant ones. Of the sutras translated after Kumarajiva's death, the Flower Garland Sutra (Avatamsaka-sutra) is most im-portant. However, all those Mahayana sutras—the Perfection of Wisdom sutras, the Lotus Sutra, the Vimalakirti Sutra (Vimala-kirti-nirdesha-sutra), the Sutra of Infinite Life (Sukhavati-vyuha), and the Flower Garland Sutra—were translations of early-period Mahayana sutras, which were compiled in India before the third century A.D.

Soon after the death of Kumarajiva, middle-period Mahayana sutras began to be translated. Included among those sutras are the six-fascicle Sutra of the Great Decease (Mahaparinivana-sutra) jointly translated by Fa-hsien and Buddhabhadra; the Sutra of the Tathagata Treasury (Tathagatagarbha-sutra) translated by Buddhabhadra; the Mahayana Mahaparinirvana-sutra, the Great Collection of Sutras (Maha-samnipata-sutra), the Sutra of a Bodhisattva's Spiritual States (Bodhisattvabhumi), and others translated by Dharmakshema; and the Shrimala Sutra (Shrimala-devi-simhanada-sutra), the Sutra of the Appearance of the Good Doctrine in [Sri] Lanka (Lankavatara-sutra), the Sutra of the Continuous Stream of Emancipation (Hsiang-hsü chieh-t'o-ching), and others translated by Gunabhadra (394–468) around the middle of the fifth century A.D., some time after Dharmakshema's works. The translations of that era include many of the most important middle-period Mahayana sutras.

The most distinguished translators of the period following Kumarajiva were Buddhabhadra and Dharmakshema. Buddhabhadra, who was active in central China in the valley of the Yangtze River, and Dharmakshema, who lived in Kansu Province, to the west of Ch'ang-an, experienced at first hand the turbulence of the widespread warfare among the sixteen Chinese kingdoms and various non-Chinese tribes then striving to gain ascendancy in northern China.

Buddhabhadra (359–429) is said to have been descended from the Shakya clan of Kapilavastu, where Shakyamuni was born. His father, a trader, took the family to northern India, where Buddhabhadra was born and reared. When Buddhabhadra was only three years old, his father died, and just two years later his mother also died, leaving the boy to be cared for by relatives. At the age of seventeen he was ordained a monk.

Buddhabhadra had a very good memory, and it is said to have taken him only one day to memorize material that other people usually spent a month memorizing. Since he was enthusiastic about scholarly studies, the practice of *dhyana* (or meditation), and keeping the precepts, during his youth he was already known for his *dhyana* practice and observance of monastic rules. He studied under the great teacher Buddhasena, who was active in northwestern India at that time. When Buddhabhadra had finished his discipline, attaining the level of enlightenment called *anagamin* (meaning that it was unnecessary for him to experience another rebirth into this world), he wanted to travel outside India to propagate Buddhism and to see the things and customs of other countries.

At that time the Chinese monk Chih-yen was staying in the area, and he observed the Buddhists there initiating serious discipline and missionary activities. Wanting to take their teaching to his own country, he asked for a suitable person to convey it. Buddhabhadra was recommended, and Buddhasena himself told Chih-yen that Buddhabhadra was the most appropriate person to reform the Chinese monks' attitudes and mode of living and to instruct them. Eager to have Buddhabhadra teach the Chinese monks, Chih-yen asked him to come to China. Buddhabhadra agreed and left for China by sea, eventually arriving in Shantung Province.

Kumarajiva was active in Ch'ang-an at that time, and Buddhabhadra followed him there, reaching Ch'ang-an in about 408. Kumarajiva was delighted at Buddhabhadra's arrival, and the two of them discussed Buddhist doctrine together, searching for the essence of Buddhism and thus coming to understand one another. In enlightenment and understanding of Buddhism, Buddhabhadra was somewhat superior, so Kumarajiva was occasionally enlightened by him. Once Buddhabhadra asked Kumarajiva, "Why do you have such a good reputation, though there is nothing special in your preachings?" Kumarajiva answered, "Because of my advanced age. I have no especially good talent." His answer reflects his humility, but his reputation was probably due to his character and great intelligence.

Emperor Yao Hsing, a devout follower of Buddhism, offered meals to three thousand monks, including Kumarajiva, but Buddhabhadra, serious in his observance of the precepts, declined Yao Hsing's generosity and continued to live a mendicant's life alone in the city. His refusal may have been an expression of his disapproval of the life of ease led by Kumarajiva, in violation of the precepts that ordained monks vowed to honor. Kumarajiva could understand Buddhabhadra's attitude, but the people close to Kumarajiva were displeased by Buddhabhadra's behavior, which they thought insincere.

Buddhabhadra possessed both scholarly ability and an excellent character gained through uncompromising discipline, and as his reputation for instruction on *dhyana* practice grew, many people gathered around him, wanting to become his disciples.

Once Buddhabhadra prophesied to his disciples: "Five ships are sailing to China from India." When Buddhabhadra's words became known to others, Kumarajiva's disciples considered the prophecy a fraud, and they attacked Buddhabhadra as an impostor. But even before the prophecy of the five ships, which later came true, Buddhabhadra had at times exhibited mysterious paranormal powers achieved through his training.

Buddhabhadra's disciples began to disperse when they sensed potential danger to themselves from Kumarajiva's disciples. Realizing that he would never be fully accepted in Ch'ang-an, Buddhabhadra left for the south with some forty-odd close disciples, including Hui-kuan. About a thousand monks and lay believers saw him off with sadness, and Yao Hsing also seemed regretful.

Buddhabhadra visited Hui-yüan at Mount Lu, and the two men agreed completely in their views on keeping the precepts. Buddhabhadra stayed at Hui-yüan's monastery long enough to translate such Zen writings as the Dharmatara-dhyana-sutra (Yogacharabhumi-sutra) for Hui-yüan. At about the same time, Emperor Wu Ti (r. 420–22) of the brief Liu Sung dynasty (420–79) invited Buddhabhadra to live in the temple Tao-ch'ang in Nanking, the Liu Sung capital. Buddhabhadra accepted, and because he engaged mainly in giving instruction in *dhyana* practice there, he was called either Zen Master Tao-ch'ang or Zen Master Buddha. But since his *dhyana* was meditation in the context of Hinayana Buddhism, it is considered inferior to the *dhyana* of Chih-i (538–97), founder of the T'ien-t'ai sect, and of Bodhidharma (fl. ca. 520), founder of the Chinese Zen school.

When Fa-hsien returned from India, he went to Nanking, and with the help of Buddhabhadra he completed the translation of several sutras, including the Mahasanghika-vinaya and the six-fascicle Sutra of the Great Decease. But it is as translator of the sixty-fascicle Flower Garland Sutra that Buddhabhadra is most famous. The original was brought from Khotan by one Chih Fa-ling, and Buddhabhadra, who was highly regarded for his scholarship and ability, was asked to translate it. He completed his superb translation about three years later, in 421, under the first emperor of the Liu Sung dynasty. His disciple Hui-kuan, who assisted him, was also very active in explaining Buddhist doctrine at that time.

Dharmakshema (385–433) was born in central India. His father died when Dharmakshema was only six, and he and his mother were forced to live in reduced circumstances, subsisting on the money his mother earned at weaving wool. When his mother saw people paying respect and giving many offerings to the virtuous, learned Buddhist priest Dharmayashas, she decided she wanted her son to grow up to be such a person and asked the priest to accept Dharmakshema as his disciple.

Dharmakshema distinguished himself from around the age of ten, becoming familiar with both Hinayana Buddhism and more general scholarship, and it is said that no one could give better lectures on the sutras or discuss the teachings more reasonably than he. From the Zen master known to us as Pai-t'ou he learned of Mahayana Buddhism, which he began to study seriously. By the time he was twenty he had already studied an enormous number of both Hinayana and Mahayana Buddhist sutras. He devoted himself not only to learning but also to actual discipline, and as a result he developed remarkable paranormal powers and came to be called the Great Divine Master.

Dharmakshema went to northwestern India, taking original copies of Mahayana sutras with him, but in that area only Hinayana Buddhism was studied and practiced, and the people were not receptive to Mahayana Buddhism. So he crossed the Himalayas into Central Asia, passing through Kucha on his way to Ku-tsang, the Liang-chou capital, in Kansu Province, where he lodged at an inn. Because wars were still being waged and robbers and thieves abounded, Dharmakshema feared that his sutras would be stolen, and he used them as a pillow at night.

During the night, however, someone pulled at the sutras beneath his head. This also happened on the following two nights, and he thought that a burglar was responsible, but on the third night he heard a disembodied voice asking him why he slept with his head on valuable sutras that preach the emancipation of the Buddha. He felt great remorse and immediately put the sutras on a high shelf before going back to sleep. Burglars did intrude that night to steal the sutras, but they could barely lift them. The following day, the robbers saw Dharmakshema easily pick up the sutras, and, awed by his obvious sanctity, they bowed politely and left.

The Northern Liang kingdom had been established in Liang-chou by the devout Buddhist Chü-ch'ü Meng-hsün (r. 401–33). Hearing of Dharmakshema, Meng-hsün invited him to accept the hospitality of the court and also asked him to translate the sutras he had with him. The high priests of the area, who knew of Dharmakshema's distinguished scholarship and virtue, worked with him in translating a number of sutras, including the Sutra of the Great Decease and the Great Collection of Sutras, most of which were not yet known in China.

Of all the sutras he took with him, Dharmakshema thought most highly of the Sutra of the Great Decease. Its Sanskrit original, written on bark, had been given to him in his youth by the Zen master Pai-t'ou. Dharmakshema translated it first, but he found he had only the initial portion of the original, so his ten-fascicle translation was incomplete. He returned to India to obtain a complete manuscript, staying for over a year, during which time his mother died. He acquired the middle portion of the sutra at Khotan and returned to the Northern Liang capital, where he made another ten-fascicle translation. He sent an envoy to Khotan to bring back the final portion of the sutra, and in this way the Sutra of the Great Decease in three parts, forty fascicles altogether, was completed in 421, seven years after Dharmakshema had begun his translation.

The translation was still incomplete, however, because the original complete manuscript contained thirty-five thousand lines, whereas Dharmakshema's translation contained only a little over ten thousand lines. The original sutra had probably been expanded gradually, for the sutra Fa-hsien first brought home was a small work of only six fascicles, while Dharmakshema's later translation grew to forty fascicles. Still later, Hui-yen and others of the Liu Sung dynasty (420–79) integrated and amended the translations of Fa-hsien and Dharmakshema as a single edition of thirty-six fascicles. That version is called the Southern Text of the Sutra of the Great Decease, while Dharmakshema's own translation is called the Northern Text.

During the time that Dharmakshema was active as a translator, the Northern Liang state came under frequent attack by the non-Chinese T'o-pa tribe, which had styled itself the Northern Wei dynasty, conquered the Later Ch'in state, and taken over the Later Ch'in capital of Ch'ang-an, where Kumarajiva and so many other translators had worked. In time, the Northern Wei emperor heard of Dharmakshema and sent messengers to invite him to Ch'ang-an. However, fearing that the T'o-pa would somehow make use of Dharmakshema's magical skills and usurp the Northern Liang throne, the ruler Meng-hsün refused to permit Dharmakshema to travel to Ch'ang-an.

Meng-hsün's fear helps to explain his response when Dharmakshema sought permission to travel to the west to seek additional versions of the Sutra of the Great Decease. Meng-hsün feigned consent and even gave Dharmakshema money for the journey, but he had his men waylay and kill Dharmakshema.

Though Dharmakshema foresaw the ambush, he accepted his unavoidable destiny and set out pretending ignorance of the king's plot. He was forty-eight years old at his death. Both Buddhabhadra's persecution at Ch'ang-an and Dharmakshema's murder might be considered ineluctable acts of fate.

There is some evidence that Dharmakshema resorted to artifice, and we doubt whether he was a truly enlightened person like Buddhabhadra; but his perseverence in making a complete translation of the Sutra of the Great Decease must be admired, and he is remembered for conveying Mahayana precepts to China.

FIVE

Hsüan-tsang, the Law Seeker

THE EARLY YEARS AND
THE JOURNEY TO INDIA
Kumarajiva, Paramartha, Hsüan-tsang, and Amoghavajra are the most renowned of the roughly two hundred notable translators who were responsible for the translation of several thousand Buddhist works into Chinese in the eleven hundred years between the second century A.D. and the thirteenth.

At the beginning of the fifth century, Kumarajiva translated important sutras and philosophical works that permitted the Chinese to understand the true meaning of Buddhism and that later had a great influence on Japanese Buddhism. Because of the far-reaching effects of Kumarajiva's work, his achievements and his contribution to the history of scriptural translation are respected more highly than those of any other translator.

In his influence on later Buddhist thought and development, Hsüan-tsang was second only to Kumarajiva, and he translated more scriptures than any of the other translators. Of the thirty-two volumes of scriptures included in the monumental *Taishō Daizōkyō* (the definitive collection of the Chinese canon) almost seven full volumes, or more than one-fifth of all the surviving Chinese translations of sutras, are attributed to Hsüan-tsang. In comparison, Kumarajiva's extant translations amount to about one-fourth of the number ascribed to Hsüan-tsang.

Of the four preeminent translators all but Hsüan-tsang were

Indians or Central Asians to whom Indic languages were familiar. Hsüan-tsang was Chinese, but despite this potential handicap he rendered more and better translations than any of the others.

Most of the sutras and philosophical works conveyed to China by Kumarajiva were the documents of early-period Mahayana Buddhism, which presented the true aim of Buddhism centered on practice of the faith. Early-period Mahayana Buddhism was studied earnestly by Kumarajiva's disciples and others in the period of the Northern and Southern dynasties (317–589), and later, in the Sui dynasty (581–618), the fruits of their study contributed to the development of the doctrines of the T'ien-t'ai sect and the San-lun (Three Treatises) school.

Middle-period Mahayana Buddhist works, however, were not translated until after Kumarajiva's death in 413. Middle-period Mahayana Buddhism emphasized philosophical theory rather than the practice of faith, but not all its sutras and philosophies had been transmitted by the beginning of the Sui dynasty, nor was its study fully developed by then. Moreover, in India the middle-period Mahayana doctrine of Vijnanavada (Consciousness Only) was interpreted differently by different groups of its adherents, and when it was brought to China, scholars there added their own interpretations to the doctrine. Various conflicting theories thus developed.

Paramartha (499–569) was the most outstanding translator of middle-period Mahayana Buddhist sutras and philosophical texts during the Liang and Ch'en dynasties (502–89) of the Northern and Southern dynasties period, but because political conditions in southern China forced him to wander from state to state during that time, he was not able to exercise his excellent scholarly abilities as fully as he could have done under more settled circumstances. Paramartha did manage to translate the Treatise on the Seventeen Stages of Spiritual Development (Saptadasha-bhumika-shastra), a partial translation of the Yogacharabhumi-shastra (the basic scripture of the Yogachara school), but that translation was lost in the wars.

Thus, although the study of early-period Mahayana Buddhism was quite exhaustive by the time of the reunification of China under the Sui dynasty, the study of middle-period Mahayana Buddhism was still incomplete because of a lack of texts. And this was the state of Chinese Buddhism at the time of Hsüan-tsang's birth, around 596.

Hsüan-tsang was born into a family of scholars that lived near Loyang, to the east of Ch'ang-an. His grandfather had been a National Preceptor, and his father had been well versed in Confucianism at an early age. It was said that his father and older brother were more handsome and had better physiques than most people and carried themselves with dignity but that in Hsüan-tsang those qualities were even more apparent.

His father was appointed to a provincial governorship at the end of the reign of Yang Ti (r. 604–18), the last emperor of the Sui dynasty, but since he did not want to serve in the government of the new dynasty, he resigned his post and retired. With the loss of his father's income, the family experienced financial difficulties, and Hsüan-tsang's older brother left home to become a monk at Ching-t'u Temple in Loyang, receiving the religious name Ch'ang-chieh at ordination. He earned an excellent reputation for his outstanding lectures on the sutras.

Because Hsüan-tsang's family became increasingly poor, Ch'ang-chieh brought his younger brother into the temple to pursue the same vocation. Both brothers entered the monkhood in order to secure a living and not out of a genuine desire to seek after the truth. Nonetheless, Hsüan-tsang became interested in the sutras and by the age of eleven he was already able to read the Vimala-kirti Sutra, the Lotus Sutra, and others with ease. It is said that he was so intent in his study of sutras and philosophical works that he did not join the other monks when they took time to chat or relax and that the young Hsüan-tsang attended all the lectures on sutras and commentaries given at Hui-jih Temple in Loyang.

By the time he was fifteen and had begun to study at an advanced level, his abilities had become evident and even people far from Loyang had heard of him. When he had learned all he could in Loyang, he went to Chuang-yen Temple in Ch'ang-an in search of an able teacher, but his trip was fruitless. Fleeing the widespread warfare and famine in that part of the country, Hsüan-tsang and his brother made their way to the west, eventually settling in the mountains of Szechwan Province. Finding Buddhism studied widely there, the brothers were content to remain.

The study of Buddhism in Szechwan centered on the philosophical theories of Hinayana Buddhism. Hsüan-tsang became well versed in the philosophies and theories of both Mahayana and Hinayana Buddhism, and later, when he returned to China after studying in India, many of the works he brought back with him and translated were related to the philosophical theories of these two streams of Buddhism. (While in India he studied primarily the middle-period Mahayana Buddhist doctrine of Consciousness Only, or Vijnanavada.)

During his years in Szechwan Hsüan-tsang acquired all the knowledge of Buddhism possible in that area. He never forgot what he read or heard in his studies, and he had a profound understanding of what was being conveyed. He studied systematically, pondering what lay hidden in the texts of the preachings. The learned monks all marveled at his discourse, so well supported by his broad knowledge, excellent memory, and logical thinking.

Having learned all that he could in Szechwan, Hsüan-tsang, just twenty-one years of age, left to visit several places in central China but found no outstanding scholars in that region. He made his way to Chao-chou in the north, where for ten months he studied the Ch'eng-shih theory of nonsubstantiality with the scholar Tao-shen. After that, he spent eight months in Yeh studying Mahayana and Hinayana doctrines under the high priest Hui-hsiu. The priest recognized Hsüan-tsang's intellectual superiority and refused to permit Hsüan-tsang to regard him as a teacher. In fact Hui-hsiu seemed to gain more than Hsüan-tsang from their study together.

Through his travels, Hsüan-tsang visited most of the high priests and learned scholars throughout China to study Buddhism until at last there were no more teachers he could seek in China. When Hsüan-tsang was about twenty-nine, the emperor ordered him to take up residence at Chuang-yen Temple in Ch'ang-an, but he refused because he was not yet confident in his knowledge and understanding of Buddhism. Hsüan-tsang decided there was no course left to him but to go to India for firsthand study in order to comprehend the essence of Buddhism. Although he repeatedly requested the T'ang emperor's permission to travel to the west, he was refused because relations between the T'ang court and regions to the west were strained.

In 629, however, when Hsüan-tsang was around thirty, severe frosts caused food shortages and famine in several cities, including Ch'ang-an and Loyang, and the government permitted and encouraged people to leave the stricken areas and search for food. Joining the hungry refugees, Hsüan-tsang finally set out for the west without permission from the government.

The next sixteen years of Hsüan-tsang's life were spent in travel and study. In his prime both physically and mentally, Hsüan-tsang was well able to endure the hardships of deserts, cold mountains, hunger, and thirst, which would have overwhelmed a less vigorous man. He was able to master various Central Asian and Indic languages and to acquire a large store of Buddhist knowledge.

Very early in his travels Hsüan-tsang stopped at Turfan, where the king was so impressed with him that he would not allow him to leave. The king asked him to settle there and accept an appointment as spiritual preceptor and to spread the Buddha's teachings, but Hsüan-tsang finally convinced the king that his first duty was to seek the Law. Swearing they would always be brothers, the king sent Hsüan-tsang on his way with provisions, treasures, guards, letters of introduction to neighboring rulers, and a military escort to ensure his safety.

With but minor differences, Hsüan-tsang enjoyed much the same hospitality wherever he stayed. When compared with the lot of Fa-hsien, who was already above sixty years of age and had little linguistic ability when he made his way to India some two hundred years earlier, Hsüan-tsang's journey was blessed with good fortune.

Despite the fact that he had left China illegally, when Hsüan-tsang was at last ready to return home, he implored the T'ang emperor T'ai Tsung (r. 626–49) for permission to bring back with him many sutras and images of the Buddha. Greatly pleased by Hsüan-tsang's return, the emperor received him like a victorious general, and it is said that Hsüan-tsang and his party could not pass through the hundreds of thousands of people lining the last ten kilometers of the road into Ch'ang-an, the T'ang capital.

Pleased by and respectful of Hsüan-tsang's knowledge and attitude, T'ai Tsung urged him to leave the monkhood and accept
a ministerial post. Hsüan-tsang refused, however, because he was
anxious to translate the sutras he had brought back with him. Yet
T'ai Tsung, eager to learn all he could from Hsüan-tsang about the
countries to the west, often interrupted Hsüan-tsang's work to question him. Hsüan-tsang may have written and presented his twelve-
fascicle *Record of the Western Regions (Ta-T'ang hsi-yü-chi)* to the
emperor in July 646 in order to preclude further interruptions that
would take him away from the work to which he wished to devote
all his energies.

In his travels he had recorded all his experiences and all he had
heard from the time of his departure until his return to China. No
other traveler had yet written about India in such detail, and his
record provided very important information on the geography and
history of India and Central Asia in the seventh century, as well as
on the religions, cultures, customs, politics, and economics of that
time.

According to Hsüan-tsang's journals, apart from his own account
of his travels, one of his disciples, Hui-li, later wrote a ten-fascicle
biography of Hsüan-tsang called *Ta-tz'u-en-ssu San-tsang Fa-shih-
chuan,* which has proved very useful to scholars and historians.

Hsüan-tsang mentioned over one hundred and thirty countries
in his *Record of the Western Regions.* Although he did not visit them all,
he did record whatever he learned of neighboring countries wherever he went and described conditions in Central Asia and India in
surprisingly accurate detail. He also made notes on Buddhist pilgrimage sites and on each of Asoka's pillar edicts, some of which
we have yet to discover. Archaeologists have found Hsüan-tsang's
journal a valuable guide in planning excavations.

THE INDIAN YEARS AND   Hsüan-tsang did not resume his stud-
THE RETURN TO CHINA   ies until after he had passed through
                         Central Asia and reached India. He
stayed in the Kashmir region of northwestern India for a time,
studying both Hinayana treatises, such as the Great Commentary

(Abhidharma-mahavibhasha-shastra) and the Abhidharma Store-house Treatise (Abhidharmakosha-shastra), and logic from Hina-yana scholars there and also learning Indic grammar. The time in Kashmir was only in preparation for later studies, but he was ad-mired there for his linguistic ability and understanding of the texts.

Hsüan-tsang began serious study of Buddhist philosophy in Ma-thura, in central India, and at the great Nalanda monastery, to the east. Buddhist students from throughout India gathered at the monastic university of Nalanda to study the teachings of the Yoga-chara (Yoga Practice) and Madhyamika (Doctrine of the Middle Way) schools of middle-period Mahayana Buddhism under promi-nent scholars. Four thousand monks lived at the university, and a total of six thousand people, including secular researchers and non-Buddhist scholars, pursued studies there.

Hsüan-tsang's reputation preceded him, and when he reached Nalanda, more than a thousand monks and lay believers welcomed him. He was provided with living quarters, and then twenty monks escorted him to Shilabhadra, the university's foremost scholar. Shilabhadra, already one hundred and six years old at the time of Hsüan-tsang's arrival, was an authority on the doctrine of Con-sciousness Only (Vijnanavada), and his knowledge had earned him the sobriquet Treasury of the True Law.

After greeting Hsüan-tsang, Shilabhadra asked where he came from. Hsüan-tsang replied that he had come from China and wished to study the Treatise on the Stages of Yoga Practice (Yogachara-bhumi-shastra) and other works. On hearing this, Shilabhadra wept and asked his disciple Buddhabhadra (who was not related to the great translator of the same name) to tell a particular story.

Buddhabhadra said, "My teacher suffered from a serious illness three years ago. He had a sharp pain, as if he were being pierced by a sword, and, resolving to die, he stopped eating. In a dream, however, a golden being with the appearance of a shining buddha or bodhisattva appeared and said, 'You must not lay down your life. In a previous existence you were a king and abused many people. Because of this, you now suffer pain. A Chinese monk is now on his way to India to study, and he will be here in three years. You should teach him the Law so he can disseminate it in China. If you do this, your pain will disappear. I am [the Bodhisattva] Manjushri, and I am here to encourage you.' ''

When asked how long ago he had left his country, Hsüan-tsang replied that he had left three years earlier. Hsüan-tsang's departure was just as the dream had foretold, and Shilabhadra's attendants were astonished by the correspondence, while rejoicing at the prospect of his recovery. Shilabhadra installed the young Hsüan-tsang among the ten great people of virtue at the university and furnished him with four attendants and choice food. When Hsüan-tsang went out, he rode in a howdah borne by an elephant and was accompanied by thirty companions. He enjoyed cordial generosity from the beginning of his stay at Nalanda.

Hsüan-tsang asked Shilabhadra to lecture on the one-hundred-fascicle Yogacharabhumi-shastra, the basic Yogachara scripture, only a portion of which had been transmitted to China. Thus for fifteen months Shilabhadra gave a series of lectures to an audience of several thousand, but when he had finished, Hsüan-tsang asked the great teacher to lecture on the scripture again, which he did for another nine months.

Hsüan-tsang remained with Shilabhadra for five years, mastering the doctrines of the Yogachara school and also studying other Mahayana and Hinayana Buddhist doctrines. Although Hsüan-tsang wanted to study further, Shilabhadra persuaded him that he must return home as soon as possible to disseminate the teaching and gave him many sutras and philosophical texts.

Heeding his teacher's advice, Hsüan-tsang left Nalanda and went to various regions in the east, south, and west of India. In western India he studied the doctrine of the Sammatiya school of Hinayana Buddhism for two years. He spent another two years studying Mahayana teachings under the great scholar Vijitasena at the mountainside center at Yashtivana, where several hundred monks and lay believers attended lectures every day. Thus Hsüan-tsang absorbed all facets of Buddhism while in India.

At that time India was divided into many kingdoms, but since each was weak, there were few wars, and peace prevailed. Of all the kings, Harsha (606–47), in north India, was the most powerful. Harsha had established his capital at Kanyakubja (present-day Kannauj), on the middle reaches of the Ganges, and his influence extended into central and eastern India.

Although King Harsha protected various Indian religions, he was a devout Buddhist. Once every four years the benevolent Harsha held an assembly, lasting seventy-five days, in order to give away gold, silver, jewels, clothing, and grain to religious people, philosophers, and the needy. For Harsha this was a practical way to dispose of surplus goods stockpiled in his warehouses and to help his people at the same time.

Around the time that Hsüan-tsang was to return to China, King Harsha asked the rulers of various countries to gather for a religious assembly, to which he invited tens of thousands of *shramanas,* or ascetics, and Brahmans from all over India. Harsha erected large buildings in which to lodge his religious guests. At the time that Harsha convened his assembly, Hsüan-tsang was in remote Kamarupa (modern Assam), in northeastern India, where he had been invited to teach Buddhism to King Kumara. King Harsha had heard that Hsüan-tsang was in Kamarupa and sent a messenger to invite him to Kanyakubja. King Kumara himself accompanied Hsüan-tsang to Harsha's capital.

By that time Hsüan-tsang's reputation was excellent, and he was addressed by the respectful title Mahayanadeva (Great-Vehicle Deity). King Harsha had Hsüan-tsang debate publicly with the people of religion and the philosophers in attendance at the assembly. Such contests were often held in India in those days; and since generous awards of gold, silver, and jewels were presented to the winner, winning was a singular honor. The debates between Hsüan-tsang and his opponents lasted eighteen days, during which time Hsüan-tsang disproved his opponents' arguments, gaining the admiration of the foremost scholars in India.

With nothing left to study, Hsüan-tsang asked permission to return to his country. Various kings, including Harsha, attempted to detain him, but at last understanding his firm resolve, they gave him elephants and made handsome gifts of gold and silver so he could travel in comfort. He refused most of the gifts, accepting only a single elephant and feed for it, a little money for expenses, and provisions. The elephant was large enough to carry eight people and everything Hsüan-tsang had collected, including sutras and images of the Buddha.

With several companions Hsüan-tsang made his way north, receiving the hospitality and protection of the king in each country through which he passed and eventually arriving safely near the border of India. Hsüan-tsang crossed the upper reaches of the Indus River on his elephant, but he put some of the sutras and statues and the seeds of unusual flowers in a boat. As the boat left the shore, the wind began to rise. The boat almost sank, and fifty boxes of Hsüan-tsang's goods fell into the river.

The king of Kapisa, waiting on the opposite bank to greet Hsüan-tsang, surveyed the damage and asked if Hsüan-tsang had loaded Indian flower seeds on the boat. Hsüan-tsang replied that he had, and the king said, "Since ancient times a ship carrying Indian flower seeds has been sure to sink or be capsized to prevent such seeds from leaving India."

The sutras that fell overboard comprised the Tripitaka of the Kashyapiya school of Hinayana Buddhism. They were only a small part of the sutras Hsüan-tsang had collected, but since he had gone to the trouble of obtaining them, he delayed his journey for over fifty days in order to collect other copies of them.

When they were finally ready to resume their journey, Hsüan-tsang and his companions packed their goods on the elephant, ten mules, and four horses. They encountered many hardships in the Himalayas before crossing the Pamirs, making their way into Central Asia and at last reaching Khotan, where the elephant drowned in a river. Because Hsüan-tsang had no other means of transporting all the goods the elephant had carried, he sent a messenger with a letter to the T'ang emperor asking help.

It took about six months for the messenger to return, and during that time Hsüan-tsang lectured on Buddhism every day to the king, monks, and lay believers in Khotan. The T'ang emperor asked the king of Khotan to supply Hsüan-tsang with transportation, and his sutras and images of the Buddha were loaded on twenty horses. Hsüan-tsang's party passed through the Takla Makan Desert safely, and in January 645, they entered Ch'ang-an and were greeted by the viceroy, Fang Hsüan-ling. Hsüan-tsang was at that time around forty-six years old. The monk who had left the country without his emperor's permission was welcomed home with a procession befitting a triumphant general.

THE TRANSLATION YEARS   Hsüan-tsang had brought back with him 150 grains of the Buddha's relics, gold and silver images of the Buddha, 6 carved sandalwood images of the Buddha obtained in various parts of India, and some 658 sutras and related writings, which had been packed in 527 boxes to be carried by the twenty horses. The Mahayana works he had gathered consisted of 224 sutras and 192 treatises. He also had with him writings from a number of Hinayana schools: 15 Theravada sutras, *vinayas,* and treatises; 15 Mahasanghika sutras, *vinayas,* and treatises; 15 Sammatiya sutras, *vinayas,* and treatises; 22 Mahishasaka sutras, *vinayas,* and treatises; 17 Kashyapiya works; 42 Dharmaguptaka sutras, *vinayas,* and treatises; and 67 Sarvastivadin sutras, *vinayas,* and treatises. In addition, he had obtained 36 general works on logic and 13 works on grammar. Once he was safely home, Hsüan-tsang's greatest wish was to translate as many of these sutras as possible.

When Hsüan-tsang arrived at Ch'ang-an, the T'ang capital, Emperor T'ai Tsung was at Loyang, a little to the east. T'ai Tsung, engaged in consolidating his empire and extending Chinese suzerainty over countries to the west, was unable to travel to Ch'ang-an to see Hsüan-tsang at once, although he wanted to do so. About a month after Hsüan-tsang's return to China, Emperor T'ai Tsung invited him to the palace at Loyang. T'ai Tsung was eager to hear directly from Hsüan-tsang about Central Asia and India, and they spoke together frequently. Though T'ai Tsung, very impressed with Hsüan-tsang, pressed the monk to return to secular life and accept a government post, Hsüan-tsang firmly refused because he wanted to translate sutras.

Nonetheless, the two had much to talk about, and once when one of his expeditionary forces was about to depart, T'ai Tsung, feeling he still had not heard everything from Hsüan-tsang, proposed that they continue their discussion along the way. Hsüan-tsang begged off, pleading that a skin disease he had contracted on the long journey from India rendered him unfit for further travel. When Hsüan-tsang explained in detail his plan to translate the sutras, T'ai Tsung at last understood Hsüan-tsang's dedication and generously advised him to go to Hung-fu Temple in Ch'ang-an and work in the quiet meditation hall that had been built there for his late mother. Thus Hsüan-tsang's translation work was sanctioned by the emperor and was later to be supported financially by other members of the imperial family.

In March 645, Hsüan-tsang returned to Ch'ang-an from Loyang to prepare to translate at Hung-fu Temple. All the arrangements were made by the viceroy of Ch'ang-an, Fang Hsüan-ling, and high priests and able scholars were to be gathered from all over the country to collaborate on the translations. In June, the priests and scholars were selected, and capable assistants were chosen. The twelve high priests who examined the translations to ensure that the meaning was correct were Ling-juen, Wen-pei, Hui-kuei, Ming-yen, Fa-hsiang, P'u-hsien, Shen-fang, Tao-shen, Hsüan-chuang, Shen-t'ai, Ching-ming, and Tao-yin. The nine high priests responsible for editing and copying the translations were Ch'i-hsüan, Ming-chün, Pien-chi, Tao-hsüan, Ching-mai, Hsing-yu, Tao-chuo, Hui-li, and Hsüan-tse. The high priest Hsüan-ying confirmed the correctness of each Chinese ideogram in the translations, and the high priest Hsüan-mo verified the Sanskrit characters and sentences in the translations. Many other priests were summoned to participate in transcribing Hsüan-tsang's dictation, making fair copies, and so on.

In the first year, that extraordinary assembly produced a number of worthy translations, including the twenty-fascicle Bodhisattva Treasury Sutra (P'u-sa-tsang-ching), the one-fascicle Buddha-stage Sutra (Fo-ti-ching), and the one-fascicle Sutra of the Dharani of the Six Gates (Shanmukhi-dharani-sutra). The translation of the shortest sutra was completed in a single day.

In the following year, 646, Hsüan-tsang translated the sixteen-fascicle Exegesis on the Collection of the Mahayana Abhidharma (Mahayanabhidharma-samucchaya-vyakhya) and presented to the emperor the twelve-fascicle *Record of the Western Regions*. As we have noted, it is possible that the *Record of the Western Regions* was written expressly to give the emperor all the information Hsüan-tsang possessed on India and Central Asia because Hsüan-tsang feared that the emperor's constant interruptions with questions about the regions to the west would delay his translation work.

In the same year, Hsüan-tsang also began translating the one-hundred-fascicle Yogacharabhumi-shastra, which he completed in May 648. Since the main purpose of his journey to India had been to acquire, study, and then introduce into China the original manuscript of the Yogacharabhumi-shastra, he devoted about two years to making his careful translation.

In that same spring T'ai Tsung returned from his expedition and went to Yü-hua Palace, in the mountains remote from the capital, inviting Hsüan-tsang to join him so they could talk. The emperor still had not abandoned the idea of persuading Hsüan-tsang to leave his religious community and accept an imperial appointment, but through their discussions at this time, the emperor finally came to understand Buddhism and to develop faith. As expressions of his new-found faith he donated robes to high priests and permitted state-supported priests to be ordained throughout the country. In spite of his faith, however, he never left Hsüan-tsang to himself, so that he remained a hindrance to Hsüan-tsang's work.

When the emperor and Hsüan-tsang returned to Ch'ang-an from Yü-hua Palace, in October, the emperor built the retreat Hung-fa-yüan near his palace so he could always have Hsüan-tsang close by. During the day he invited Hsüan-tsang to the palace to talk, and Hsüan-tsang had to make his translations at night, after leaving the imperial palace. Because his work was being delayed, Hsüan-tsang began to worry.

In the same year the crown prince constructed in Ch'ang-an the temple Ta-tz'u-en, in which he included a wonderful building for translation work. Moreover, the prince appointed more people to assist with the translations in order to permit Hsüan-tsang to dedicate himself fully to translating sutras, although he was not actually able to do so because of the emperor's frequent interruptions. In April of the following year, 649, T'ai Tsung took Hsüan-tsang to Ts'uei-wei Palace, far from the capital. There Hsüan-tsang

gradually brought the emperor to a full understanding of the meaning of the Buddha's teachings, at which point the emperor regretted
having met Hsüan-tsang so late in life. From that time on, the emperor's health deteriorated, and he died at the palace in May. The
crown prince succeeded to the throne and styled himself Kao Tsung
(628–83).

After the protracted funeral observances for T'ai Tsung, Hsüan-
tsang returned to the Ta-tz'u-en temple the following year and
was at last able to devote himself solely to translating sutras. He
made it a rule to complete the portion he had planned to translate
each day, and if for some reason he could not finish it during the
day, he continued into the night until he had finished. For the many
monks who traveled great distances to learn from him, Hsüan-tsang
lectured twice each day and answered questions on the work in
progress.

In the course of his translation work, Hsüan-tsang made about
two hundred images of the Buddha, and he often conferred the sixteen bodhisattva precepts on government officials, lay believers,
and clerics, who came from throughout the country. He also met
frequently with the imperial family and people in government.
Despite his busy life, Hsüan-tsang continued to translate sutras in
his fifties with as much energy as ever and remained in good health.
In what spare time he had, he also translated writings on Indian
logic and non-Buddhist philosophies.

As they grew older, both Kao Tsung and his empress, Wu Hou
(625–705), came to respect Hsüan-tsang more deeply, and, like his
father before him, the emperor wanted Hsüan-tsang to be his con-
versational partner. In 657, Hsüan-tsang had very little time for
translation because of accompanying the emperor to the Loyang,
Chi-ts'uei, and Ming-te palaces, and he finally asked Kao Tsung
for permission to translate at the quiet Shao-lin Temple on Mount
Shao-shih, to the south of the capital.

It was not until autumn that Hsüan-tsang at last went to the
temple, but full-time work on translation did not last long, for in
January of the following year he had to follow Kao Tsung back to
Ch'ang-an. That fall a new temple, named Hsi-ming, was built in
Ch'ang-an for Hsüan-tsang, but a year later he asked the emperor

if he could stay at Yü-hua Palace, away from the capital, in order to translate the Great Perfection of Wisdom Sutra (Mahaprajna-paramita-sutra) as his final undertaking. He received permission, and on the first of the following January he began translating the six-hundred-fascicle Great Perfection of Wisdom Sutra.

This sutra is extremely long: its Sanskrit original contained 200,000 verses (some 6,400,000 characters), and the Chinese translation comprises three full volumes of the *Taishō Daizōkyō*. Of all the Chinese translations, the Great Perfection of Wisdom Sutra is by far the longest. The next longest is the two-hundred-fascicle Great Commentary (Abhidharma-mahavibhasha-shastra), also translated by Hsüan-tsang, but it fills only one volume of the *Taishō Daizōkyō*.

Hsüan-tsang was already about sixty-two when he began work on the Great Perfection of Wisdom Sutra, and he devoted all his remaining energy to its translation. In translating the sutra, he and his disciples relied on three different Sanskrit manuscripts that he had brought with him from India. Because the sutra was long and repetitious, his disciples felt it would not appeal to the literary tastes of the Chinese, and they suggested that it would be better to concentrate on the essence of the sutra and to eliminate repetitions, as Kumarajiva had done. Hsüan-tsang wondered if he should follow their advice and abridge the translation.

During the time he was considering this question, Hsüan-tsang began to suffer nightmares. In his dreams, he had to climb a steep and dangerous mountain road or was attacked by fierce animals. Whenever he had such dreams, he would wake in a cold sweat. He told his disciples about his dreams and at last decided to translate the sutra just as it was in the original rather than to delete the repetitive portions of it. In his dream that night, the Buddha and bodhisattvas appeared, emitting rays of light from between their eyebrows, and showed their great joy to him, and he reverenced them with incense and candles.

Hsüan-tsang then began his translation of the complete original, referring to the three versions of the manuscript when necessary. It is said that not only Hsüan-tsang but also the disciples assisting him with the translation had many auspicious dreams and saw favorable signs. For instance, at one point a mango tree outside the translation building blossomed out of season. Realizing that his life was drawing to an end, Hsüan-tsang committed himself to the translation, working both by day and at night, so that the six-hundred-fascicle translation was completed at the end of November 663. He had spent almost four years on the work.

On the day the translation was completed, Hsüan-tsang told his disciples with great joy, "This sutra has a deep bond with China. I came to Yü-hua Palace because of the power of the sutra. Earlier, in the capital, where I was occupied with unrelated tasks, I could do nothing, but now I have finally managed to finish the translation. This is due only to the divine protection of the buddhas and the help of heavenly beings. This Great Perfection of Wisdom Sutra is the scripture that brings peace to and protects the country and is the greatest treasure of human beings and heaven." It is said that at that moment the Great Perfection of Wisdom Sutra emitted rays of light, the heavens rained flowers, and everyone heard music and smelled extraordinary perfume.

All Japanese Buddhists, except followers of the Pure Land and Nichiren sects, generally recite the Heart of Wisdom Sutra (Prajnaparamita-hridaya-sutra), in which the essence of the Great Perfection of Wisdom Sutra is distilled into two hundred and sixty ideograms. This short sutra is also Hsüan-tsang's translation and expresses in the simplest form the basic Buddhist concept "All is void."

On the first day of the following year, 664, Hsüan-tsang's disciples pleaded with him to translate the Sutra of the Great Accumulation of Treasures (Maharatnakuta-sutra). After translating only a few lines, however, the illustrious translator realized that he no longer had the stamina to translate such a lengthy sutra, and he stopped. During the night of February 5 of that year, according to the lunar calendar, his extraordinary life came to an end.

SIX

The Chinese Court and Buddhism

PROTECTION AND
PERSECUTION

The period of the Northern and Southern dynasties (317–589) was one of the most tumultuous in Chinese history. During the years from 304 to 439 a number of non-Chinese and Chinese peoples, the Sixteen Kingdoms, vied for control of northern China. In 311 the nomadic Hsiung-nu destroyed Loyang, and in 316 they took Ch'ang-an. Refugees from the defeated northern court made their way as far south as Nanking, where they founded the Eastern Chin dynasty (317–420). The first of the Southern dynasties, the Eastern Chin was succeeded by the Liu Sung, Southern Ch'i, Liang, and Ch'en dynasties before the country was reunited by the first Sui emperor.

The Northern Wei dynasty (386–535), established by the non-Chinese T'o-pa tribe, labored to bring the Sixteen Kingdoms of northern China under control. By 439 the Northern Wei dynasty had destroyed the last of its rivals and unified northern China under a single court.

The Northern Wei flourished for about one hundred years afterward, but disagreements between court and army led to revolts that split the northern court once more: into the Eastern Wei dynasty (534–50) and the Western Wei dynasty (535–57). Through usurpations the Eastern Wei was succeeded by the Northern Ch'i (550–77), and the Western Wei by the Northern Chou (557–81).

These dynasties too were ruled by peoples of non-Chinese origin.

Although the Northern Chou conquered the Northern Ch'i in 577 and again unified northern China, the ineptitude of the Northern Chou emperor, court intrigues, and the court's persecution of Buddhism culminated in the usurpation of the Northern Chou throne in 581 by the court official who established the Sui dynasty (581–618). When the Sui conquered the Ch'en dynasty of southern China in 589, the country was finally reunified under a single emperor.

During the two hundred and seventy years of the Northern and Southern dynasties, Buddhism generally prospered, and Buddhist scriptures were translated in both northern and southern China. From the fourth century until the founding of the Sui dynasty, the Northern dynasties were ruled by non-Chinese invaders who came mostly from Central Asia. The people of Central Asia, having accepted Buddhism very early, had a deeper faith in it than did the Chinese, and they retained their faith and continued to practice their religion after assuming control of northern China. In China they supported monks, constructed Buddhist monasteries, and encouraged the translation of sutras.

In southern China, Prince Ching-ling (459–94) of the Southern Ch'i dynasty (479–502), who was a devout Buddhist, applied himself to research and composed thirty-six abridgments of well-known sutras in order to make the doctrines more comprehensible. Buddhism gradually prospered in southern China because Prince Ching-ling took a personal interest in a number of prominent monks, providing for and nurturing them, and those monks played an active role in supporting Buddhism during the succeeding Liang dynasty (502–57).

Liang-dynasty emperor Wu Ti (r. 502–49) and his son became ardent Buddhists and built temples and treated monks well, thus contributing to the increasing popularity of Buddhism. But around the end of the Liang dynasty and during the succeeding Ch'en dynasty (557–89), the political situation became ever more unstable in both northern and southern China, and in northern China, the Northern Chou emperor, also named Wu Ti (r. 561–77), attempted to sweep Buddhism from the country.

At that time all China was in turmoil, and the final period of the decay of Buddhism was thought to have arrived. Cleaving to the doctrine "one thousand years of the True Law, five hundred years of the Counterfeit Law," the Chinese believed the final period of Buddhism would come fifteen hundred years after the death of the Buddha. The year 573, the year preceding the start of Wu Ti's active persecution of Buddhism, was thought to be the fifteen hundredth year after the Buddha's death. But when China was reunified under the Sui dynasty, Buddhism was once again adopted to help maintain public peace and to ease the hearts of the people.

The first Sui emperor, Wen Ti (r. 581–604), an earnest Buddhist, set about both the construction of new Buddhist temples and the reconstruction of those that had been destroyed under Wu Ti. It is said that five hundred thousand men were ordained to the priesthood during Wen Ti's reign.

Wen Ti's decision to establish Buddhism as the country's principal religion had a great influence on Japan. Prince-Regent Shōtoku (574–622), who cultivated friendly relations with China, was so impressed with Wen Ti's support of Buddhism as China's national religion that he resolved to base Japan's government and material and spiritual culture on Buddhism. Shōtoku believed that, in order to elevate Japanese culture and to meet with China as an equal, it was necessary for Japan to adopt the Buddhist faith. He was himself a very devout Buddhist who had a correct understanding of the doctrines, and his great ambition was to unite Japan and bring all its people together in harmony through the spirit of the Buddha's Law.

Major efforts to suppress Buddhism in China, spanning several hundred years, are attributed to three emperors named Wu and one named Tsung: the Northern Wei emperor Wu Ti (r. 424–51), the Northern Chou emperor Wu Ti (r. 561–77), the T'ang emperor Wu-tsung (r. 840–47), and the Later Chou emperor Shih-tsung (r. 954–59). Of these emperors, only Wu Ti of Northern Wei and Wu Ti of Northern Chou concern us here.

The earliest persecution of Buddhism was undertaken by the Northern Wei emperor Wu Ti on the advice of his minister Ts'ui

Hao (381–450), a zealous Confucian, and of K'ou Ch'ien-chih (d. 448), an equally zealous Taoist. Ts'ui Hao's ambition was to establish a Confucian state ruled by indigenous Chinese rather than by the foreign "barbarians," while K'ou Ch'ien-chih envisioned a Taoist empire of which he would be the religious leader. Although their objectives differed, they joined forces against the foreign relion, Buddhism, which by then had spread throughout northern China.

In 446, the persecution of Buddhism crested when Emperor Wu Ti went to Ch'ang-an to put down a rebellion and found corruption widespread in the monasteries there. Wu Ti's discovery resulted in an edict decreeing both death for all Buddhist monks and the destruction of all Buddhist stupas and sutras. The monks were not seized immediately, however, so that most were able to escape, although many temples and sutras were destroyed. Both K'ou and Ts'ui died soon afterward, and the suppression of Buddhism gradually subsided. After Emperor Wu Ti's death in 454, Buddhism prospered once more.

The persecution of Buddhism carried out between 574 and 578 under the Northern Chou emperor Wu Ti, however, was more far-reaching and more devastating. For over a century the Taoists had declared that their founder, Lao-tzu, had gone from China to India, where he converted the people and became the Buddha, thereby rendering Shakyamuni both inferior in stature and later in time. The Buddhists had countered by postulating their own impossibly early date for the Buddha's birth in order to establish his position as clearly superior to that of Lao-tzu.

Descended from non-Chinese ancestors and eager to embrace all things Chinese, Wu Ti opposed Buddhism, which he regarded as a foreign influence. In 573, Emperor Wu Ti declared Confucianism the national religion, and in 574 he issued a decree proscribing Buddhism. The number of monks and nuns harassed and forced to quit their monasteries during his reign was said to total two million in the areas of Ch'ang-an and Loyang and three million in the region centering on Yeh, to the east.

Fearing that with the destruction of their temples and sutras the Law would be lost forever, Buddhists began engraving the sutras on rocks in order to preserve them and to transmit the Law to posterity. Thus the initial impetus for the carving of sutras in stone in China lay in the suppression of Buddhism during the Northern Chou dynasty.

The carved sutras that survive in northern China are engraved on polished stone and rock, on cavern walls, and on slate tablets. Among the sutras carved in the faces of great cliffs in Shantung and Shansi provinces in northern China are the Great Perfection of Wisdom Sutra, the Diamond Wisdom Sutra, the Flower Garland Sutra, the Great Collection of Sutras, the Shrimala Sutra, the Lotus Sutra, and the Sutra of the Great Decease. The practice of engraving sutras on rock, begun in a crucial period in the history of Chinese Buddhism, continued long after the cessation of persecution by the Northern Chou emperor Wu Ti.

The Vimalakirti Sutra and the Shrimala Sutra, among others, were carved in the caverns of Hu-shan, a mountain in the northern part of Honan Province. These carvings are well preserved, and from the dedicatory inscriptions we know they were engraved with the intention of handing the Law down to posterity.

The most immense carving project in China is found in Hopei Province at Mount Fang, which people refer to as the stone-sutra mountain. Near the beginning of the reign of the second Sui emperor, Yang Ti (r. 604–18), the Buddhist priest Ching-yüan (d. 639) called for preparations against possible future persecution and the decline of the Law. He had a chamber hewed in the living rock of the mountain and then engraved sutras on the walls. Before sealing the chamber, he also deposited in it slate tablets on both sides of which sutras had been carved.

Emperor Yang Ti's consort supported Ching-yüan's work, contributing generously toward it, and ordinary citizens also helped by donating money and goods. Ching-yüan completed only four chambers before his death, but construction was continued for generations afterward. By the early days of the T'ang dynasty (618–907) the stone cavern was composed of seven large chambers, in which such sutras as the seventy-fascicle Sutra of Stability in Contemplation of the True Law, the forty-fascicle Sutra of the Great Decease, the eighty-fascicle Flower Garland Sutra, and the first portion of the five-hundred-and-twenty-fascicle Great Perfection of Wisdom Sutra had been carved.

Eventually the balance of the Great Perfection of Wisdom Sutra was engraved, along with eighty-five other scriptural texts, including the one-hundred-and-twenty-fascicle Sutra of the Great Accumulation of Treasures, the Treatise on the Great Perfection of Wisdom Sutra, the Treatise on the Establishment of the Doctrine of Consciousness Only, and the Collection of the Mahayana Abhidharma. The great carving work continued for almost five hundred years, not ceasing until 1094. Even during the persecutions under Emperor Wu-tsung in 845 and Emperor Shih-tsung in 955, the Buddhists continued their patient labors to protect the sutras that form the foundation of the teachings of Shakyamuni Buddha and, with them, the Buddha's Law.

TRANSLATION SPONSORS   A number of the monks prominent during the period of the Northern and Southern dynasties (317–589) journeyed from India and Central Asia to northern China in the first half of the sixth century. It is said that in those days over ten thousand non-Chinese monks lived and worked in Ch'ang-an and Loyang. The most eminent translators of the early sixth century were Bodhiruchi (fl. ca. 508–35) and Ratnamati (fl. ca. 508), who had come from northern India, and Buddhashanta, who had come from central India. Of the three, Bodhiruchi was the most prolific, translating a total of thirty works in more than one hundred fascicles, including such important sutras as the Diamond Sutra (Vajracchedika-prajnaparamita-sutra), the Sutra of Profound and Mysterious Emancipation (Shen-mi chieh-t'o-ching), the Sutra of the Appearance of the Good Doctrine in [Sri] Lanka (Lankavatara-sutra), and the Sutra on Neither Increasing Nor Decreasing (Pu-tseng pu-chien-ching), as well as such important commentaries as the Treatise on the Sutra of the Ten Stages (Dashabhumika-sutra-shastra), the Treatise on the Lotus Sutra (Miao-fa lien-hua-ching-lun), and the Treatise on the Sutra of Eternal Life (Wu-liang-shou-ching-lun).

The leading translator of sutras in southern China was Paramartha (499–569), who was said to be the greatest of the four outstanding translators in sixth-century China. Paramartha was born in western India, where he mastered the Buddhist doctrines. In his late forties he traveled to China by a southern sea route, arriving in the Liang-dynasty capital Nanking in 546. Soon after his arrival, however, a rebellion arose. Unable to concentrate on his translations, Paramartha went in search of a more tranquil atmosphere in which to work but met only disappointment. At that time he almost gave up and returned to India, but because his disciples begged him to stay, he remained in China. Even after the Liang dynasty was succeeded by the Ch'en dynasty in 557, Paramartha was unable to establish a permanent residence. He spent a wretched life translating sutras while wandering from place to place, accompanied by a small band of disciples.

If Paramartha had been able to work under the salutary conditions enjoyed by Kumarajiva and Hsüan-tsang, he could have produced several times the number of translations that he actually did. However, during the period of the Liang and Ch'en dynasties he did translate such works as the Golden Light Sutra (Suvarnaprabhasa-sutra), the Diamond Sutra, the Sutra on Emancipation (Fo-shuo chieh-chieh-ching), the Treatise on the Seventeen Stages of Spiritual Development (Saptadasha-bhumika-shastra), the Treatise on the Buddha-nature (Fo-hsing-lun), and the Abhidharma Storehouse Treatise (Abhidharmakosha-shastra). Many of the treatises translated by Paramartha were commentaries previously unknown in China. Altogether Paramartha's translations amounted to over fifty works in more than one hundred and twenty fascicles. Although it was also said that he compiled more than twenty fascicles of commentaries for use in explaining and lecturing to his disciples about the sutras and Indic commentaries while translating them, those commentaries have all been lost. Many of Paramartha's translations were of middle-period Mahayana scriptures, and they are extremely important to modern-day research on Buddhist doctrines.

Since the distinguished translators (whether native-born Indian, Central Asian, or Chinese) possessed not only excellent knowledge and skills in both Chinese and Indic languages but also a full understanding of Buddhism, the task of translating the scriptures was not especially difficult for them.

One of the greatest translators preceding Kumarajiva was Dharmaraksha (231–308?). Of Central Asian ancestry, he was born in Tun-huang and may have been familiar with as many as thirty-six Indic and Central Asian languages. Dharmaraksha translated more than one hundred and fifty works in over three hundred fascicles with only a little assistance in transcription. In the sixth century, Paramartha also translated sutras into Chinese with little help.

At the time that Kumarajiva, Hsüan-tsang, and Amoghavajra were making translations—in the fifth, seventh, and eighth centuries —the situation was quite different. Translation work was carried out with government support, and translators had the assistance of as many scholars as they required.

For example, when Kumarajiva translated the Perfection of Wisdom Sutra in Twenty-five Thousand Lines at the beginning of the fifth century, he worked in the company of many other learned monks. Kumarajiva translated the original Sanskrit manuscript into Chinese and at the same time explained the meaning of the sutra. Emperor Yao Hsing himself held other translations of the same sutra (one made by Dharmaraksha in 286 and another made by Wu-ch'a-lo in 291), which Kumarajiva was using for comparison to ensure accuracy. About five hundred high priests and scholars, including Hui-kung, Seng-lüeh, Seng-ch'ien, Pao-tu, Hui-ching, Fa-ling, Tao-liu, Seng-jui, Tao-hui, Tao-piao, Tao-heng, and Tao-ts'ung, assembled detailed explanations for the new translations and refined the writing style. They then made fair copies of the manuscript, which they also proofread. This is but one example of the thoroughness of the government-sponsored translation bureaus.

When Hsüan-tsang made his one-hundred-fascicle translation of the Treatise on the Stages of Yoga Practice (Yogacharabhumi-shastra), he himself translated the Sanskrit manuscript into Chinese, a recorder transcribed the oral Chinese translation, a Sanskrit reader verified the correctness of the Sanskrit characters, an ideogram corrector confirmed the accuracy of the written Chinese, a meaning verifier carefully studied and discussed the meaning of the individual translated sentences, and a sentence arranger put them in the correct order. In addition, a revision supervisor oversaw the whole project. Because of this system Hsüan-tsang's translations were extremely accurate.

After Hsüan-tsang's time the government translation projects grew to even more imposing dimensions. In the Sung dynasty (960–1126), a nine-phase system was established in the state-supported translation bureau.

The first person concerned was the man who had brought the Sanskrit manuscript to China. He would read it aloud in Sanskrit, and a copyist transcribed not the Chinese translation but the Sanskrit as it was read from the original manuscript. (Copyists had also been employed in the time of Kumarajiva to transcribe the recitations of people who had memorized sutras in Sanskrit.) A translator then translated the Sanskrit into Chinese. (Since Kumarajiva and Hsüan-tsang had known both Sanskrit and Chinese and possessed original manuscripts, they immediately began to make their own translations.)

Next in the government system, the Chinese translation was verified by comparing it with the Sanskrit original. This task was delegated to men who made certain the meanings in the Sanskrit original had been correctly translated by the translator and to men who confirmed that the significance of its content had been correctly understood by the translator of the Chinese version.

Next, officials edited the Chinese translation so that it would read smoothly, embellishing it somewhat to make it appeal to Chinese readers. Kumarajiva's translations were widely read not only because the original meanings were fully conveyed in his translations but also because his translations were so polished that they were smooth and lyrical to read, as well as pleasant to hear.

Literary embellishment had been a tradition since the works of the Chinese translator Chih Ch'ien of the Wu dynasty (222–80). In the prose sections of sutras, Chih Ch'ien divided the sentences into meaningful phrases or units and attempted to translate individual phrases into the four- or six-syllable phrasing then regarded as the most elegant literary style in Chinese. Conforming to this literary convention, most of the prose in Kumarajiva's translations was rendered lyrically into phrases of four or six syllables. Such embellishment should not be accepted if it masks or distorts the correct meaning of the original, but Kumarajiva's works are ideal translations because he not only produced graceful prose but also conveyed the correct meaning of the original.

The sixth group of translation-bureau functionaries examined the sutra translations for correctness of content and for inconsistencies. The seventh group chanted the Sanskrit original, a ritual that was performed at the commencement of scriptural translation work or lectures on the Law. The chanting of sutras was probably not associated with scriptural translation in earlier times, but later, as translation work became formalized, the chanting became a necessary ritual.

Next, if the sutra being translated had ever been translated into Chinese before, officials referred to the earlier translation to assess the merits or demerits of the former translation and to discover any errors in content so that the new translation would be more reliable. (This practice was also followed by Kumarajiva and Hsüan-tsang, and, as it happens, Hsüan-tsang pointed out many errors in Paramartha's translations of sutras that Hsüan-tsang also translated.)

The final group supervised and inspected the whole translation project at each stage and was responsible for its smooth progress.

SUTRA CATALOGUES AND LATE TRANSLATIONS
With so many prolific translators at work, the number of Chinese versions of Buddhist sutras gradually increased, and sutra catalogues began to be compiled during the Northern and Southern dynasties period. As I mentioned on page 50, in northern China more than five hundred of the sutras that had been translated between the first century A.D. and the beginning of the fourth century were listed by Tao-an in his 374 compilation Tsung-li chung-ching mu-lu (Comprehensive Catalogue of the Sutras), which is generally known by its abbreviated title, An-lu (An's Catalogue).

Sutra catalogues also began to appear in southern China at about the same time. For example, the two-fascicle Chung-ching pieh-lu (Independent Catalogue of the Sutras) is thought to have been compiled during the Liu Sung dynasty (420–79), and Shih Wang-tsung completed his two-fascicle Chung-ching mu-lu (Catalogue of the Sutras) during the Southern Ch'i dynasty (479–502). During the subsequent Liang dynasty (502–57), Seng-chao compiled his four-fascicle Hua-lin fo-tien chung-ching mu-lu (Hua-lin Fo-tien Catalogue of the Sutras) in 515, and Pao-ch'ang completed his four-fascicle Liang-shih chung-ching mu-lu (Liang Dynasty Catalogue of the Sutras) in 518. Both of these catalogues have been lost, perhaps because they were so quickly displaced by the monumental fifteen-fascicle Ch'u san-tsang chi-chi (Collection of Records Concerning the Tripitaka), edited by Seng-yu (445–518), which was completed around 518.

The oldest extant sutra catalogue, the Ch'u san-tsang chi-chi is an outstanding work. With its record of more than two thousand works—over forty-five hundred fascicles of sutras—it is far more comprehensive than the two catalogues it superseded. In addition to its exhaustive lists of sutras, it contains introductory essays on the sutra translations and biographies of the early translators, making it the most complete and reliable early reference work known. Even today the Ch'u san-tsang chi-chi is indispensable to the study of ancient sutra translations and translators.

The cataloguing of sutras was not being neglected in northern China during this period. Li K'uo completed his one-fascicle Yüan-Wei chung-ching mu-lu (Northern Wei Dynasty Catalogue of the Sutras) between 532 and 534, and about forty years later, between 570 and 576, Fa-shang compiled his one-fascicle Kao-Ch'i chung-ching mu-lu (Northern Ch'i Dynasty Catalogue of the Sutras). Unfortunately, however, neither of these works has survived.

Because there was little communication between north and south during the Northern and Southern dynasties period, the translation of sutras and the compilation of catalogues were carried out independently in the two regions. However, when the country was reunited under the Sui dynasty and Buddhism became the state religion, the collecting of sutras from various districts in both northern and southern China was undertaken as a national endeavor. In order to facilitate the collecting of the sutras, a comprehensive catalogue of Chinese-language sutras was compiled by referring to all the catalogues that had appeared up to then in both northern and southern China.

That compendium, the seven-fascicle Chung-ching mu-lu (Catalogue of the Sutras), known to us as Fa-ching's Catalogue, was compiled in 594 by twenty great masters led by Fa-ching. The catalogue's systematic arrangement listed 2,257 works in 5,310 fascicles, believed to be the total number of sutras then extant in China. According to the compilers, these sutras were to be gathered from throughout the country so that an accurate catalogue could be prepared.

The new catalogue, the Sui-chung-ching mu-lu (Sui Dynasty Catalogue of the Sutras), which is generally called Yen Tsung's Catalogue, was completed eight years later, in 602. Compiled by a number of translators, including Yen Tsung, the five-fascicle catalogue recorded some 2,109 works in 5,059 fascicles, although only 688 works numbering 2,533 fascicles were actually then extant. Those extant sutras comprised only about sixty percent of the 1,076 extant works in 5,048 fascicles listed in the twenty-fascicle government-sponsored K'ai-yüan shih-chiao-lu (K'ai-yüan Era Buddhist Catalogue) compiled by Chih-sheng more than one hundred years later, in 730. The discrepancy between the two catalogues was the result not only of the addition of new translations but also of the rediscovery of translations long thought to have been lost.

During the interlude between the publication of Fa-ching's Catalogue, in 594, and Yen Tsung's Catalogue, in 602, a privately edited catalogue made its appearance. The Li-tai san-pao-chi (History of the Three Treasures in Successive Reigns and Catalogue of the Sutras), also known as Ch'ang-fang's Catalogue, was fairly massive, consisting of fifteen fascicles. The first three fascicles contained a Buddhist chronology, and the remaining twelve fascicles contained a record of sutras.

Fei Ch'ang-fang, the layman who compiled the catalogue in 597, had earlier participated in government-sponsored sutra translations. Ch'ang-fang had at one time been a monk but had been compelled to leave the priesthood sometime between 574 and 578, during the years that Buddhism was being persecuted under the Northern

Chou dynasty emperor Wu Ti. Grieved by the crushing blows dealt to Buddhism, Ch'ang-fang blamed Taoism for the decline of Buddhism, since it was Taoist influence in the imperial court that had led to the suppression of Buddhism. Ch'ang-fang compiled his catalogue in an effort to protect the Law and demonstrate that Buddhism was superior to Taoism.

Ch'ang-fang's Buddhist chronology was the first ever set down. It was not a credible scholarly work, however, since it was compiled in an effort to prove that Shakyamuni predated Lao-tzu (in order to disprove the Taoist claim that Lao-tzu had been reborn in India as Shakyamuni) and to attest to the great number of Buddhist sutras that had been translated into Chinese since the time of the Later Han emperor Ming Ti (r. A.D. 57–75). In his eagerness to protect the Law, Ch'ang-fang gave an unreasonably early date for the Buddha's death and inflated the number of translated sutras by citing some sutras two or three times. He also credited translators at random with sutras that earlier catalogues had listed as the work of unknown translators, and he changed the dates of some translations to make them appear older than they actually were.

For example, it is believed that when Buddhism was first introduced into China, during the reign of the Later Han emperor Ming Ti, the only sutra that had been translated into Chinese was the Sutra of Forty-two Chapters, but Fei Ch'ang-fang listed 5 works in 16 fascicles in addition to that sutra. He also inflated the number of translations attributed to An Shih-kao (d. ca. A.D. 170), the translator of the oldest extant Chinese translations. Ch'ang-fang credited An Shih-kao with 176 works, totaling 197 fascicles, although according to reliable early catalogues, he is believed to have translated only 34 works in 40 fascicles.

It is thought that Ch'ang-fang's indiscriminate altering of facts was known to scholars of his time but was tacitly accepted by them because of his sincere desire to protect the Law. Some fifty or sixty years later, in the time of Hsüan-tsang, the portraits of well over one hundred earlier translators were painted on a wall of the building in which Hsüan-tsang made his translations at the temple Ta-tz'u-en, in Ch'ang-an. When the titles of the translators' works were written above their portraits, the inflated attributions of Fei

Ch'ang-fang were recorded instead of the more reliable traditional attributions found in earlier catalogues.

After it appeared prominently in wall paintings in a structure built by the government for translators, the twaddle of the Li-tai san-pao-chi became accepted as fact, and the misrepresentations of the Li-tai san-pao-chi influenced later sutra catalogues. No doubt the catalogue based upon those wall paintings, the Ku-chin i-ching t'u-chi (Record of the Paintings of Ancient and Modern Sutra Translations), which was made by Ching-mai and is also known as Ching-mai's Catalogue, did much to help perpetuate the aberrations of the Li-tai san-pao-chi.

Even Chih-sheng's catalogue, the K'ai-yüan shih-chiao-lu, which became the standard reference and a model for later catalogues, contained fundamental errors because of Fei Ch'ang-fang's flights of fancy, although Chih-sheng did correct many of Ch'ang-fang's flagrant exaggerations. Because all later sutra catalogues, including those contained in the modern *Taishō Daizōkyō*, were based on the K'ai-yüan shih-chiao-lu, some of Fei Ch'ang-fang's falsifications have been perpetuated to the present day and are still accepted as fact by scholars.

A number of government-supported sutra catalogues also appeared during the period between the completion of Yen Tsung's Catalogue, in 602, and the completion of the K'ai-yüan shih-chiao-lu, in 730. The work of the eminent translator Hsüan-tsang had a direct effect on the compilation of catalogues, for within a relatively brief period his prodigious output greatly increased the number of Chinese-language scriptures, making new catalogues necessary. In 664, the year of Hsüan-tsang's death, the five-fascicle Chung-ching mu-lu (Catalogue of the Sutras) compiled by Ching-t'ai was completed. That work, known as Ching-t'ai's Catalogue, was a complete record of all Chinese-language sutras stored at the temple Ching-ai-ssu in Loyang. Ching-t'ai's Catalogue contained 816 entries, comprising 4,066 fascicles, and, in addition to the then-extant 741 works in 2,731 fascicles recorded in an earlier catalogue, it included Hsüan-tsang's recent translations, which numbered 75 works in 1,335 fascicles.

At the same time, in 664, Tao-hsüan (596–667), who had participated in Hsüan-tsang's translation work, edited the ten-fascicle Ta-T'ang nei-tien-lu (Catalogue of T'ang Dynasty Buddhist Sutras), a record of all the sutras stored at the temple Hsi-ming-ssu, which had been built in Ch'ang-an for Hsüan-tsang. In his catalogue, Tao-hsüan included more detailed information than was found in Ching-t'ai's work. Both catalogues, however, record even the number of sheets of paper required for copying individual sutras, which gives us a fairly accurate indication of the length of specific sutras.

After the death of Hsüan-tsang a number of monks from India continued adding new translations to the growing body of Chinese-language scripture. Following the death of the third T'ang emperor, Kao Tsung, in 683, his empress, Wu Hou, who was favorably disposed toward Buddhism, began exercising control of the imperial court. In 690 she usurped the throne in her own name, proclaiming herself empress and changing the dynastic name to Chou, a dynasty that survived only until 705, the year of her death.

Taoism and Buddhism had competed fiercely for supremacy during the early years of the T'ang dynasty (618–907), with Taoists going so far as to insist that since the imperial family and the founder of Taoism, Lao-tzu, shared the same surname—Li—they were descended from the same ancestors. Accepting this flimsy argument, the imperial family had officially favored Taoism over Buddhism, and it was through Taoist intrigues that Buddhism had suffered persecution in the reign of the first T'ang emperor, Kao Tsu (r. 618–26).

However, Empress Wu, who had been instructed in Buddhism by Hsüan-tsang and had long been a believer, actively supported the religion during her reign. In 695 Ming-shuan and more than twenty other monks compiled the comprehensive fifteen-fascicle Ta-Chou k'an-ting chung-ching mu-lu (Chou Dynasty Catalogue of the Sutras) in order to bring the imposing quality and quantity of Chinese-language scriptures to the attention of the public. But this catalogue, which included works translated after the death of Hsüan-tsang, was on the whole rather slipshod and not entirely accurate.

After the publication of the Ta-Chou k'an-ting chung-ching mu-lu, excellent translations continued to appear from the hands of such Indian monks as Shikshananda (652–710), Bodhiruchi (672–727), Vajrabodhi (671–741), and Shubhakarasimha (637–735). Shiksha-nanda is remembered for his translation of the eighty-fascicle Flower Garland Sutra (Avatamsaka-sutra) and of the seven-fascicle Sutra of the Appearance of the Good Doctrine in [Sri] Lanka (Lankavatara-sutra). Bodhiruchi, who was not related to the early-sixth-century translator of the same name, translated the Sutra of the Great Accumulation of Treasures (Maharatnakuta-sutra), which Hsüan-tsang had been unable to complete before his death. Vajrabodhi, Shubhakarasimha, and Amoghavajra (705–74) are noted for introducing and translating Esoteric Buddhist sutras. Shubhakarasimha, for example, translated such important works as the seven-fascicle Great Sun Sutra (Mahavairochana-sutra), a basic text of the Tantric school, and the three-fascicle Sutra of Good Ac-complishment (Susiddhikara-sutra).

Also active at about this time was the Chinese monk I-ching (635–713), who translated the many sutras he had brought back to China from India. By the age of fifteen he had already decided to journey to India in order to experience at first hand the discipline and environment described earlier by Hsüan-tsang. With scores of other monks I-ching left China in 671, taking a southern sea route to India. I-ching was the only member of the group to reach India, since his companions elected to remain in Java, Sumatra, and other island countries along the way. I-ching visited many holy places in India and studied Buddhism at the great monastery at Nalanda before finally returning to China in 695 with almost four hundred sutras, commentaries, and other works. Of the writings he took home with him, he eventually translated forty-six works, consisting of two hundred and thirty fascicles.

One of I-ching's most important translations is the one-hundred-and-seventy-odd-fascicle Vinaya-pitaka of the Mulasarvastivadin school, containing Indian Buddhist injunctions on keeping the pre-cepts, which he felt was most important for him to obtain in India. He also translated the ten-fascicle Sutra of the Most Honored King (Suvarnaprabhasottamaraja-sutra), which has been very highly re-garded in Japan, as well as a number of philosophical works.

I-ching also wrote several works still known to us. His two-fascicle *Biographies of Eminent T'ang Dynasty Monks Who Sought the Dharma in the Western Regions* (*Ta-T'ang hsi-yü ch'iu-fa kao-seng-chuan*) is a record of the sixty-odd Chinese and Korean monks who traveled to India. His four-fascicle *Record of the Buddhist Kingdoms in the Southern Archipelago* (*Nan-hai chi-kuei nei-fa-chuan*) records the practices and customs of monks at the monastery at Nalanda. Since the state of Indian Buddhism at that time is described in I-ching's preface to this work, scholars of Buddhism value it as highly as the journals of Fa-hsien and Hsüan-tsang.

Because such a great number of translations were produced in China during the seventy years following Hsüan-tsang's death, Chih-sheng edited his monumental catalogue in 730. The twenty-fascicle K'ai-yüan shih-chiao-lu (K'ai-yüan Era Buddhist Catalogue), which listed 1,076 then-extant works totaling 5,048 fascicles, is still considered the definitive catalogue of the time. Chih-sheng estimated that 1,148 works in 1,980 fascicles had already been lost by his time. Although the K'ai-yüan shih-chiao-lu had minor faults, its organization was perfect, and it later served as a model for other catalogues.

During the seventy years after the compilation of the K'ai-yüan shih-chiao-lu, additional translations were made by Dharmachandra, Amoghavajra, and Prajna, among others, leading Yüan-chao to compile a new catalogue in 800. The 30-fascicle Chen-yüan hsin-ting shih-chiao mu-lu (Chen-yüan Era Buddhist Catalogue) listed 5,390 fascicles of then-extant works, 342 fascicles more than listed in Chih-sheng's catalogue. Yüan-chao's catalogue recorded some 110 Esoteric Buddhist scriptures in 143 fascicles, including the 3-fascicle Diamond Peak Sutra (Vajrashekhara-sutra) rendered by the great translator and master of Esoteric Buddhism Amoghavajra.

A native of Sri Lanka, Amoghavajra went to China and became a disciple of Vajrabodhi at the age of fourteen and was ordained at the Loyang temple Kuang-fu-ssu at the age of twenty. When Vajrabodhi died in 741, Amoghavajra carried out his teacher's wishes and left for India and Sri Lanka. Amoghavajra, familiar with Indic languages, was also well versed in Chinese after having lived in China more than twenty years.

At the time of Amoghavajra's journey, Esoteric Buddhism was flourishing at the Nalanda monastery and in Sri Lanka, where numerous Esoteric Buddhist sutras were preserved. Amoghavajra studied Esoteric Buddhism in Sri Lanka for three years, winning the devotion of the king there, and then went on to India, where he visited many holy sites. When he returned to China in 746 he took with him a variety of goods, including sutras and ritual implements. During the following thirty years, Amoghavajra gained the respect and devotion of the T'ang imperial house and served as National Preceptor to three successive emperors: Hsüan Tsung (r. 713–55), Su Tsung (r. 756–62), and Tai Tsung (r. 763–79).

SEVEN

Scriptural Controversy

AUTHORIZED SCRIPTURE   From earliest times Buddhists were anxious to preserve and protect the sutras, in which are recorded the teachings of Shakyamuni, the historical Buddha. That desire was the impetus for the convening of the Buddhist councils, which settled questions of orthodoxy. In the beginning the Buddhist councils, charged with compiling sutras and correctly transmitting the teachings of the Buddha, were usually convened when disputes among different schools of Buddhism had reached the crisis level and schism threatened to sunder the religion. According to traditional Southern Buddhist reckoning, six Buddhist councils have been convened in the twenty-five centuries since the Buddha's death.

As I mentioned in chapter one, after Shakyamuni's death there were some among his disciples who asserted that with the Buddha gone they were no longer required to observe the burdensome Buddhist precepts and that they were free to order their monastic lives as they wished. It was to silence the claims of such misguided monks that five hundred *arhats,* or enlightened disciples, assembled near Rajagriha shortly after Shakyamuni's death and at that First Buddhist Council together compiled and edited the historical Buddha's teachings.

The Second Buddhist Council met at Vesali (Vaishali) around 380 B.C., one hundred years after the Buddha's death, because of a dispute between liberal Buddhists, who favored a broad interpretation of the precepts established by the Buddha, and conservative Buddhists, who adhered rigidly to traditional orthodoxy. The conservatives summoned seven hundred *arhats* to the Second Council in order to hand down the traditional teachings unchanged. The liberals, however, called a rival council and edited their own sutras. In time the conservatives became known as the Theravada school, and the liberals became known as the Mahasanghika school.

Roughly one hundred years after the Second Buddhist Council the great emperor Asoka (ca. 274–ca. 236 B.C.), a devout Theravada Buddhist, adopted the Buddha's Law as his guide in ruling a unified India. Although he protected other religions as well, Emperor Asoka supported and encouraged belief in Buddhism, and it is said that he erected eighty-four thousand stupas in and beyond India to house fragments of the Buddha's relics. Many people took advantage of Asoka's high regard for Buddhism and joined the Buddhist Order not out of genuine faith but simply as a means of securing a livelihood. The influence of such "believers" eventually led to dissent within the Buddhist Order and gave rise to manifold heretical teachings.

To eliminate confusion and establish orthodox Buddhist teachings, one thousand *arhats* assembled at Pataliputra (present-day Patna) to participate in the Third Buddhist Council, some two hundred and thirty years after the Buddha's death. Under the aegis of Emperor Asoka, the sutras compiled at that council were transmitted to Sri Lanka by Theravada emissaries, including Asoka's son Mahinda. Those teachings, which gave birth to Southern (or Theravada) Buddhism as we know it today, were embraced by the people and successive rulers of Sri Lanka. By the fifth century A.D., some seven or eight hundred years after its introduction into Sri Lanka, Southern Buddhism had been carried to Burma, Thailand, and Cambodia. However, Theravada was not the only form of Buddhism conveyed to Sri Lanka. Other Hinayana sects, as well as various Mahayana teachings, were also imported, and even Vajrayana (Diamond Vehicle) teachings were disseminated for a time.

As early as the first century B.C. conflict arose in Sri Lanka between the Mahavihara (Great Monastery) and Abhayagiri-vihara

(Mount Fearlessness Monastery) sects of Buddhism, culminating in the oppression of the conservative Mahavihara sect by the liberal Abhayagiri-vihara sect in the fourth century A.D. Even though the Abhayagiri-vihara sect alone prospered during the ensuing five or six centuries, the Mahavihara sect faithfully continued to preserve and protect its own teachings.

In the twelfth century Sri Lanka's greatest king, Parakrama Bahu I (r. 1153–86), ascended the throne. Uniting the island country under a single ruler, he did much to reform the economy of the country and make its might felt abroad. Parakrama Bahu, who also took steps to improve discipline in the Buddhist Order, discovered that the precepts, study, and practice of the Abhayagiri-vihara sect had become corrupt. Though the sect appeared to be flourishing, its priests proved to be taking orders merely to assure themselves of a living. As a result of these revelations Parakrama Bahu sanctioned the untarnished Mahavihara sect as the national religion.

In conjunction with a reformation of discipline in the Buddhist Order, the Mahavihara sect convened the Fourth Buddhist Council and compiled and edited both the sutras traditionally regarded as genuine and the commentaries of the one thousand *arhats* in attendance. Today's Southern Buddhist sutras and commentaries are the products of that council.

In the sixteenth century European traders in search of profit began making regular journeys to India and Southeast and East Asia, and they were quickly followed by eager companies of Christian missionaries. By the mid-nineteenth century the Indian subcontinent was effectively under British control, and by the end of 1885 three closely spaced wars had brought Burma into the British Empire.

Long before the British conquered Burma, the Burmese had feared for the future of their culture under British rule. In 1868 Buddhist groups, apprehensive of the destruction of Buddhism under the British, convened a council at Mandalay, then the Burmese capital, in order to preserve true Buddhism for posterity. As a result of this Fifth Buddhist Council, which met for four years altogether, Buddhists engraved all the Pali sutras on stone tablets and built four hundred and fifty pagodas in which to house them. Those sutra stones still survive, in perfect condition.

The Sixth Buddhist Council, which sat for three years, was convened in 1954 in Rangoon, the modern capital of Burma. Participants in that council included Buddhist scholars from throughout the Southern Buddhist countries. Following the Sixth Council, the Pali canon and commentaries on the scriptures were published in Burmese script on the twenty-five hundredth anniversary of Shakyamuni Buddha's death (according to Southern Buddhist reckoning), apparently to commemorate both the Buddha's death and the postwar independence of the countries in the region.

GENUINE AND SPURIOUS SUTRAS — As we have already noted, extant Buddhist scriptures—even some of the Agama sutras, the oldest of extant scriptures—contain discourses apart from the sermons preached by the Buddha himself. Some scriptures include the discourses of ordained or lay followers of the Buddha; some contain discourses by Brahma or Indra, or by various demons; and some record incidents that occurred after the Buddha's death. Moreover, a number of sutras that are assumed to have been uttered by the Buddha have undergone considerable change during several hundred years of oral transmission.

Some of the extant scriptures were already being recited by disciples during the Buddha's lifetime, for instance, the Meaningful Chapter (Atthakavagga), which is one of the oldest of all surviving sutras. The Meaningful Chapter is recorded in the Suttanipata (Collection of Discourses), the famous collection of sutras that forms part of the Agama sutras, and it is also quoted in various Mahayana and Hinayana sutras and commentaries on sutras. For example, the following story about that sutra is found in both the Udana (Solemn Utterances of the Buddha) and the Vinaya-pitaka (Ordinance Basket).

Maha-Kacchayana, who became one of the chief disciples of the Buddha and was recognized as the foremost interpreter of the Buddha's teachings, was the son of a minister of the powerful kingdom of Avanti, in western India. In time word that Shakyamuni was a great man of religion reached Avanti; and the king, wishing to hear Shakyamuni's teachings, sent seven retainers, including Maha-Kacchayana, to Magadha to invite him to Avanti. But when Maha-Kacchayana heard Shakyamuni preach, he was so moved that he immediately requested permission to become a monk.

In his zeal, Maha-Kacchayana—who attained the eminent enlightenment of an *arhat* through diligent practice—forgot that he had been commanded to invite Shakyamuni to Avanti. Although Maha-Kacchayana did at last recall and perform his mission, it seems that Shakyamuni never journeyed to Avanti, and it has been assumed that Shakyamuni sent the enlightened Maha-Kacchayana to western India in his stead. In any event, Maha-Kacchayana eventually returned to Avanti, where he converted the king and numerous less exalted people to Buddhism. As a result of Maha-Kacchayana's dedicated teaching efforts, other western kingdoms also embraced Buddhism, and Ujjeni, the capital of Avanti, became one of the major centers of Buddhism in western India after Shakyamuni's death.

Maha-Kacchayana did not find it easy to pursue his teaching ministry alone in Avanti. In particular he was hindered by the fact that, although a single monk could confer the simple precepts on new lay believers, ten monks were required in order to ordain monks. Maha-Kacchayana's young attendant in Avanti, Sona, had become a lay believer and was eager to receive the precepts of a monk, but it was three years before Maha-Kacchayana was able to summon the necessary additional monks from various places and confer the monk's precepts on Sona.

Sona, earnest and steadfast in his practice of the monk's disciplines, cherished the desire to meet with Shakyamuni as a disciple. When Sona told Maha-Kacchayana of his longing, the elder monk readily gave Sona permission to leave Avanti and entrusted him with a message to be delivered to Shakyamuni.

Sona journeyed to northern India to the Jetavana Monastery at Savatthi, the capital of Kosala, where he met Shakyamuni and delivered Maha-Kacchayana's message. Delighted by Sona, Shakyamuni told his great disciple Ananda to prepare a bed for the young monk in Shakyamuni's own room. Sona practiced meditation with Shakyamuni until quite late that night before retiring. On the following morning Shakyamuni asked Sona if he was disposed to preach the Law, and Sona replied that he was. Sona then preached to the assembled monks the entire sixteen stanzas of the Atthakavagga (Meaningful Chapter) and was praised warmly by Shakyamuni.

This story, found in two different sources, makes it clear that the two-hundred-and-ten-verse Atthakavagga—compiled from Shakyamuni's sermons—was already known during Shakyamuni's lifetime and was being learned by his disciples. Another sutra as old as the Atthakavagga is the Parayanavagga (Chapter on the Way to the Other Shore), which is also recorded in the Suttanipata. Because both of these sutras are often quoted or mentioned in other sutras—especially in such ancient sutras as the Samyukta-agama (Kindred Sayings) and the Ekottara-agama (Gradual Sayings)—we know that they are both genuine and the oldest among extant Buddhist scriptures.

Yet even these venerable sutras were most likely not preached by the Buddha in exactly the form in which they have been handed down to us, and still less do the Mahayana scriptures, composed much later, contain the Buddha's exact words. Nonetheless, both primitive sutras and Mahayana sutras are considered Shakyamuni's genuine teaching because they embody the true spirit of Buddhism. Thus, whether primitive or Mahayana, all the sutras composed in Indic languages and later translated into Chinese have been revered as genuine records of the Buddha's word.

In Chinese Buddhism, however, there appeared sutras that were not translations into Chinese but that actually originated in China. Among those sutras there was one kind that was accepted as genuine and another that was deemed spurious.

It is thought that the "genuine" Chinese sutras were compiled because the sutras translated from Indic languages often did not accord with Chinese thought or with Chinese understanding of Buddhism. Nor could the Chinese find in those translated sutras what they considered ideal ways of preaching Buddhism. Hence the "genuine" Chinese sutras were compiled in an effort to make Buddhism more comprehensible to the people of the time. Like their Indian counterparts, the Chinese authors are unknown, but they must have composed their sutras with the intention of disseminating the teachings of Buddhism more correctly.

Those sutras, therefore, are in complete harmony with the fundamental spirit of Buddhism. They contain no equivocal teachings when examined in the light of the three great truths known as the Seal of the Three Laws—all things and phenomena in the universe constantly change ("All things are impermanent"); all things in the universe exist in interrelationship with one another ("Nothing has an ego"); and the ultimate freedom is to be rid of greed, aggression, and self-delusion ("Nirvana is quiescence"). Undoubtedly certain Buddhists were aware that these sutras had not been translated from Indic originals, but they did not condemn the works as spurious because they recognized the importance of making Buddhism more understandable to the populace. These sutras, which were widely circulated, were considered to be as genuine as those translated from Indic originals, and a surprising number of them became the subjects of commentaries or interpretations by distinguished monks and by the founders of various Chinese Buddhist sects.

Numbered among the "genuine" sutras produced in China are the Sutra of the Perfect Net (Fan-wang-ching) and the Sutra on a Bodhisattva's Original Action (P'u-sa ying-luo pen-yeh-ching), which together set forth a system of discipline and spiritual attainment of bodhisattvas that had not yet been codified even in India. Other original Chinese sutras include the Sutra of Meditation on Amitabha Buddha (Kuan wu-liang-shou-ching), one of the three scriptures of the Pure Land sect of Buddhism; the Sutra of Innumerable Meanings (Wu-liang-i-ching), traditionally known as the "opening sutra" of the Threefold Lotus Sutra; and the Sutra of Diamond Meditation (Chin-kang san-mei-ching), the Sutra of Perfect Enlightenment (Yüan-chüeh-ching), and the Heroic Marching Sutra (Shou-leng-yen-ching), all scriptures associated with Zen Buddhism. Chinese and Japanese Buddhists have looked on the Sutra of the Perfect Net as the principal sutra expounding both Ma-

hayana precepts and the training and spiritual attainment of bodhisattvas, and those Buddhists have esteemed that sutra as a translation by Kumarajiva from an Indic original.

All the Chinese sutras accepted as genuine were included in the
complete Chinese canon and survive to the present day in such
works as the *Taishō Daizōkyō*. Although since the late nineteenth
century Japanese scholars of Buddhism have pointed out that those
sutras are not translations from Indic scriptures but are Chinese
compositions, they have not denied the doctrinal validity of the
sutras.

The spurious sutras produced in China are readily distinguishable
from the "genuine" sutras and fall into four rough categories: (1)
sutras expounded by someone in the throes of some sort of fanatic
possession claiming to reveal the word of the Buddha, (2) sutras
expounded in order to take advantage of Buddhism for some
purpose, (3) sutras created in order to palm folk beliefs off as the
word of the Buddha, and (4) sutras that were merely simplified
abridgments of the more complex, repetitive translated sutras.

Because the spurious sutras either fail to encompass the true spirit
of Buddhism or include statements patently inconsistent with the
Buddha's teaching, on the whole they are manifestly not genuine
sutras. Although a loose interpretation might admit the abridged
sutras as the teaching of the Buddha, their use was forbidden because they garbled the Buddha's words and corrupted the Indic-
language originals.

In the early days of translating sutras from Indic languages,
spurious sutras may have been fabricated to interpret Buddhism in
the terms of the philosophy of the fifth-century B.C. founder of
Taoism, Lao-tzu, and of the revered late-fourth- and early-third-
century B.C. Taoist writer Chuang-tzu. Such fabrication seems to
have been effected in good faith in order to fuse Buddhism with
Taoism in the *ko-i* form of Buddhism I mentioned on page 48; however, since the resulting sutras distorted the Buddha's teachings,
they must be declared spurious. But we should bear in mind that
spurious sutras are found throughout the ages in China.

As we have seen, extant sutras in China were compiled in a
number of catalogues of the complete Chinese canon, or Tripi-

taka. Some ten-odd catalogues survive to the present day to inform us on Chinese Buddhist scripture. While the catalogues list and categorize all genuine sutras (of both Indic and Chinese origin), all the spurious sutras were catalogued separately in order to prevent their being mistaken for genuine sutras, and as an added precaution a notice was included to the effect that the spurious sutras must not be relied upon.

Let us look briefly at an example of spurious sutras expounded in the throes of religious fervor. A nun named Seng-fa (b. 489), who came of a scholarly family, had since childhood indulged in ecstatic meditation while seated quietly with her eyes closed, and when in such rapture she fluently recited various sutras as if she had long been acquainted with them. When people asked Seng-fa to repeat sutras they had heard and copied down weeks earlier, she changed not a word. People thought this performance marvelous, and her ability became so widely known that the enthusiastic Buddhist founder of the Liang dynasty, Emperor Wu Ti (r. 502–49), heard of her and summoned her to his palace to recite for him.

Between the ages of nine and thirteen, in her transports Seng-fa had recited numerous spurious sutras (some at one time accepted as "genuine" and some with the same titles as works translated from Indic languages)—including the Sutra of the Treasure Summit (Pao-ting-ching), the Pure Land Sutra (Ching-t'u-ching), the Sutra of the True Summit (Cheng-ting-ching), the Lotus Sutra (Fa-hua-ching), the Sutra of the Herbs (Yao-ts'ao-ching), and the Sutra of Attaining Perfect Wisdom (Pan-jo te-ching). In 505, at the age of sixteen, Seng-fa recited for Emperor Wu Ti. Seng-fa's accomplishments added to the Chinese canon some twenty-one spurious sutras comprising thirty-five fascicles.

Let us now turn to examples of abridged sutras. It is said the Southern Ch'i prince Ching-ling (459–94), who was devoted to Buddhism and supported and encouraged many Buddhist scholars, himself compiled thirty-six abridged sutras in one hundred and twenty-two fascicles so that his father's subjects could easily read and understand them. Among his works were a fourteen-fascicle Abridged Flower Garland Sutra (Ch'ao hua-yen-ching); a twelve-fascicle Abridged Great Collection of Sutras (Ch'ao fang-teng ta-chi-ching); a twelve-fascicle Abridged Sutra of a Bodhisattva's Spiritual States (Ch'ao p'u-sa-ti-ching); a one-fascicle Abridged Story of the Bodhisattva Medicine King (Ch'ao fa-hua yao-wang-p'in), chapter twenty-three of the Lotus Sutra; and a single-fascicle Abridged Sutra of Meditation on the Bodhisattva Universal Virtue (Ch'ao p'u-hsien kuan-ch'an hui-fa), the "closing sutra" of the Threefold Lotus Sutra. Although these abridgments were originally made in an honest desire to disseminate Buddhism, they nonetheless had to be discredited as spurious sutras, because they could so easily have been confounded with the genuine translations of Indic sutras.

The A.D. 730 catalogue K'ai-yüan shih-chiao-lu (K'ai-yüan Era Buddhist Catalogue) lists some 392 sutras in 1,055 fascicles as spurious and another 14 works in 19 fascicles as being of doubtful authenticity. That catalogue also includes a detailed description of each of these sutras. When we compare the number of spurious sutras with the number of genuine translated sutras (which comprise 1,076 works in 5,048 fascicles), it is obvious that there are a great many more genuine sutras. However, since the spurious sutras total well over one-third the number and one-fifth the fascicles of the genuine sutras, it is apparent that many spurious sutras were in common use, distorting the Buddha's Law.

Having considered the differences between genuine and spurious sutras, I should like to mention briefly an original concept of the great Zen master Dōgen (1200–1253), founder of the Sōtō Zen sect of Japanese Buddhism. During the Southern Sung dynasty (1127–1279), Dōgen went to China seeking the true Law of the Buddha, and at the age of twenty-six he finally found an excellent teacher, Ju-ching (1163–1228).

Dōgen devoted himself to discipline day and night and at the same time took questions to his teacher without hesitation. Once he went to his teacher and commented that the Heroic Marching Sutra and the Sutra of Perfect Enlightenment, which were frequently read by lay Buddhists, were considered to be sutras that expressed the essence of Buddhism as conveyed from India. In studying those sutras, however, Dōgen found that both of them contained questionable material and that their content was both different from and inferior to that of Mahayana sutras in general, though they bore some similarities to the philosophies of the six great non-Buddhist teachers and other sages of Shakyamuni's time. When asked his opinion, Ju-ching agreed with Dōgen, saying that the Heroic Marching Sutra had long been suspected of being a spurious sutra and the Sutra of Perfect Enlightenment was composed in the same style.

Obviously the young Dōgen had a superb eye that enabled him to see through the falsity of the two sutras. In the T'ang dynasty (618–907), Tsung-mi (780–841), a distinguished Zen scholar and the fifth patriarch of the Hua-yen (Flower Garland) sect, wrote a number of commentaries on the Sutra of Perfect Enlightenment, saying that it best stated the theory and practice of Buddhism. Hence Zen Buddhists of the Sung (960–1126) and Southern Sung dynasties frequently relied on the Sutra of Perfect Enlightenment and the Heroic Marching Sutra, quoting liberally from them.

According to Dōgen, if a person who had truly attained enlightenment quoted from these spurious sutras in order to preach true Buddhism, that quotation could be considered the true teaching of the Buddha. In Dōgen's opinion, not only are the Buddhist scriptures and even secular writings considered sutras by the person who has attained true enlightenment, but also everything in nature —the sun, moon, stars, mountains, water, trees, stones—is considered a sutra in itself.

This idea is voiced many times in Dōgen's principal work, *Shōbō-genzō*, or *The Eye Storehouse of the True Law*. For example, in the section "On Buddhist Sutras" Dōgen says: "In seeing the peach blossoms, there is enlightenment to the Way; in hearing the echo of bamboo there is enlightenment to the Way; and in seeing the morning star, enlightenment to the Way. The sutras [the world of nature] help people of wisdom to grow. . . . Such sutras are the whole world in ten directions, which is nothing but sutras. . . . We receive sutras from mountains, rivers, and the great earth, and we preach them. We receive sutras from the sun, moon, stars, and heavenly bodies, and we preach them."

Dōgen believed that if our eyes are open we can read or hear sutras in our everyday affairs and in nature. If the meaning of the sutras and of the Buddha's preaching is interpreted as broadly as possible, we are able to hear the Buddha's preaching in everything around us. In other words, the Buddha is in everything around us.

THE AUTHENTICITY OF   Because it was more than three or four
MAHAYANA SUTRAS   centuries after the Buddha's death that
                        the Agama sutras, which we call prim-
itive sutras, were compiled in the form in which we know them today, strictly speaking they cannot be called the Buddha's direct
teachings. The Mahayana sutras were composed even later than
the Agama sutras and certainly cannot be considered the Buddha's
direct words. Historically, however, the primitive sutras did arise
from the Buddha's preachings, although the Mahayana sutras did
not begin to appear until some five centuries after the Buddha's
death.

Mahayana sutras often mention demons, in the guise of monks,
who slander Mahayana, saying it is not the Buddha's teaching.
Those demons may represent people who believed in Hinayana
Buddhism and thus recognized only the primitive sutras as the word
of the Buddha. For example, the Perfection of Wisdom Sutra in
Twenty-five Thousand Lines, an early Mahayana sutra translated
by Kumarajiva, says, "A demon disguising himself as a monk and
wearing [a Buddhist monk's] robes came to a bodhisattva and said,
'What you have heard is not the Buddha's teaching but is all
embellished and adulterated. What I shall teach you is the Buddha's
true teaching.' "

Elsewhere it is recorded that a demon confronted a bodhisattva,
saying, "The perfect enlightenment of which you have heard is
false: it is not that which the Buddha preached. You should
abandon this vow [of Mahayana]. You must not fall into evil paths
through prolonged suffering or uneasiness."

The Treatise on the Great Perfection of Wisdom Sutra, attributed
to the second-century A.D. Indian Mahayana Buddhist philosopher
Nagarjuna, says, "By reciting the Buddha's preachings, the Buddha's disciples compiled [Mahayana] sutras. [Thus,] ignorant
people are guilty of slander when they say, 'This [Mahayana] is

not the Buddha's preaching. It was made by [Mara—the Evil One] or Mara's followers, and it was also written by people with false views.' "

The Mahayana scripture the Sutra of the Great Accumulation of Treasures states, "At that time . . . assuming the form of a monk in order to deceive the people, Mara went to a certain place and said, 'These sutras are the products of people trying to make worldly words seem righteous. Why do I say this is not what the Tathagata [Shakyamuni] preached? Because you cannot obtain merit and benefit through it.' " Similar statements are found in other sutras.

Mahayana Buddhist believers maintained that the Mahayana teachings are true Buddhism and comprise the true words of the Buddha. Calling their own school Mahayana, literally, "Great Vehicle"—indicating their confidence in the supreme worth of their teachings—the Mahayana Buddhists referred to the Abhidharma school as Hinayana (literally, "Small Vehicle") Buddhism, scorning Abhidharma Buddhism as inferior and worthless.

The Diamond Hermit's Treatise (Chin-kang-hsien-lu), a commentary on the Perfection of Wisdom Sutra, sets forth four important points in Mahayana Buddhism: (1) the essence of Mahayana Buddhism embraces all merits, avoiding the lesser destinies of the five vehicles of human beings, celestial beings, *shravakas, pratyekabuddhas,* and bodhisattvas;* (2) through the Mahayana vehicle great bodhisattvas can attain the same enlightenment as the Buddha; (3) all buddhas ultimately comprehend (and accomplish) the (Mahayana) teachings; and (4) all the buddhas exist eternally in order to teach and to bring salvation to all sentient beings.

The arguments of the Diamond Hermit's Treatise and the Perfec-

---

* More fully, the five vehicles are: (1) human beings, or lay believers, who rightly receive and keep the lay precepts and are reborn as celestial beings; (2) celestial beings, who rightly practice prescribed good deeds, ensuring rebirth in a higher realm; (3) *shravakas* (meaning "those who hear the Buddha's voice"), who rightly understand the Four Noble Truths and through diligent practice become *arhats;* (4) *pratyekabuddhas* (meaning the "self-enlightened," because they attain buddhahood through independent practice, without a teacher), who rightly understand the Law of the Twelve Causes; and (5) bodhisattvas, those who become bodhisattvas (or beings in the final stage prior to attaining buddhahood) as a result of religious practice over countless years.

tion of Wisdom Sutra represent Indian debate on whether Mahayana scriptures are authentic records of the Buddha's teaching. However, from the beginning it was principally Mahayana teachings that were introduced into China, so that Mahayana Buddhism became the recognized school in China. Since the Chinese believed that the Mahayana sutras undeniably recorded the Buddha's true teaching and that the Hinayana sutras were inferior, quarrels between Mahayana and Hinayana Buddhists were rare in China.

Mahayana sutras were nevertheless criticized by certain people in China who were ignorant of the true meaning of Mahayana scriptures because of an initial paucity of information. In the fifth century, for instance, three Buddhist monks were outspoken: Hui-tao expressed doubts about the teachings in the Perfection of Wisdom Sutra in Twenty-five Thousand Lines, T'an-le disparaged the Lotus Sutra, and Seng-yüan belittled the Mahayana Sutra of the Great Decease. All these monks, however, were censured by Buddhist scholars of the day.

Seng-jui (378–444?), one of Kumarajiva's four great disciples, said that Buddhist scriptures, whether Mahayana or Hinayana, were preached because of the need for them and that, for example, the Hinayana Tipitaka eliminates bondage, the Perfection of Wisdom Sutra drives out falsehood, the Lotus Sutra discloses the Buddha's highest teaching, and the Mahayana Sutra of the Great Decease instructs on true faith. Seng-jui also stated that notions of superiority or inferiority depend on the individual, that profundity or shallowness reflects a person's level of enlightenment, and that a person can practice only to the limit of his capacity for understanding. Seng-jui went on to say that people are responsible for the survival of the Law and that both disparaging the true teaching and deliberately ignoring instructions on true faith imperil its survival.

Speaking of the three dissenting monks, Seng-jui asserted that Hui-tao would not attain salvation because he denied the validity of the Perfection of Wisdom Sutra in Twenty-five Thousand Lines and revered only the Tipitaka. Seng-jui reported that T'an-le felt justified in denying the worth of the Lotus Sutra and went on to say that even though Seng-yüan doubted the true teaching in the Mahayana Sutra of the Great Decease and did not regard it as leading to enlightenment, the true worth of the sutra would itself disprove his slander.

A final example of the controversy over whether the Mahayana sutras are genuine involves one Chu Fa-tu, who was born in China around the fifth century A.D. The son of a merchant, Chu Fa-tu became a monk in the Hinayana tradition and preached that Hinayana Buddhism was the Buddha's only true teaching and that people should not read Mahayana sutras because they were not the word of the Buddha. Denouncing the Mahayana sutras, Chu Fa-tu followed the way of Hinayana Buddhism, and some nuns from a noble clan, deeply moved by his sermons, came to believe his teaching.

The monk Seng-yu (445–518) said that the offense Chu Fa-tu committed was like causing people to drink poison and that women tended to be unintelligent although they were steadfast in their belief. Seng-yu also said that once the nuns accepted Chu Fa-tu's false teaching they persisted in it, and therefore several Ch'ang-an temples (along with their nuns) were poisoned by this false teaching. Seng-yu went on to say that an evil path is easy to open and that he feared the poison could not be stopped. He thought that demons had used the nuns in order to extinguish Mahayana Buddhism.

Since Japanese Buddhism developed under the influence of Chinese Buddhism, in Japan too the Mahayana sutras were recognized as the Buddha's true preaching. However, in the eighteenth century non-Buddhists participated in discussions denying Mahayana as the Buddha's preaching.

The first advocate of this theory was Tominaga Nakamoto (1715–46), the son of a merchant in Osaka, where his family had owned a soy-sauce company for generations. The company had prospered until his grandfather's generation, but because his parents were interested more in acquiring knowledge than in managing the company, his family's fortunes dwindled during his youth.

Under his parents' influence, Tominaga read scholarly works during his childhood, and at the age of ten he entered a private school that his father had founded. At school he studied the teachings of the eminent neo-Confucian philosopher Wang Yang-ming (1472–1529).

A gifted child with a nimble mind and an exceptional memory, Tominaga is said to have written at the age of fifteen a book in which he asserted that all the time-honored theories of Confucianism and of Chinese philosophers and their schools were wrong. The book no longer exists, but he said that the ideas of Confucianism and of other philosophers were born, developed, and improved upon according to the tides of history and thought. He went on to say that although Confucian teaching proclaimed that only Confucius was outstanding (and that all other teachers advocated heretical doctrines) this mistaken view disregarded historical fact.

Today Tominaga's opinion seems reasonable, but at that time scholars regarded it as heretical. It is remarkable that at the age of fifteen Tominaga had read everything available on Confucianism and other Chinese philosophies and on the basis of the history of thought correctly traced the relationships among various theories. Yet one could hardly expect such a radical theory to be accepted by Confucianists in those days, and Tominaga seems to have been expelled from his school and gone on to study Chinese poetry.

When he was about twenty he married, and since he had to make a living, he went to Kyoto, where he worked printing the Ōbaku Edition of the Tripitaka, still preserved at the temple Mampuku-ji. More than fifty years earlier the Ōbaku Edition of the Tripitaka, a copy of the Chinese Wan-li Edition of the Tripitaka, had been carved into wooden printing blocks at the direction of the Japanese Zen master Tetsugen (1630–82). The Ōbaku Edition consisted of some sixty thousand blocks containing over sixteen hundred works in about sixty-two hundred fascicles, and it was Tominaga's task to print each of those blocks by hand.

Tominaga had a thorough knowledge of Chinese ideograms and could read and understand all the sutras he worked on. It seems that he jotted down words and thoughts and that by comparing ideas, words, and phrases he observed the development of the sutras, from the simple to the complex. He edited the material he had collected and wrote a book entitled *Shutsujō Kōgo* (Words After

Meditation), which appears to indicate that through meditation he came to understand the circumstances of the compilation of the sutras and that he was able to write about the sutras after this meditation.

Tominaga's book, published when he was thirty, just a year before his death, discussed the composition of sutras from the Agama, or primitive, sutras down to the Mahayana sutras. He approached his subject in much the same way that contemporary scholars do. For instance, he pointed out accurately and in copious detail that the Mahayana sutras were compiled piecemeal about five hundred years after Shakyamuni's death and that they were not the direct word of the Buddha.

Tominaga's book was well written, but the Chinese ideograms he used were obscure and his argument was so erudite that only outstanding scholars could follow it. Buddhist scholars of his day seem not to have responded to his work at all. Much later, Buddhist scholars did reply to the book, but their words were insufficient to refute Tominaga's assertions.

Quite some time after its publication, Tominaga's book caused a stir among scholars outside the field of Buddhism. For example, the Japanese scholar Hattori Ten'yū (1724–69) was so impressed by the book that he himself studied the sutras and wrote a book in which he simplified Tominaga's discourse, making it easier to understand.

The Shintoist and scholar of Japanese classics Hirata Atsutane (1776–1843) learned of Tominaga's work through a book written by another scholar of Japanese classics, Moto-ori Norinaga (1730–1801). With some difficulty Hirata obtained a copy of Tominaga's book, which impressed him greatly, and eventually wrote his own seven-volume work *Shutsujō Shōgo* (Laughter After Meditation). For Hirata, who despised Buddhism, Tominaga's book was an excellent source of support in attacking Buddhism and describing its weak points. Unlike Tominaga's work, Hirata's book, which was filled with derision and a hatred of Buddhism, was not at all scholarly. After the Meiji Restoration of 1868, a number of Hirata's followers started a movement to abolish Buddhism.

Since Tominaga's book thus gave impetus to an attempt to destroy Buddhism, some Buddhist scholars regarded the book as a great threat. However, Tominaga's purpose in writing was not to deride Buddhism but to expose it to the light of historical investigation. Although he did express a certain respect for Confucianism and Buddhism and state that they were superior to Taoism, he did not feel that Buddhism and Confucianism were necessary for the world at that time. He studied both religions with the scientific detachment of Western scholars, without trying to grasp their true inner spirit. Needless to say, a superficial study of this sort will not lead to discovery of the true values of Buddhism because the sutras must be understood not merely intellectually but through practice and actual faith.

EARLY MODERN CONTROVERSY   In the mid-nineteenth century, under the influence of Western scholarship, Japanese scholars began historical study of Buddhist doctrine and of the formation and development of the sutras. For example, they saw Shakyamuni Buddha as a historical person who lived in India about twenty-five centuries earlier, not as some symbolic entity. In their study of the sutras they tried to distinguish between what was actually uttered by the Buddha and what was composed after Shakyamuni's death. This approach was almost identical to that of Tominaga Nakamoto in the mid-eighteenth century.

Most famous among the many Japanese scholars who undertook such study in the late nineteenth and early twentieth centuries were Dr. Murakami Senshō (1851–1929) and Dr. Maeda Eun (1855–1930). Adherents of the Pure Land sect of Buddhism (Dr. Murakami was a monk of the Higashi Hongan-ji branch, while Dr. Maeda was a monk of the Nishi Hongan-ji branch), the two men are considered representative of Buddhist scholars of the time. Dr. Murakami lectured on Indian philosophy at the University of Tokyo and became the first head of that university's department of Indian philosophy. Dr. Maeda taught at such institutions as the University of Tokyo and was active in the publication of two monumental collections of sutras: the *Dai Nippon Kōtei Zōkyō*, or *Manji-zōkyō* (published between 1902 and 1905), and the *Dai Nippon Zoku Zōkyō*, or

Manji-zokuzō (published between 1905 and 1912), which together comprise over three thousand sutras.

In July 1901, the publication of the first of the five volumes of Dr. Murakami's *Bukkyō Tōitsu Ron* (On the Unity of Buddhism) revived the controversy among Buddhists over whether the Buddha actually taught Mahayana doctrines. That initial volume of his collected University of Tokyo lectures contained an outline of the doctrines of various Japanese Buddhist sects.

In his book Dr. Murakami stated that Shakyamuni is the sole historical Buddha and that Amitabha Buddha—in whom followers of the Pure Land sects believe—never existed as an actual being but was merely an abstract inhabitant of an ideal world. In Murakami's view, there is no absolute proof either that Shakyamuni did or that he did not preach Mahayana doctrines, but Murakami went on to point out that clearly the statement that Shakyamuni did not expound Mahayana teachings is consistent with historical evidence.

On the surface, Murakami's statements are tantamount to denials of the orthodoxy of the teachings of the Pure Land sects and of the Higashi Hongan-ji branch (to which he belonged), since he was so explicit in his assertions that Amitabha Buddha was nothing more than an abstract concept from an ideal world and that the Mahayana sutras on which the Pure Land sects base their teachings are not in fact records of the Buddha's preaching. Such an interpretation of Murakami's work would also, of course, deny the orthodoxy of all other Mahayana sects.

Bukkyō Tōitsu Ron aroused a great deal of comment, both favorable and unfavorable. Many of Dr. Murakami's fellows in the Higashi Hongan-ji branch disagreed with his views, and finally, fearing that his continued presence would only aggravate dispute, Murakami renounced the office of monk. Various newspapers and magazines published discussions of Murakami's theory—both pro and con—and he received numerous letters expressing negative criticism. The magnitude of the sensation caused by Murakami's book is indicated by the fact that within months of its publication several works critical of it, including a collection of criticisms, appeared on the market.

Murakami's theory that the historical Buddha himself did not preach the Mahayana sutras was not propounded in order to attack or destroy Mahayana Buddhism. Murakami simply wanted to clarify the place of each type of Buddhism in the light of historical evidence. As a devout Buddhist, he hoped to demonstrate the concord between true Buddhism and the spirit of the Buddha's teachings and thus to show that even teachings that had not actually been preached by the Buddha could be identified with him.

Dr. Murakami's assertion that the historical Buddha had not preached the Mahayana sutras was based on three premises. First, Shakyamuni Buddha as he appears in Mahayana sutras and in treatises on those sutras is not the historical Buddha but a figure larger than life, a superhuman being. Second, with the exception of the Bodhisattva Maitreya, the various bodhisattvas mentioned in Mahayana sutras as members of the Buddha's audiences are all personifications of the qualities or attributes of bodhisattvas. Hence if the bodhisattvas who listened to the Buddha's sermons are all symbolic figures, then the Buddha who preached to them could not be the Shakyamuni Buddha who actually lived. Third, Mahayana sutras cannot be considered true records of the Buddha's teaching, since there is no historical evidence to support any of the myths included in them.

Murakami did not restrict himself to a historical examination of Mahayana sutras, however; he also examined them from the more important standpoint of doctrine. In Murakami's opinion, the fact that the historical Buddha did not actually preach Mahayana teachings could not be interpreted to mean either that they do not represent true Buddhism or that they do not embody the spirit of the Buddha's teachings. Murakami felt that the question of whether Mahayana Buddhism is the Buddha's direct teaching should be considered from both the historical and the doctrinal viewpoint. He emphasized that in saying that the Mahayana sutras are not the teaching of the historical Buddha he was speaking purely from a historical point of view, since from a doctrinal point of view they clearly must be accepted as the teaching of the Buddha.

Unquestionably, Mahayana orthodoxy does represent true Buddhism and does manifest the spirit of the Buddha's teaching. Dr.

Murakami held that a person who could lose faith in Buddhism simply because the Mahayana sutras are not the actual words of the Buddha could not have had genuine faith: the question of whether the Buddha in fact preached Mahayana teachings has nothing to do with engendering faith in Buddhism.

In 1903, just two years after the appearance of Dr. Murakami's book, Dr. Maeda Eun's *Daijō Bukkyō-shi Ron* (On the History of Mahayana Buddhism) was published. Although Dr. Maeda's book did not create as much of a sensation as Dr. Murakami's, it was an important work whose scholarship was highly praised. Dr. Maeda, long a student of Buddhism, had made an exhaustive study of the Tripitaka, or complete canon, in an effort to discover some concrete evidence that Mahayana sutras are the Buddha's teachings, and his findings were set forth in *Daijō Bukkyō-shi Ron*.

First, in Dr. Maeda's opinion, Alara-Kalama and Uddaka-Ramaputta—the two hermit-sages under whom Shakyamuni had studied meditation after renouncing the world—were adepts of the Sankhya school, whose doctrines resemble Mahayana teachings. Thus, through the influence of those teachers, Shakyamuni had already acquired somewhat of a Mahayana view before beginning his own teaching mission. (Although there are some minor, superficial similarities between Sankhya and Mahayana philosophies, their basic tenets are quite different; hence Dr. Maeda's argument here is weak.)

Second, the Buddha's teaching is so profound that each person who hears it comprehends it at a different level, according to his or her intellectual capacity. In this way Hinayana and Mahayana thought emerged simultaneously from the preachings of the Buddha, rather than arising as separate schools of Buddhism only after Shakyamuni's death. Since it is evident that certain embryonic Mahayana teachings were already accepted among Shakyamuni's disciples during his lifetime, it is indeed likely that he did expound Mahayana teachings. (Certainly the seeds of many Mahayana beliefs are to be found in the Agama sutras, which were compiled well before the formal division of Buddhism into Hinayana and Mahayana schools.)

Third, Mahayana and Mahayana-like teachings are frequently

recorded in Chinese-language versions of the Ekottara-agama (Gradual Sayings), and its introductory chapter on the First Buddhist Council states, "The Buddha's teachings differ from one another. Thus are bodhisattvas aroused to attain buddhahood and led to follow Mahayana [teachings]. The Tathagata [Shakyamuni] proclaims the distinctions between his teachings, and followers reverently preach [the teaching of] the Six Perfections."*

Since other Chinese translations of stories of the First Council also mention the compilation of Mahayana-like sutras, Dr. Maeda believed he had found proof that the Buddha did expound Mahayana teachings. However, because later Mahayana Buddhists are responsible for numerous additions to the Chinese Ekottara-agama, it is difficult to accept the historical accuracy of these and other Chinese works that claim Mahayana sutras were compiled at the First Buddhist Council.

Even though he failed in his attempt to prove conclusively that the historical Buddha did in fact expound Mahayana teachings, Maeda recognized that in terms of doctrinal orthodoxy Mahayana Buddhism is the teaching of the Buddha. As it happens, it is utterly impossible to find in the Buddhist canon any proof that Mahayana sutras are records of the Buddha's actual words.

In order to "prove" that Mahayana doctrines are the Buddha's teaching, it is necessary, first, to insist that even if the historical Buddha did not actually expound Mahayana teachings they should still be regarded as his word because they embody the Truth of Buddhism and, second, to make clear that the Mahayana sutras merely explain in greater detail the many elements of Mahayana belief that are described but briefly in the Agama sutras, which are accepted as reliable records of the Buddha's words.

With regard to this second point it should be noted that the extant Agama sutras do not necessarily contain all the Buddha's teachings and that a number of important teachings seem to have already been lost or become corrupt by the time these sutras were finally recorded in writing. Nonetheless, many of the teachings

* The Six Perfections (or Six *Paramitas*) are the six kinds of practice a bodhisattva should follow to attain enlightenment: donation, keeping the precepts, perseverance, assiduity, meditation, and wisdom.

that later developed into Mahayana doctrine do appear in the Agama sutras, even if at times only as fragments or in rudimentary form.

The question of whether or not the Buddha preached Mahayana doctrines is no longer discussed much in Japan for two reasons. First, it has been accepted that it simply is not possible to prove that Mahayana doctrines are the direct teaching of the historical Buddha; and second, although the Mahayana sutras were compiled more than five centuries after the death of Shakyamuni, they do embody his original teaching and contain more profound teachings than the Agama sutras. For these reasons Japanese Buddhologists came to a tacit agreement some time ago that Mahayana sutras are the word of the Buddha.

Modern scholars have instead turned increasingly to historical investigation of the formation of the Mahayana sutras. In such research it is important to examine the close relation of thought in the Mahayana and Agama sutras and in fundamental Buddhism. The renowned Dr. Anesaki Masaharu (1873–1949) in fact made an invaluable study of Mahayana and Hinayana sutras along just these lines.

Dr. Anesaki, who established the University of Tokyo's department of religious studies, was an outstanding scholar whose fields of expertise included Buddhism and other Indian religions, Christianity, and Christianity in Japan. His comparative study of the Five Nikayas of the Pali canon and their equivalents in the Chinese canon—the Four Agamas—received international recognition after its publication in 1908 and remains a useful work today.

EIGHT

Scriptural Interpretation and Doctrinal Distinctions

SUTRA STUDIES AND THE CLASSIFICATION OF DOCTRINES

As I have mentioned, when Buddhist sutras were first translated into Chinese, in the early centuries of the Christian Era, the Chinese found Buddhist doctrines almost impossible to comprehend because the sutras introduced both terminology and philosophical concepts unknown in China. A similar situation obtains even today both in Japan and in the West, in that people who have no background in Buddhist studies generally find a great deal of Buddhist terminology quite incomprehensible. Present-day students of Buddhism, however, enjoy advantages undreamed of by those early Chinese students: dictionaries, commentaries, and other reference works that clarify obscure points.

At the time that Buddhism was first introduced into China, not only were even rudimentary reference works completely lacking, but there were no standard, agreed-upon translations of fundamental terms and concepts. As I explained on page 48, some scholar-translators had attempted to make Buddhism and Buddhist thought intelligible by employing the more familiar vocabulary of Taoism, which shares certain superficial similarities with Buddhism. The form of Buddhism relying on Taoist terminology, which came to be known as *ko-i* Buddhism, was eventually rejected, however, since Buddhism cannot be understood through comparison or analogy with Taoism because of significant irreconcilable differences between their philosophies.

Because of such inadequate translations as those of *ko-i* Buddhism, even the great teacher Tao-an (312–85)—who lived when the history of Buddhist translation in China was already some two hundred years old—was unable to attain a full, correct understanding of Buddhism despite his dedication and outstanding intellect. Unable to realize his desire to study under the eminent scholar and translator Kumarajiva, Tao-an despaired of being able to truly perfect his already remarkable knowledge of Buddhism. Thus he prayed for rebirth in Tushita (the heaven of the Bodhisattva Maitreya, who Buddhists believe will be the next Buddha) so that he might be able to learn true Buddhism directly from Maitreya himself.

The degree of Tao-an's discouragement over the state of Buddhist studies in China in his time may be gauged from the fact that he and eight of his disciples prayed before an image of the Bodhisattva Maitreya, expressing their earnest desire to be reborn in Tushita.* It is said that as a result of those supplications Tao-an was granted a vision a few days before his death, in which he saw celestial beings descend to a heavenly shrine and heard them play glorious music there; and it is further said that at death he experienced rebirth in a blessed state in Tushita.

It was not until after Kumarajiva (344–413) reached China in 401 and began teaching and translating that Buddhist doctrines were correctly transmitted and understood in that country. Nevertheless, very few among the three thousand disciples credited to Kumarajiva fully comprehended the Buddhist teachings, and those who did are known to us variously as the Four Great Men or the Eight Heroes. Numbered among the handful of Kumarajiva's accomplished disciples are Seng-chao (374–414), a renowned master

---

* I might mention here that it is believed that the Bodhisattva Maitreya, the future Buddha, will be reborn in the world in which we live, will attain enlightenment, and will become the next Buddha only after having lived five billion six hundred and seventy million years in his heaven, Tushita. Faith in the Bodhisattva Maitreya was at one time widespread in India, China, and Japan. Adherents of that sect of Buddhism hoped only to be permitted to learn true Buddhism from Maitreya after they died.

of the Madhyamika (Doctrine of the Middle Way) teachings, and Tao-sheng (d. 434), who was also a disciple of Hui-yüan.

As I mentioned earlier, when he was about fifty Tao-an's disciple Hui-yüan (334–416) went into seclusion at Mount Lu, in southern China. Hui-yüan was already at least seventy when he and Kumarajiva, who was then in Ch'ang-an, began their lengthy correspondence on questions of doctrine, and it is presumed that various circumstances, including Hui-yüan's advanced age, prevented their meeting in person to discuss the sutras and doctrine.

Thus it was not only through Kumarajiva's superb, reliable translations of various sutras but also through his teaching that Buddhism was for the first time correctly understood in China. As we have already seen, in the years of the Northern and Southern dynasties period (317–589) following Kumarajiva's death, middle-period Mahayana and other sutras previously unknown in China were translated into Chinese, and they were quickly followed by translations of sutras from other schools and periods and of philosophical works.

As the body of translated sutras increased, Chinese Buddhists observed that the sutras expounded various doctrines and philosophical concepts that seemed to contradict and conflict with one another. Seriously disturbed by the apparent discrepancies between Mahayana and Hinayana sutras—which presented the same religion and recorded the teachings expounded during the long ministry of the same Buddha—the Chinese Buddhists wanted those contradictions and discrepancies reconciled.

In order to resolve the differences they had noted, Chinese Buddhists developed the system known to us as *chia-hsiang p'an-shih* or *p'an-chiao* for classifying the scriptures. Briefly, *p'an-chiao* (meaning "judging the teachings") was the Chinese method of organizing and classifying scriptures according to the period of the Buddha's life in which they were expounded and the doctrines they transmitted. Relying on internal evidence in the sutras themselves, *p'an-chiao* represented an attempt to bring order and unity to the growing, ambiguous corpus of Buddhist scripture in Chinese.

When it first became popular, during the latter part of the Northern and Southern dynasties period, *p'an-chiao* was employed simply to determine the historical place of particular sutras and doctrines within the teaching career of Shakyamuni in order to put an end to confusion and dispute. Later, however, during and after the Sui and T'ang dynasties (581–907), *p'an-chiao* degenerated into mere value judgments of the doctrines and philosophical concepts expounded in the sutras and treatises: it was reduced to a system for proving that the scriptures embraced by one's own sect were the best—supreme among all Buddhist scriptures.

Examples of this later form of *p'an-chiao,* which I shall discuss more fully below (see pages 151–55), include the T'ien-t'ai sect's classification according to the "five periods and eight teachings"; the "five teachings and ten sects" classification employed by the Hua-yen (Flower Garland) sect; and the "ten spiritual stages" favored by the Japanese Shingon (Chen-yen, or True Word) sect, which is founded on Chinese Buddhist thought. Here, however, I should like to look briefly at the *p'an-chiao* system as it was originally applied, during the Northern and Southern dynasties period.

Roughly speaking, the early *p'an-chiao* system incorporated the following two views of the reason that various Buddhist sutras expounded tenets that appeared to be contradictory.

First, Shakyamuni's teachings were preached on differing levels at different times, according to the intellectual capacities of the people assembled to listen to him. Just as a physician prescribes different medications for different patients, depending on their ailments, Shakyamuni preached his message variously to people, in the form most suitable to leading them to enlightenment. In Buddhist terminology this flexible approach to teaching is known as the eighty-four thousand teachings preached in proportion to the eighty-four thousand illusions. (Like other very large numbers used in Buddhist scriptures and commentaries, eighty-four thousand here simply indicates a vast or infinite number.)

Second, Shakyamuni preached a single message to all of his listeners, but because of their differing capacities for understanding, different listeners interpreted the same message differently. In the Vimalakirti Sutra, for example, it is said that the Buddha speaks the same words when preaching the Law but that people's understanding varies according to their intellectual capacities. Sutra interpretations based on this thinking are known as *p'an-chiao* of the "one voice [word] teaching."

To account for the discrepancies among sutras, people most often adopted the first explanation cited above, giving rise to a number of distinctions among doctrines. For instance, according to the *p'an-chiao* system called the "teaching of a half word [imperfect teaching] and the teaching of a full word [perfect teaching]," the Buddha preached a half-word teaching (Hinayana) to people of inferior intellect and a full-word teaching (Mahayana) to people of superior intellect. And the *p'an-chiao* system of "instantaneous-enlightenment teaching and gradual-enlightenment teaching" held that to people of superior intellect the Buddha preached teachings producing instantaneous enlightenment while to people of lesser intellect he preached teachings producing gradual enlightenment in order to raise them from their low plane to a higher one.

As early as the second century A.D., the great Indian Buddhist philosopher Nagarjuna had expressed somewhat similar views on discriminating among teachings when in his Treatise on the Great Perfection of Wisdom Sutra (Mahaprajnaparamita-upadesha) he introduced the Four Siddhantas as criteria for classifying the teachings of the Buddha and the doctrines in the sutras. Nagarjuna's Four Siddhantas are: the World Siddhanta, the Varying Siddhanta, the Healing Siddhanta, and the First-Principle Siddhanta.

World Siddhanta refers to Shakyamuni's method of preaching relative to the cravings of his listeners, whereby he preached first on worldly matters to those who were attached to worldly thought and found Buddhist philosophy difficult to accept. In this use, World Siddhanta may be looked on as a simplification of the law of cause and effect devised for the average person. Although worldly concerns are of little importance in Buddhist thinking, they may be paramount to people unversed in Buddhist thought.

Varying Siddhanta indicates the method of preaching relative to the differing intellectual capacities, character, and desires of the listeners. In order to guide each individual on the path to true faith, it is necessary to take these differences into consideration so that all may come to enjoy a correct understanding of and genuinely embrace the Buddha's teaching.

Healing Siddhanta signifies the method of preaching by perceiving the imperfections of the listeners in order to free them of their failings. Through the Healing Siddhanta Shakyamuni preached the doctrine of nonexistence to those who adhered to existence and the doctrine of the Middle Path, which is neither existence nor nonexistence, to those who adhered to nonexistence. It is because of the Healing Siddhanta that Buddhism contains a number of teachings that appear to be diametrically opposed.

First-Principle Siddhanta denotes Shakyamuni's practice of preaching the ultimate truth (first principle) of his profound teaching to people of highly developed intellect in order to deepen their faith. Even though the First-Principle Siddhanta is the eventual goal of Buddhism, it is fruitless to preach Shakyamuni's most profound teachings to everyone because those teachings are so difficult to comprehend that they are worthless to beginning students or people of undeveloped intellect.

As this brief introduction to the Four Siddhantas indicates, certain teachings in the sutras were expounded from more than one viewpoint. In order to instruct and guide as many people as possible, Shakyamuni found it necessary to expound his teaching in a variety of ways, which occasionally makes the records of certain teachings appear contradictory. A prosaic example of a similar approach to imparting information can be found in our modern educational system, in which primary-school mathematics texts, for example, differ from those used in secondary schools and are still more different from university-level texts, and the advanced texts may sometimes appear to contradict the elementary texts.

Since the Buddhist sutras, treatises, and commentaries are essentially textbooks of faith and spiritual matters, it is necessary that they present the Buddha's teaching and other information in various ways in order to be suitable for people of all degrees of faith and spiritual development. By employing *p'an-chiao* classifications, the Chinese Buddhists were able to understand and explain the reasons for the discrepancies and contradictions they had found among the doctrines recorded in the sutras, and they reappraised the worth of Buddhism.

When analyzing Buddhist sutras and doctrines, however, one

should bear in mind that there are important differences from the systems of Western philosophy or science and even from the common-sensical approach we take in addressing the problems of everyday life. In science, for example, demonstrable empirical proof of a hypothesis is the important criterion for determining the validity of that hypothesis. In formal logic a variety of reasoning methods or arguments, such as the syllogism, are adopted for testing the validity of a statement, and the common-sense judgments we make in everyday life are based on assessments very like those of formal logic.

Buddhist sutras, however, contain numerous discrepancies and contradictions that cannot be explained adequately in terms of formal logic alone. Because the ways of expounding various Buddhist teachings differ with the degree of faith or spiritual development of the listeners, those teachings cannot be analyzed from only one point of view or on the basis of a single criterion; hence they do not admit of testing by the arguments of formal logic. Buddhist treatises and commentaries—and even sutras—mention a multidimensional view of the teachings.

From the standpoint of science or formal logic (both of which are given to single-perspective judgments based on a single criterion), this multidimensional view could be regarded as an extremely complicated system of non-order or non-logic. Yet such a multidimensional view is necessary in order to fully comprehend a mental state as something dynamic and mutable.

INTERPRETING THE SUTRAS As I mentioned above, from the time that *p'an-chiao* (or *chia-hsiang p'an-shih*) was developed, in the latter part of the Northern and Southern dynasties period, and up until around the time that the Sui dynasty was established, in 581, the *p'an-chiao* system was a popular means of presenting rational explanations of the apparent contradictions in Shakyamuni's teachings that became noticeable as more and more sutras were translated into Chinese. Most of these contradictions and discrepancies resulted from the necessity of preaching certain teachings in a variety of ways, according to the differing intellectual capacities of listeners. Today that flexible method of teaching is generally called expedient teaching. (Because of his mastery of expedient teaching, Shakyamuni was referred to by one of the ten epithets of a buddha: Understander of the World, indicating that the Buddha has perfect understanding of the minds of all human beings.)

During the period of the Northern and Southern dynasties, Chinese Buddhists came to understand the expedient teachings of Shakyamuni through their studies of sutras. Thus, when studying and interpreting a particular sutra, Chinese Buddhists discussed it not in isolation but in relation to all other sutras known to them. In other words, aware of the enormous body of Shakyamuni's preachings and of the essence of Buddhist doctrine, Chinese Buddhists considered each sutra from the broad perspectives of its place within the preachings expounded by Shakyamuni during his forty-five-year ministry, its relation to the fundamental doctrines of Buddhism, and its significance and value in the Buddhist canon.

When we consider studies and interpretations of the Lotus Sutra, for instance, we find that it had already been studied closely by many of the disciples of Kumarajiva, its greatest translator; however, study of this scripture burgeoned during the Liang dynasty (502–57), near the end of the Northern and Southern dynasties period. In particular, Fa-yün (467–529), chief abbot of the temple Kuang-che-ssu in the Liang capital Nanking and regarded as one of the three outstanding priests of the period, excelled in study of the Lotus Sutra. His carefully annotated eight-fascicle Miao-fa lien-hua-ching i-chi (Commentary on the Lotus Sutra) is the second-oldest extant Lotus Sutra commentary produced by a Chinese scholar— the oldest is the two-fascicle commentary of Tao-sheng (d. 434). (A four-fascicle commentary on the Lotus Sutra written in Japan by Prince-Regent Shōtoku [574–622] is said to have been based on Fa-yün's work.)

In his commentary Fa-yün examined the Lotus Sutra on the basis of an established *p'an-chiao* system. It is believed that a number of *p'an-chiao* systems were in common use at the time that Fa-yün was writing, but he seems to have been most influenced by the system devised by Hui-kuan during the Liu Sung dynasty (420–79). Although Hui-kuan had been a disciple of the great translator Buddhabhadra (359–429) at the temple Tao-ch'ang in Nanking, he had also studied earlier under Kumarajiva in Ch'ang-an.

Hui-kuan classified all Buddhist teachings as either teachings of instantaneous enlightenment or teachings of gradual enlightenment. He further organized the teachings of gradual enlightenment according to the period in which they had been expounded, assigning them to one of five periods: that of the Agama sutras, the Perfection of Wisdom sutras, the Vimalakirti Sutra, the Lotus Sutra, or the Sutra of the Great Decease. The *p'an-chiao* of the "five periods and eight teachings" used by the T'ien-t'ai sect of Chinese Buddhism is a later elaboration of the five-period system introduced by Hui-kuan.

During the Sui dynasty (581–618) interpretations of and commentaries on sutras became increasingly precise, incorporating ever-finer distinctions in their analyses. It was during this period that the classes of commentaries known as *hsüan-i* (profound meaning) and *hsüan-lun* (profound treatise), which examined sutras as a whole from broad perspectives, first made their appearance. Examples of such commentaries include the ten-fascicle Miao-fa lien-hua-ching hsüan-i (Profound Meaning of the Lotus Sutra) by Chih-i (538–97), patriarch of the T'ien-t'ai sect, and the ten-fascicle Fa-hua-ching hsüan-lun (Profound Treatise on the Lotus Sutra) by Chi-tsang (549–623), the great master of the San-lun (Three Treatises) school.

In examining both the Lotus Sutra and other scriptures, Chih-i adhered to the method of analysis called *wu-chung hsüan-i,* or five profound ways of expounding sutras. Briefly, *wu-chung hsüan-i* consists of five questions to be addressed in commenting on a sutra: (1) *shih-ming,* or the meaning of the title of the sutra; (2) *pien-pen,* or the purpose of the sutra; (3) *ming-tsung,* or the essential teaching of the sutra; (4) *lun-yung,* or the sutra's influence on people; and (5) *p'an-chiao*—that is, classification of the scripture—here meaning specifically the value of the sutra and the historical position it occupies within the great body of scripture expounded during Shakyamuni's lengthy ministry.

It should be noted that during the Northern and Southern dynasties period sutra interpretations and commentaries were undertaken principally as intellectual or academic exercises, not as guides to the practice of faith or the attainment of enlightenment. This scholarly approach—very apparent in Fa-yün's Miao-fa lien-hua-ching i-chi, written during that period—is still found later in Chi-tsang's Fa-hua-ching hsüan-lun, written during the Sui dynasty. However, the four-fascicle commentary on the Lotus Sutra written by the Japanese prince Shōtoku was not the product of such scholarly inquiry: it was intended both as a practical religious guide and as a vindication of his vision of imperial governance. (In Prince Shōtoku's commentary certain passages of the Lotus Sutra admit of political interpretations supporting both defined relationships between an emperor and his subjects and the rule of a country united under a single emperor, important to Shōtoku because undivided rule of Japan was still at issue in his day.)

Buddhist scholarship eventually became debased during the Northern and Southern dynasties period, however, and while Buddhist learning continued to mature, religious practice of the Buddhist faith declined. At about that time, Buddhists began making efforts to check the decline. The Ch'an, or Zen, school of Buddhism, formally introduced into China by its first Chinese patriarch, Bodhidharma (who arrived there from India in 520), is regarded as a significant example of such efforts.

During the Later Han dynasty (A.D. 25–220), Hinayana Zen and Mahayana Zen, precursors of the Zen Buddhism of Bodhidharma, had been introduced into China. Those early forms could be called superficial Zen, since their adherents could not have attained enlightenment through either understanding or practice of their teachings. Yet even the T'ien-t'ai patriarchs Hui-ssu (515–77) and Chih-i profited greatly from Zen disciplines, such as *dhyana* (meditation) focusing on contemplation of the Lotus Sutra and the Middle Way. However, because Chih-i excelled both in practice and in philosophical comprehension of such disciplines, succeeding disciples felt compelled to delve into abstruse doctrines and theories and eventually neglected the practical teachings that Chih-i had valued. Around the time of these disciples there appeared a Ch'an, or Zen, sect that advocated only zazen (seated meditation).

When Bodhidharma arrived in China, Buddhism there centered

on scholarly inquiry, almost to the exclusion of religious experience and practice. The Zen Buddhism of Bodhidharma emerged as a part of the effort to remedy that imbalance. Within so-called Bodhidharma Zen, the people who learned doctrine and theory from the sutras and commentaries were referred to as *chiao-chia*, or sutra-family people, while those who actually practiced Zen teachings were called *Ch'an-chia*, or Zen-family people.

The Erh-ju ssu-hsing-lun (On the Twofold Entrance to the Way and the Four Types of Practice), a treatise attributed to Bodhidharma, describes the Zen adherent's approach as "to become enlightened to the fundamental spirit of Buddhism revealed in the sutras." This statement means that Zen believers must discover the fundamental import of Buddhism for themselves and implies that at that time the followers known as the *chiao-chia* were unable to comprehend the fundamental meaning of the sutras despite diligent study.

Bodhidharma's attitude, as exemplified by the statement quoted above, provoked the animosity of the *chiao-chia;* and according to later legend, Bodhidharma was intensely resented by such prominent Buddhist priests as Bodhiruchi (fl. ca. 508–35) and Hui-kuang (468–537) and was murdered by poisoning. It may have been at the instigation of the *chiao-chia* that robbers set upon Hui-k'e (487–593), Bodhidharma's disciple and the second Zen patriarch in China, and cut off one of his arms. (Although Zen writings usually claim that Hui-k'e cut off his own arm to prove his sincerity to Bodhidharma, the attack by robbers is the more credible explanation.) By the Sung dynasty (960–1126), however, Zen overshadowed all other forms of Buddhism in China because of the piety and purity of its priests' views on the sutras. One example of such priests during the T'ang dynasty (618–907) is Hui-neng (638–713), the sixth Zen patriarch.

A simple woodcutter, Hui-neng was completely illiterate, yet he was outstanding at comprehending the essence of a sutra. While peddling firewood in his village one day, Hui-neng heard a mendicant priest chanting the Diamond Sutra, and that impelled him to enter the priesthood and become a monk.

Before long Hui-neng had devoted himself to the practice of Zen under the fifth patriarch, Hung-jen (602–75), who trained him well. Among the seven or eight hundred priests practicing under Hung-jen, some were highly accomplished in knowledge of all kinds of sutras and in other Buddhist learning, but it was to the unlettered Hui-neng that Hung-jen handed on the Law, making him the sixth patriarch in the Chinese Zen lineage established by Bodhidharma.

Hung-jen's designation of Hui-neng as his successor was confirmation that Hui-neng saw with the eye of the spirit and was able to perceive the true nature of a sutra. Some years after Hui-neng became the patriarch, a priest called Fa-ta, who made it a practice to recite the Lotus Sutra, was unable to fathom its meaning and asked Hui-neng for guidance. It is said that Hui-neng had only to read a small portion of the Lotus Sutra in order to grasp its essence and be able to enlighten Fa-ta.

From around the end of the Northern and Southern dynasties (317–589), Pure Land Buddhism, with its emphasis on the practice of *nien-fo*—invoking the name of Amitabha Buddha in order to be reborn in his Pure Land, or paradise—also became widely accepted. T'an-luan (476–542), Tao-cho (562–645), and Shan-tao (613–81), the three early Pure Land masters who were instrumental in popularizing the practice of *nien-fo,* all understood the true meaning of the sutras through direct spiritual experience, without the hindrance of slavish preoccupation with subtle interpretations of each word they contained. Of the many Buddhist sects once popular in China, only Zen and Pure Land Buddhism still flourish today, and their survival can be attributed to the simplicity and purity of their approach to the sutras.

We have seen that although a great many sutras were translated into Chinese and studied by Chinese Buddhists, a number of those scriptures accorded neither with Chinese philosophical thought nor with the Chinese understanding of Buddhism, and greatly revised or simplified versions of those works were produced in order to make them more comprehensible to ordinary believers. The Zen and Pure Land priests, however, did not presume to compose similar new sutras and instead interpreted the existing sutras rather freely.

It should be noted that the free, nondogmatic interpretations of the Zen and Pure Land priests did represent the true spirit of Buddhism. In his will the Indian monk Gunavarman (377–431), who went to China early during the Northern and Southern dynasties, left counsel that supports less rigid interpretation: "Although various kinds of teachings [such as Mahayana, Hinayana, Provisional, and Real] are found [in the sutras], there is no difference in the way of practicing [the faith]. [Moreover,] while many [scholars] cling to their own views and discuss the correctness or flaws of others' views, no dispute arises among those who achieve [the true spirit of Buddhism]."

Nevertheless, because many of the sutras translated into Chinese did not adequately meet the needs of the people, the Chinese came to produce their own original Chinese-language sutras, the "genuine" and spurious sutras discussed in the previous chapter. As we have seen, although a number of these sutras were fabricated for wholly dishonorable reasons, some of them were composed out of a genuine desire to communicate the true meaning of Buddhism.

The most famous of these well-intentioned spurious sutras were written by Hsin-hsing (540–94). Hsin-hsing, who founded the Sect of the Three Stages (San-chieh-chiao), based on the theory of three periods of the Law—that is, the period of the True Law, the period of the Counterfeit Law, and the period of the Decay of the Law—is regarded as a follower of Fa-yün, whose influential commentary on the Lotus Sutra we have already considered.

Like Seng-ts'an (d. 606), the third Zen patriarch in China, Hui-wen (fl. ca. 550), the seminal thinker who contributed so much to the eventual founding of the T'ien-t'ai sect, and the great Pure Land teacher Tao-cho (562–645), Hsin-hsing experienced at first hand the persecution of Buddhism between 574 and 578 instituted by the Northern Chou dynasty emperor Wu Ti. Hsin-hsing believed that Buddhism was made to suffer so heavily at that time because Buddhists had become corrupt and strayed far from the True Law. Maintaining that in order to resuscitate Buddhism priests must devote themselves to sincere practice of the Law rather than to academic investigation, Hsin-hsing himself actively practiced Zen meditation.

Although Hsin-hsing has been called a Zen master, he fostered belief in the Three Stages (San-chieh) of the Buddhist Law in the conviction that if Buddhist practice were not amended it would be unable to ensure the salvation of the world. According to Hsin-hsing's view, in the period of the True Law the doctrine of the one vehicle (comprising both Hinayana and Mahayana teachings) was preached; in the period of the Counterfeit Law the doctrine of the three vehicles (that is, the vehicles of the hearer, who exerts himself to attain enlightenment by practicing the Buddha's teachings; of the self-enlightened person, who attains enlightenment for himself without a teacher; and of the bodhisattva, who dedicates himself to the attainment of enlightenment for all) was preached; but in the period of the Decay of the Law, fifteen hundred years after the death of the Buddha (in the sixth century A.D. by Hsin-hsing's reckoning), few people would rightly view or preserve the Law. Hence, Hsin-hsing urged people to accept the universal Law as he taught it, asserting that only his teachings offered the possibility of salvation in the period of the Decay of the Law.

In later years Hsin-hsing forsook the monastic precepts that Buddhist monks and nuns vowed to keep and took up manual labor as a layman. He led a simple life, eating but one meal a day and devoting himself to the practice of the Bodhisattva Never Despise (Sadaparibhuta), who paid respect to and commended everyone he saw. Because Hsin-hsing's honest life, preaching, and conduct were in perfect accord with the Buddha's Law, many believers and patrons—some of them quite prominent people—gathered around him. A number of Buddhist temples were built by his followers, and more than forty sutras and works on the Three Stages teachings were composed and gained widespread popularity among lay believers.

However, some among Hsin-hsing's followers and disciples held that Mahayana sutras—such as the Lotus Sutra and the Sutra of Infinite Life—were harmful, useless teachings in the period of the Decay of the Law and further asserted that people who recited those sutras would descend into hell. The Sect of the Three Stages followers were so resolute in prohibiting the use of such Mahayana scriptures that they earned the enmity of other Buddhist sects, who denounced the Three Stages teachings as heresy. Thus, although the scriptures and writings of the Sect of the Three Stages had at one time been included in records of the complete Chinese Buddhist canon, the sect's teachings were eventually repudiated and stricken from the accepted Chinese canon. The sect finally died out completely around the middle of the ninth century, during the persecutions under the T'ang-dynasty emperor Wu-tsung (r. 840–47).

SECTARIAN *P'AN-CHIAO*   In Japan the Buddhist priest Gyōnen (1240–1321), of the temple Tōdai-ji in Nara, wrote *Sangoku Buppō Dentsū Engi* (A History of the Transmission of the Buddha's Law Through Three Countries), in which he traced the history of Buddhism in India, China, and Japan. Gyōnen stated that by the end of the Heian period (794–1185) eight Buddhist sects had been established in Japan, while thirteen schools and sects had been established in China between the Southern and Northern dynasties (317–589) and the T'ang dynasty (618–907).

The thirteen Chinese schools were of roughly two types: those of a scholarly bent, which emphasized the doctrinal theories of Buddhism, and those that were pragmatic and emphasized religious faith and practice. In general, the intellectually oriented sects were established during the Northern and Southern dynasties, and the more practical sects appeared during the Sui (581–618) and T'ang dynasties. There is a clear relationship between these two types of sects and the major streams of *p'an-chiao* that I mentioned earlier, since scholarly *p'an-chiao* systems were popular during the Northern and Southern dynasties, while sectarian systems came into favor during the Sui dynasty.

As we have noted, during the Northern and Southern dynasties the *p'an-chiao* systems for classifying the scriptures concentrated on scholarly investigation to determine the correct historical place of individual sutras and doctrines within the great body of Shakyamuni's teachings. Reflecting this approach, the P'i-t'an (Abhidharma), Ch'eng-shih (Completion of Truth,) Nieh-p'an (Nirvana), Ti-lun (Stage Treatise), and She-lun (Comprehensive Treatise) schools—all founded during the Northern and Southern dynasties— were what we could call intellectual schools, for they were ardent in their detailed examination of the place that the then-ascendant philosophies and sutras occupied within the whole corpus of Buddhist scripture.

The P'i-t'an school studied Abhidharma philosophy, which posits a fairly common-sensical theory of existence and reality. The Ch'eng-shih school adhered to the Treatise on the Completion of Truth (Satyasiddhi-shastra), which presents theories critically opposed to Abhidharma thought. The Nieh-p'an school turned to the Mahayana Sutra of the Great Decease (Mahaparinirvana-sutra), which teaches that all sentient beings possess the buddha-nature, or potential for attaining buddhahood, and that even the most depraved of beings can attain buddhahood. The Ti-lun school espoused the Shih-ti-ching-lun, or Treatise on the Sutra of the Ten Stages (Dashabhumika-sutra-shastra), composed by the fourth- or fifth-century A.D. Indian master Vasubandhu, while the She-lun school followed the Comprehensive Treatise on Mahayana Buddism (Mahayanasamgraha), written by Asanga, Vasubandhu's elder brother. Both of these works expound abstruse Mahayana Buddhist teachings.

The tradition of scholarly inquiry exemplified by these schools continued up to the T'ang dynasty and the founding of the Fa-hsiang (Dharma Characteristics of Existence) school, based on such works as the Ch'eng wei-shih-lun, or Treatise on the Establishment of the Doctrine of Consciousness Only (Vijnaptimatratasiddhi-shastra), which had been transmitted to China and translated by Hsüan-tsang in the seventh century. We may perhaps look on the San-lun (Three Treatises) school, born during the Sui dynasty, and the Hua-yen (Flower Garland) sect, established during the T'ang dynasty, as transitional schools, for while they indeed wholeheartedly embraced philosophical theory and inquiry, they were also solidly founded in religious practice. The later T'ien-t'ai sect could also be viewed as transitional, since even though it was based on a highly developed philosophical analysis of Buddhism, it emphasized the practice of faith.

The history of Chinese Buddhism clearly demonstrates that a sect that simply expounds a philosophical theory (regardless of how distinguished that theory may be) is unlikely to prosper if that theory is not put into practice. The Chinese sects that flourished in later ages all emphasized religious practice more than philosophical theory.

Of the thirteen Chinese sects identified by Gyōnen, the P'i-t'an, Ch'eng-shih, Ti-lun, She-lun, San-lun, and Fa-hsiang schools had been established principally on the basis of philosophical treatises. They were all scholarly sects that approached Buddhism from a philosophical viewpoint. Even though the Nieh-p'an school was founded on a sutra, rather than a treatise, it too was philosophical in its orientation. It is worth noting that none of these sects has survived to the present.

However, the T'ien-t'ai, Hua-yen (Flower Garland), and Chen-yen (Shingon, or True Word) sects—all founded during the Sui and T'ang dynasties—were established primarily on the basis of sutras and offered theory supported by practice. Other sects centered on faith were the Pure Land sect, which stressed the practice of *nien-fo* while also following the Pure Land sutras, and the Zen sect, which sought to practice the true spirit of Buddhism, although it did not espouse any particular sutra as its basic scripture. In addition, one sect—the Lü (Precepts) sect—focused on the precepts for believers and attempted to bring unity to the views of the precepts held by various sects.

Six of these thirteen Chinese sects—the Ch'eng-shih school, the San-lun school, the Fa-hsiang school, the Kosha school (a minor school within the Fa-hsiang school), the Hua-yen sect, and the Lü sect—were established in Nara, then Japan's capital, during the Nara period (710–94), becoming known as the Six Nara Sects. Early in the Heian period (794–1185), the T'ien-t'ai (called Tendai in Japan) and Chen-yen (called Shingon) sects were brought to Japan's new capital, Kyoto (which was also known as Heian-kyō), and became known as the Two Heian Sects. During the Kamakura period (1185–1336), the Pure Land and Zen sects became widely popular in Japan, and they continue to flourish today. Thus at one time all of Japanese Buddhism was represented by eight sects: the Six Nara Sects and the Two Heian Sects. To these eight sects, the priest Gyōnen later added the Pure Land and Zen sects and stated that Japanese Buddhism was composed of ten sects.

As I have said, during the Sui and T'ang dynasties the various Chinese Buddhist schools and sects employed *p'an-chiao* systems of classifying scriptures simply as a means of proving their own scriptures, doctrines, and practice were superior to those of any other school or sect. A similar penchant for proclaiming the superiority of one's own beliefs can be seen in early Indian Buddhism in the Yogachara (Yoga Practice) school, for example.

According to the Yogachara school—the forerunner of the Fa-hsiang school in China—Shakyamuni's sermons expounded both the teaching "All is actual existence" and the teaching "All is void"; but the Yogachara school maintained that its own teaching of Shakyamuni's Middle Way, that is, "All is neither actual existence nor void," which synthesized the first two teachings, was most correct. And in China the Fa-hsiang school classified all the Indian Buddhist doctrines according to the following eight theories.

1. *Wo-fa chü-yu-tsung,* which held that both the individual ego composed of the five aggregates and each element of the aggregates as an attribute of an individual or his environment are actual existences.* This was both a secular view and the basic theory of the Abhidharma Buddhist Vatsiputriya school, which believed that the ego is subject to transmigration.

2. *Fa-yu wo-wu-tsung,* according to which the separate elements of the five aggregates comprising individuals and the world were recognized as actual existences, but which did not affirm the actual existence of the individual ego because that existence is only transitory. The Sarvastivadin school—the Indian precursor of the Kosha school in China—subscribed to this view.

3. In the two theories above, the elements of the five aggregates are eternal existences, continuing from the past through the present and into the future. However, *fa-wu ch'ü-lai-tsung,* adhered to by a branch of the Mahasanghika school, maintained that actual existence occurs only in the present because all concrete experiences belong to the present, for the past has already vanished and the future is yet to be.

---

* The five aggregates are the elements or attributes of which every human being is composed: (1) form, or the body; (2) receptivity, sensation, feeling; (3) mental conceptions and ideas; (4) volition, or various mental activities; and (5) consciousness. The union of these five aggregates dates from the moment of birth and constitutes the individual.

4. *Hsien-t'ung chia-shih-tsung,* which stated that even phenomena experienced in the present are not all actual existences but are both actual existences and transitory existences because in both physical and mental phenomena there are elements of actual existence and elements of transitory existence, that is, elements born of actual existences and elements conceptualized from actual existences. This is the theory of the Sautrantika school, which criticized the views of the Sarvastivadin school.

5. *Su-wang chen-shih-tsung,* which observed in value terms that the actual existences in the present are to be distinguished as either true or counterfeit. The secular existences of ordinary transmigrating humans are all counterfeit, while the pure Law of those holy people making progress toward the ideal is true. This theory was propounded by several branches of the Mahasanghika school, including the Lokottaravadin school (which preached that only the world of enlightenment is true).

6. According to *wu-fa tan-ming-tsung,* however, both counterfeit existences and the true Law are merely terms or concepts. Although this view is similar to those of noumenalism and idealism in Western philosophy, Buddhist thought, unlike Western philosophy, never considered terms or concepts as existences of actual substance. Among the branches of the Mahasanghika school expounding this theory was the Prajnaptivadin school, which preached that all existences are only transitory words and philosophies.

These six theories were the products of various schools of Hinayana Abhidharma Buddhism.

7. *I-ch'ieh chieh-k'ung-tsung* was based on the Perfection of Wisdom sutras, which teach that all is void. According to these sutras, one should not become attached to existences because all existences are mutable, being called into existence only in accordance with the Law. This theory was common to both the Madhyamika (Doctrine of the Middle Way) school in India and the San-lun (Three Treatises) school in China, both of which relied on the Treatise on the Middle (Madhyamaka-shastra) and related works for explication of the theory presented in the Perfection of Wisdom sutras.

8. *Chen-te pu-k'ung-tsung* was the theory of the Yogachara school itself, and of the Fa-hsiang school in China. While Hinayana

Abhidharma Buddhism taught the theory of existence and the Perfection of Wisdom sutras and the Treatise on the Middle of early Mahayana Buddhism taught the theory of the void, the Yogachara school of middle-period Mahayana Buddhism advocated the Middle Way—the synthesis of existence and the void—and maintained that the middle path, avoiding the two extremes, is the ultimate principle of Buddhism. The Mahayana Sutra of the Great Decease, the Shrimala Sutra (Shrimaladevi-simhanada-sutra), the Sutra of the Appearance of the Good Doctrine in [Sri] Lanka (Lankavatara-sutra), and the Treatise on the Awakening of Faith in Mahayana (Mahayana-shraddhotpada-shastra) all expound the theory of the Middle Way.

This brief introduction indicates the arguments employed by the Fa-hsiang school in declaring its teachings superior to those of any other school. To these eight theories the Hua-yen (Flower Garland) sect added the following two of its own, thus arriving at the total of ten on which it based its "five teachings and ten sects" classification of doctrines.

9. *Hsiang-hsiang chü-chüeh-tsung,* which is the view that one attains enlightenment instantly through a religious experience, not through study of scripture or doctrine. This is, of course, the theory of the Zen sect, which stresses the importance of pure, direct experience in attaining enlightenment.

10. *Yüan-ming chü-te-tsung* is, as might be expected, the theory of the Hua-yen sect and sets forth an excellent teaching with a wonderful view of humanity and the world based on the Law of Causation, which explains the complex interdependent interrelationships existing among all things in the universe.* This teaching further proclaims that one's actions should be like those of a buddha, performed effortlessly, unhindered by any obstacle.

Although the Hua-yen sect expounded a truly admirable doctrine, it eventually failed like the purely intellectual schools because

* The central doctrine of Buddhism, the Law of Causation states that all phenomena in the universe are produced by causation. According to this doctrine, since all phenomena result from the relation of cause and effect, all things in the universe exist in interrelationship with one another ("Nothing has an ego") and all things and phenomena in this world constantly change ("All things are impermanent").

its philosophical theory was not adequately supported and reinforced by practice.

The T'ien-t'ai sect's classification of the "five periods and eight teachings" is no less important than the Hua-yen sect's classification according to the "five teachings and ten sects." Unlike the Hua-yen sect, the T'ien-t'ai sect strongly emphasized practice in addition to philosophical theory. This emphasis later prompted the Tendai (the Japanese pronunciation of T'ien-t'ai) sect in Japan to adopt the useful esoteric elements of T'ien-t'ai practice, which helped the sect become a significant force in the current of Japanese Buddhism following its introduction at the beginning of the ninth century. The Tendai emphasis on practice influenced the thinking of the major Japanese Buddhist sects founded in the twelfth and thirteenth centuries—the Pure Land, Zen, and Nichiren sects—and undoubtedly contributed greatly to their survival to the present day.

Because of the genius and erudition of Chih-i (538–97), who established T'ien-t'ai Buddhism and integrated into his writings a comprehensive survey of all Buddhist doctrines and theories, the T'ien-t'ai analyses and *p'an-chiao* classifications became so complex that even specialists find them difficult to understand. Moreover, Chih-i was so meticulous in his interpretations of sutras that his expositions are almost incomprehensible to the average reader.

In his Miao-fa lien-hua-ching wen-chü (Textual Commentary on the Lotus Sutra), Chih-i examined individual words and phrases of the Lotus Sutra from four points of view and further developed his thoughts in thirteen minutely considered facets. For instance, a Chinese ideogram meaning "buddha" is analyzed thoroughly from thirteen different perspectives. Such a study is invaluable from a scholar's point of view because it encompasses all Chinese views on the Buddha current at that time; however, in terms of practical value, Chih-i's commentary is so copious in its detail that it simply compounds any confusion that the average person might have been troubled with before consulting it.

In general, the following four interpretations of the word "buddha" offered by Chih-i seem to be most germane for the nonspecialist curious about the theoretical and practical meanings of the word.

1. The Buddha is one's focus of devotion in the true sense. He is the savior who delivers human beings from their sufferings and fulfills their desires and is also the figurative parent and lord of humankind. Thus one should offer prayer and reverence to him with an attitude of total dedication and of obedience to his teaching. (This is regarded as the "first-step" view of the Buddha.)

2. When considering the essence of the Buddha objectively, the discriminating person thinks of his Law (that is, of the universal, logical truth of the universe), of justice and benevolence as the basic ideal virtues of humankind, and of selfless compassion as the means of saving all sentient beings.

3. Since the second interpretation alone is not sufficient to sustain a living faith, it must be merged with the first. Thus the third interpretation unites the abstract theory of the first with the concrete practice implied by the second.

4. When one has at last arrived at a state of profound faith, one has attained unity with the Buddha and is always embraced by him even if one's awareness of the Buddha is not perfect (that is to say, not in complete accord with the union of theory and practice set forth above in the third interpretation). In this fourth interpretation one has already achieved buddhahood and sees the buddha-nature in all the objects and beings one encounters and venerates all those objects and beings as buddhas. It is at this point that the buddha-land, or paradise, becomes a reality rather than an ideal or goal.

Although the T'ien-t'ai sect enjoyed a very highly developed intellectual and philosophical appreciation of Buddhism as a religion, unlike the Hua-yen sect, for example, it also embraced a thoroughly pragmatic, down-to-earth practice of the religion that enabled it to survive while the completely academically oriented schools perished.

NINE

The Sutras in Script and Print

RECORDING THE SUTRAS   Beginning in the time of Shakyamuni, Buddhist sutras were committed
to memory and handed down orally, rather than being recorded
in writing. The oral transmission of teachings was not a custom of
Buddhists alone but was a common practice throughout India. For
instance, Orthodox Brahmanism—which possessed scriptures for
possibly a thousand years before the birth of Shakyamuni—continued to convey its sutras orally for many centuries after the
founding of Buddhism.

The Brahmans believed that memorizing scriptures and passing
them down orally was safer than committing them to writing, since
written documents can, for example, be stolen or lost through flood
or fire. Moreover, Brahmanism forbade the transmission of its
teachings to the Sudras, or slaves, who constituted the lowest of the
four major castes of India; and if the Brahmanic scriptures had
been written down and copied, they might have been seen or read
by those lowly people.

Buddhism, too, followed the tradition of reciting scriptures. The
early Buddhist *sangiti*, or councils, met not to compile or correct
written material—as they have done in more recent times—but to
recite and confirm memorized records. The original meaning of the
Sanskrit word *sangiti* is, in fact, "to recite together."

The fact that people relied on the oral transmission of information does not mean that writing was unknown in Shakyamuni's time. Some of the primitive Buddhist sutras make it clear that writing systems were generally known in the India of that day. Certain of those sutras mention, for example, a popular guessing game in which a person was to identify a letter traced on his back.

About two hundred years after Shakyamuni's death, Emperor Asoka had a number of edicts engraved on massive rocks and on stone pillars at various sites in India and neighboring countries. As I mentioned in chapter two, Asoka's edicts were written chiefly in two different scripts: Brahmi and Kharoshti. The fact that the Brahmi characters were written in varying forms in different parts of India indicates that they had been in use long enough to undergo stylistic changes, which occur only slowly. An early date for the general use of writing is further supported by the discovery of large numbers of second-century B.C. Indian coins bearing inscriptions.

In its early use, writing was confined primarily to commercial records, correspondence, and signets or seals: it was never employed for recording sacred documents. The phrase "Thus have I heard," with which so many sutras begin, is evidence that they were transmitted orally, as are the repetitive, conventionalized phrases that make the task of memorizing easier.

Nevertheless, Buddhism did eventually record its scriptures in writing—the first among all Indian religions to do so. In this sense Buddhism can be seen as a progressive religion, for its aim was to convey the Law to everyone equally, regardless of caste, and it was not reluctant to make written copies of its sutras so that all might read them.

During the time of primitive Buddhism and through the period of Abhidharma (Hinayana) Buddhism, however, sutras were not written down, presumably because there was no need to teach large numbers of people the content of the sutras, which were still at that time memorized and conveyed from one ordained monk to another in the traditional Indian manner. Yet when the sutras were taken to regions where the spoken language was different from the original language of the sutras, it would have been extremely difficult for people to memorize and preserve the sutras if they had not first been translated into the local language. Written copies of such translations may have been made at that time in order to hand the sutras down to future generations correctly.

At the time that Buddhist scriptures were first being recorded in writing in India, the leaves (or *pattra* in Sanskrit) of a type of fan palm (or *tala* in Sanskrit) were used as writing materials. But since fan palms grow only in tropical regions, birch bark, cloth, and hides were also used for written records in northwestern India and Central Asia. In some rare instances sutras were even engraved on costly sheets of copper.

When paper became more commonly available, however, sutras were recorded on paper. For example, the ancient Nepalese manuscripts written in the Siddhan script are all transcribed on palm leaves, while the later Nepalese manuscripts written in the Devanagari script are all recorded on paper. It is interesting to note that when paper came to be used for recording sutras the sheets of paper were trimmed into very long rectangles, in imitation of the earlier palm leaves, and—like the palm-leaf manuscripts—were bound in bundles tied together with cords fed through two holes punctured in the center of the sheets. In later times, when the sheets of paper were no longer tied together with cords, the two distinctive holes for the cords were retained, indicating that the paper manuscripts were replicas of or substitutes for earlier palm-leaf manuscripts.

Fan palms are common in southern India and Sri Lanka. When the early-seventh-century Chinese translator Hsüan-tsang journeyed to India, he noted there was a vast fan-palm forest, some fifteen kilometers in diameter, near Konkana in southern India, and that many people went there from other areas to pick the long, broad, glossy leaves for use in copying sutras. Since fan-palm leaves are so readily obtainable and easy to handle, they are still used today for copying sutra manuscripts in such Southern Buddhist countries as Sri Lanka, Burma, and Thailand.

Among the many kinds of fan palm to be found in Sri Lanka, the palmyra and talipot palms are generally used for manuscripts. The less durable leaves of the palmyra palm have been used for ordinary correspondence, while the tough leaves of the talipot palm —which can live for one hundred years and attain a height of twenty-five meters—have been favored for sutra manuscripts meant to be preserved. Obviously it is not mere coincidence that the name talipot is derived from the Sanskrit words *tala* and *pattra* and means, literally, "fan-palm leaf."

Today, as in the past, the leaves used for sutra manuscripts are taken from among the young leaves at the tops of fan palms. The tough, pliable, cream-colored leaves grow to lengths of three to six meters in clusters of eighty to a hundred leaves. Just before the young leaves unfurl and separate, they are reaped one by one; the harvested leaves are blanched in a cauldron, dried in the shade, and polished to a gloss on both sides. The large prepared leaves are then trimmed into rectangles twenty-five to eighty centimeters long and five to eight centimeters wide. The small manuscript leaves are used for copying short sutras, and the large leaves are used for longer sutras. Very long sutras are written on both sides of a number of manuscript leaves trimmed to the same size, which are then bound together by threading cords through two holes punched a few centimeters apart in the center of the leaves.

From ancient Mahayana palm-leaf manuscripts we know that the sutras were originally written with a brush and the carbon-based ink known variously as India ink or Chinese ink. Brush and carbon ink were also used in copying the birch-bark manuscripts in northern India and in Central Asia and later in transcribing the paper manuscripts. In Southern Buddhist countries, however, the Pali canon is recorded by first scoring the letters on a palm leaf with a metal stylus. Carbon ink is then brushed liberally over the leaf, and when the excess ink is wiped off, only the ink deposited in the etched characters remains.

The oldest historical mention of the copying of sutras indicates that sutras were being recorded in writing in Sri Lanka around the first century B.C. The Buddhism of Sri Lanka is Theravada Buddhism, introduced from India during the time of Emperor Asoka (ca. 274 to ca. 236 B.C.), and its sutras are recorded in Pali, the language in which they were brought to the country. Although Pali was not spoken in Sri Lanka, it has been retained as the Buddhist liturgical language there, and Buddhist sutras are still handed down in Pali in Sri Lanka today.

According to an ancient Sri Lankan chronicle, some two centuries after Buddhism was first conveyed to Sri Lanka the reigning king became a devout Buddhist and built a temple called Abhayagiri-vihara (Mount Fearlessness Monastery). Until that time the temple Mahavihara (Great Monastery) had served as the center of Buddhism in Sri Lanka.

The chief monk of Abhayagiri-vihara was a gregarious man who associated freely with lay believers. The monks of Mahavihara, who observed strict precepts, frowned upon the liberal attitudes accepted at Abhayagiri-vihara. Thus began a conflict between the two temples (the centers of two distinct sects) that was to continue for over one thousand years. Eventually the rigidly conservative Buddhism of the Mahavihara sect triumphed, becoming the foundation of Southern Buddhism in Sri Lanka as we know it today.

The monks of Mahavihara decided to write down their sutras to preserve them correctly for later generations, lest the true teachings be distorted by the heresies of the Abhayagiri-vihara sect. The *Mahavamsa* (Great Chronicle), a fifth- or sixth-century A.D. history of Sri Lanka written in Pali, states, "Monks of great wisdom conveyed sutras and commentaries on them by oral recitation, but seeing people stray [from the true Law], the monks met and recorded the sutras and commentaries in writing to preserve the Law forever."

In Northern Buddhism the first reference to recording sutras in written form occurs much later than the early Southern Buddhist reference mentioned above. In northern India, toward the end of the first century A.D., the great Kushan-dynasty emperor Kanishka (who, like Emperor Asoka some centuries earlier, was a devout Buddhist and protector of Buddhism) supported a council to compile sutras convened by the Sarvastivadin school, one of the eighteen or twenty schools of Hinayana Buddhism. The Great Commentary (Abhidharma-mahavibhasha-shastra), a philosophical work edited at that council, was engraved on copper plates, which were preserved at an imperial residence in Kashmir. Even though this is the earliest verifiable instance of recording scriptures in writing in Northern Buddhism, presumably the custom of copying scriptures had existed before that time in northwestern India.

Although the Agama sutras of primitive Buddhism make no mention of the practice of copying sutras, even the earliest Mahayana Buddhist sutras speak of the merit of writing out the sutras. The merits to be gained by copying the sutras are emphasized not only in the older Mahayana sutras, such as the Perfection of Wisdom sutras, but also in such later sutras as the Lotus Sutra and, in fact, in almost all Mahayana sutras. For instance, Kumarajiva's translation of the Perfection of Wisdom Sutra in Eight Thousand Lines says, "Kaushika [Indra]! If a good man or woman cannot receive and keep the Perfection of Wisdom [Sutra], read and recite it, or practice as it preaches, he or she should copy it and revere, respect, and applaud it with good flowers, scents . . ." This sutra further mentions that introducing others to the practice of sutra copying has great merit. Similar statements are found in all the Perfection of Wisdom sutras.

In the Lotus Sutra, chapter nineteen, "The Merits of the Preacher," enumerates the merits that are attained through the five kinds of practice for a teacher of the Law: receiving and keeping the sutra, reading it, reciting it, expounding it, and copying it. Chapter twenty, "The Bodhisattva Never Despise," also sets forth the merits of copying sutras and goes on to state, "Therefore all bodhisattva-*mahasattvas,* after the extinction of the Tathagata [Shakyamuni], should ever receive and keep, read, recite, expound, and copy this sutra." Chapter twenty-eight, "Encouragement of the Bodhisattva Universal Virtue," declares, "If there be any who receive and keep, read and recite, rightly remember, practice, and copy this Law-Flower Sutra [the Lotus Sutra], know that such are attending on Shakyamuni Buddha . . ." In short, in Mahayana Buddhism, copying a sutra is considered a practice equal in importance to receiving and keeping a sutra, reading, reciting, and expounding it.

The reason the Mahayana scriptures—unlike the scriptures of primitive Buddhism—preach the merit of copying sutras is found in the differences between monastic Buddhism and lay Buddhism.

Primitive and Abhidharma Buddhism made clear distinctions between monks and lay believers. Ordained monks were specialists who dedicated themselves exclusively to memorizing sutras, reading and reciting them, and expounding and practicing them. Since they transmitted their learning to the next generation of monks, sutras and other teachings of the Buddha were conveyed correctly to succeeding generations so long as these ordained monks existed. The scriptures of primitive Buddhism were transmitted in this way by the Order, or Sangha, of monks, and so long as the Order remained sound it was unnecessary to record the sutras in writing.

At the beginning of the fifth century A.D., when the Chinese monk Fa-hsien (340?–420?) made his pilgrimage to India, he found no written sutras in northwestern India—only monks in the Buddhist temples there, orally handing down the scriptures they had memorized. It was not until he went farther south, to Magadha and Sri Lanka, that he was able to obtain the written scriptures he sought. This information, recorded in Fa-hsien's journal, makes it clear that even at that late date sutras were transmitted through recitation by ordained monks. With regard to the Chinese translations of sutras in that time, we know that a number of sutras had been conveyed to China in oral versions recited by Indian monks.

Most Mahayana scriptures, however, seem to have been recorded in writing at an early date in India and Central Asia. For example, around the middle of the third century A.D. the religious scholar Chu Shih-hsing was able to obtain in Central Asia the written version of the Perfection of Wisdom Sutra in Twenty-five Thousand Lines that Wu-ch'a-lo later translated into Chinese. Such an incident demonstrates that from its inception Mahayana Buddhism maintained the custom of copying its sutras.

Mahayana Buddhism adopted this custom because, unlike Abhidharma Buddhism, it had no ordained monks charged with memorizing scripture. The greatest problem for Mahayana Buddhists, who advocated lay Buddhism, was to preserve the teachings of the Law and keep them alive. Since in its early days the adherents of Mahayana Buddhism were all lay people who had to support themselves and care for their families, none of them could dedicate themselves exclusively to teaching the Law. Even if a lay believer became distinguished for outstanding knowledge of the Law, as did Vimalakirti, there was no mechanism, such as the Buddhist Order, for educating successors.

To amend this shortcoming, Mahayana Buddhism did eventually produce ordained monks who studied the sutras, interpreted doctrine, organized scholarly theory, and instructed lay believers. Famous later Mahayana leaders (such as Nagarjuna, his disciple Aryadeva, and the brothers Vasubandhu and Asanga) were all ordained monks. But until the emergence of such teachers, there remained the problems of how to make Mahayana teachings known to people at large and how to preserve the teachings and hand them down to future generations.

To accomplish those goals, Mahayana Buddhism emphasized the merits of copying, reading, reciting, and expounding sutras. Preaching on the great merits to be obtained by simply copying the sutras ensured that the sutras would be transmitted to later generations as an act of faith even if believers had no teacher to guide them.

We have already seen how Mahayana scriptures emphasized the importance of revering and copying sutras. Beyond that, however, the scriptures also stressed that the places where written sutras were kept were to be revered as the abode of the Buddha himself and that the sutras themselves were to be revered as manifestations of the Buddha. This is preached in the Diamond Wisdom Sutra, for example, and in chapter twenty-one, "The Divine Power of the Tathagata," the Lotus Sutra states, "Whether in a place where a volume of the sutra is kept, or in a temple, or in a grove, or under a tree, or in a monastery, or in a lay devotee's house, in a palace or a mountain, in a valley or in the wilderness, in all these places you must erect a *caitya* [a pagoda in which sutras are deposited] and make offerings." Such teachings, which are characteristic of the Mahayana sutras, were of course intended to ensure the eternal preservation of the true Law.

COPYING THE SUTRAS Beginning in the T'ang dynasty (618–907), various Chinese courts authorized the compilation of a number of Tripitaka, or complete canons, called *Ta-tsang-ching* (Great Storehouse Scripture) or *I-ch'ieh-ching* (Complete Scripture) in Chinese. By imperial permission, both new translations of sutras and important Buddhist writings produced in China were included in these Tripitaka. Thus it happened that some sutras composed in China that had been included in one Tripitaka were deleted from collections compiled later. This is the reason that the writings of Hsin-hsing (540–94), founder of the Sect of the Three Stages (San-chieh-chiao), and the Biography of the Treasure Forest (Pao-lin-ch'uan), which records Zen history, are found in some Tripitaka and not in others.

The earliest Chinese Tripitaka, or complete collections of sutras, were compiled during the period of the Northern and Southern dynasties (317–589). In northern China, Emperor Hsiao-ming Ti (r. 515–28) of the Northern Wei dynasty and, in southern China, Emperor Ming Ti (r. 494–98) of the Southern Ch'i dynasty and emperors Wu Ti (r. 557–59), Wen Ti (r. 559–66), and Hsüan Ti (r. 568–82) of the Ch'en dynasty all had a number of copies of Tripitaka transcribed for enshrinement in major provincial temples. Before long it became fashionable among wealthy commoners to commission copies of the Tripitaka to be dedicated to temples.

The first Sui emperor, Wen Ti (r. 581–604), who established Buddhism as the national religion after the reunification of China, commissioned forty-six copies of the Tripitaka, which he had enshrined in various provincial temples. Tripitaka including the sutras recently translated by Hsüan-tsang (ca. 596–664) were enshrined in the temples Ching-ai-ssu in Loyang and Hsi-ming-ssu in Ch'ang-an; and Ching-t'ai's five-fascicle catalogue Chung-ching mu-lu (Catalogue of the Sutras; commonly called Ching-t'ai's Catalogue) and the ten-fascicle Ta-T'ang nei-tien-lu (Catalogue of T'ang Dynasty Sutras) compiled by Tao-hsüan (596–667) were prepared as catalogues of those collections of sutras.

In 730 Chih-sheng (658–740) compiled his monumental K'ai-yüan shih-chiao-lu (K'ai-yüan Era Buddhist Catalogue), in which some 1,076 translated sutras numbering 5,048 fascicles were methodically arranged and classified. Yüan-chao included a number of new translations in the Chen-yüan hsin-ting shih-chiao mu-lu (Chen-yüan Era Buddhist Catalogue), which he edited and completed in 800; and the information in that catalogue was brought up to date and new translations were recorded in 945 by Heng-an in his Hsü Chen-yüan shih-chiao-lu (Supplementary Chen-yüan Era Buddhist Catalogue), which listed 1,258 sutras totaling 5,390 fascicles. By the end of the T'ang dynasty the most important sutras had all been translated into Chinese, and only a small number were translated later.

In China, carbon ink was used to copy sutras on paper. The oldest extant copy of a Chinese-language sutra was transcribed during the Three Kingdoms period (220–80), and although copies of scriptures transcribed in succeeding ages also survive, many of them are only fragmentary. In the beginning there was no standard format for written sutras, but examination of extant sutras makes it clear that the practice of copying sutras in lines of seventeen ideograms was adopted at an early date.

As I mentioned earlier, some catalogues even recorded the number of sheets of paper required for copying individual sutras. The fact that the figures given for particular sutras vary little from one catalogue to another is further evidence that sutras were being copied in a fairly standardized format. A note appended to the first sutra entry in Tao-hsüan's Ta-T'ang nei-tien-lu states that a single sheet of a sutra is composed of twenty-eight lines. Although there is no mention of the number of ideograms per line, it is thought that all the sutras recorded in T'ang-dynasty catalogues were transcribed in the format of twenty-eight lines of seventeen characters each per sheet of paper. (The individual sheets of paper were afterward pasted together to form scrolls.)

Around the beginning of the Sung dynasty (960–1126) carved wood blocks began to be used to print complete copies of the Tripitaka. Though they varied somewhat in format, the most common editions from the Sung dynasty and through the Ming dynasty (1368–1662) were printed with thirty lines of seventeen characters each on one sheet of paper. (This format was used both for the sutras bound as scrolls and for the later sutras bound as books.) The most recent edition of the complete Chinese canon, the massive *Taishō Daizōkyō*, which was printed in Japan between 1924 and 1934, has three columns per page, each column composed of twenty-nine lines of seventeen ideograms each. Thus a single page of the *Taishō Daizōkyō* is roughly equivalent to three sheets of the Tripitaka as it was originally printed in China.

The copies of the Tripitaka presented to temples were stored in sutra repositories. Although these structures followed no standard design, a fixture common to most of them was the so-called round shelf—a tall, octagonal revolving cabinet in the center of the repository. According to legend, the round shelf was invented by the lay master of Buddhism Fu Ta-shih (497–569; also known as Shan-hui Ta-shih) during the Liang dynasty (502–57), and it was said that by simply turning a cabinet full of sutras around and around an illiterate person could gain merit equal to that of reciting the sutras. Legend notwithstanding, it is thought that the round shelf was invented as a convenience for readers, to reduce the amount of walking necessary to find the sutras they wished to study. Round shelves were also installed in the sutra repositories of Japanese temples, along with a devotional statue of Fu Ta-shih.

Buddhist scriptures were first brought to Japan in the mid-sixth century, when Buddhism was introduced into the country. Prince-Regent Shōtoku (574–622) himself lectured and commented on three Mahayana sutras—the Lotus Sutra, the Shrimala Sutra, and the Vimalakirti Sutra—and it is believed that he sent a mission to the Chinese court for the express purpose of bringing those sutras to Japan. Eight Sui-dynasty (581–89) scriptures belonging to the Nara temple Tōdai-ji and currently stored in the Sutra Repository of the Shōsō-in—Tōdai-ji's storehouse for its own and imperial treasures, built in 756—are believed to have been brought to Japan during the regency of Shōtoku or shortly thereafter.

It is thought that the earliest Japanese copy of the Chinese Tripitaka was transcribed at the Nara temple Kawara-dera in 673, the first year of the reign of Emperor Temmu. It appears that the scriptures included in that copy were those recorded in the Ta-T'ang nei-tien-lu compiled by Tao-hsüan in 664, indicating the rapidity with which Buddhist scriptures were making their way to Japan. During the reign of Emperor Shōmu (r. 724–49)—whose imperial treasures are stored in the Shōsō-in—the Nara monk Gembō (d. 746) journeyed to China and, in 735, brought back to Japan "over five thousand fascicles of Buddhist scriptures," which must have been the 5,048 fascicles listed in the K'ai-yüan shih-chiao-lu compiled only five years earlier by Chih-sheng.

Shōmu and his consort, Kōmyō (701–60), seem to have commanded the making of copies of the Tripitaka brought back by

Gembō. A number of those copies, along with the original scriptures from China, still survive among the imperial treasures maintained in the Shōsō-in.

Government facilities for copying sutras in Japan were established under Emperor Temmu (r. 673–86). During the reign of Emperor Shōmu the official transcription office came to be called the transcription building and was quickly separated into two facilities: one building for sutra transcription and another for commentary transcription. As the practice of copying sutras became more popular, transcription buildings were established in Nara at Tōdai-ji and at the Buddhist chapel of the imperial palace. Presumably out of belief in the merit to be gained by copying sutras and out of a desire to hand the treasure of the Law on to future generations, other temples as well as members of the nobility raised their own private transcription buildings. For instance, in 797 the great priest Saichō (767–822), who is better known in Japan by his posthumous name Dengyō Daishi, sent a number of disciples to Nara. There, with assistance from Tōdai-ji, the disciples made a complete copy of the Tripitaka to be dedicated at the temple atop Mount Hiei, outside Kyoto. They later made a copy for Emperor Kammu (r. 781–806), who is said to have conferred court rank on them.

At about this time, in 800, Yüan-chao completed his Chen-yüan hsin-ting shih-chiao mu-lu, which listed a greater number of scriptures than did the 730 catalogue K'ai-yüan shih-chiao-lu. It is said that by 833 two copies of the Chinese Tripitaka based on Yüan-chao's catalogue had been made in Japan and installed in the temple Miroku-ji in northern Kyushu and in the Kyoto temple Jingo-ji. It is further said that in the following twenty years three copies of the Tripitaka were made in the area around modern Tokyo and that those copies were installed in various government-supported provincial temples or in Miroku-ji.

During the extreme persecution of Buddhism in 845 under the T'ang-dynasty emperor Wu-tsung (r. 840–47), more than 277,000 monks and nuns were returned to lay life, and forty-seven thousand temples were destroyed. And in 955 the Later Chou emperor Shih-tsung (r. 954–59) issued a decree proscribing Buddhism. At that time over thirty-three hundred temples were destroyed, and gilt-bronze Buddhist images and bells were melted down for coin. Through these and earlier persecutions many Buddhist scriptures were lost in China; thus, at the time of the renaissance of Buddhism in the Sung dynasty (960–1126), the Chinese had to import sutras and commentaries from Korea and Japan to complete their Tripitaka.

I might mention here that it was in order to protect and preserve the original Sanskrit manuscripts, images of the Buddha, and other articles he had brought back from India that the T'ang-dynasty translator Hsüan-tsang had an enormous tiled tower, some fifty-five meters tall, built in Ch'ang-an a few years after his return to China, in 645. That structure, the Ta-yen-t'a (Great Wild Goose Tower), is still extant, though because of repairs its appearance is changed from what it must have been in Hsüan-tsang's time. Unfortunately, however, all the scriptures and religious implements originally stored in the tower have been lost owing to the proscription of Buddhism and the upheaval of war during the Ten Kingdoms and Five Dynasties period (907–79), following the T'ang dynasty.

Both before and after the time of Hsüan-tsang, a number of other Sanskrit scriptures were taken to China and carefully preserved, but they too were scattered and disappeared as a result of war and of the persecutions of Buddhism. A few Sanskrit texts that were taken back to Japan by the Japanese priests who journeyed to China during the T'ang dynasty have been preserved in temples in Japan, and those texts have been studied and published in modern times. The Sanskrit texts in Japan include the Heart of Wisdom Sutra (Prajnaparamita-hridaya-sutra), the Diamond Wisdom Sutra (Vajracchedika-prajnaparamita-sutra), and the Amitabha Sutra (Sukhavati-vyuha), which were published in the 1880s by Professor Max Müller and Dr. Nanjio Bunyiu through the Oxford University Press. It may be that Japan's long periods of internal stability and peace and the nationwide acceptance of Buddhism contributed to the survival of such ancient copies of the Buddhist scriptures.

It should be noted that the great loss of scriptures during the Ten Kingdoms and Five Dynasties period hastened the decline of the various scholarly Chinese sects and schools, which were so committed to the academic study of sutras. The Zen sect, however, which had been striving to manifest the spirit of Buddhism without depending on scripture, flourished in those uncertain times and was an influential representative of Chinese Buddhism between the T'ang and Sung dynasties.

Beginning in the tenth century the practice of copying sutras became increasingly popular in Japan, eventually giving rise to quite splendid copies, such as those executed on deep blue paper in inks compounded by blending powdered gold or silver with animal glue.

In China, the practice of copying scriptures in gold or silver ink seems to have begun around the middle of the T'ang dynasty (618–907). According to the travel diary of the Japanese Tendai priest Ennin (793–864), who journeyed to China in 838 and remained there for nine years, a magnificent Tripitaka of some six thousand fascicles transcribed in gold and silver inks on dark blue paper in 779 was installed in the sutra repository of the temple Chin-ke-ssu on Mount Wu-t'ai. And a copy of the Golden Light Sutra (Suvarnaprabhasa-sutra) preserved in Japan at the temple Jōdo-in on Mount Hiei was executed in gold ink in China in 842. During the Sung dynasty, and even afterward, the Chinese still continued to copy scriptures in gold and silver inks.

Once this manner of copying sutras was imported into Japan, it gained popularity among those who could afford the materials. For instance, among the treasures of the Shōsō-in (the eighth-century imperial storehouse at Tōdai-ji) is a copy of fascicle 463 of the Great Perfection of Wisdom Sutra (Mahaprajna-paramita-sutra) transcribed in gold ink on dark blue paper.

In 1103 the cloistered emperor Shirakawa (1053–1129) made an offering of a Tripitaka written in gold ink to the Kyoto temple Hosshō-ji, and in 1126 the nobleman Fujiwara no Kiyohira offered to Chūson-ji (in modern Iwate Prefecture) a Tripitaka copied in gold and silver inks on dark blue paper, a portion of which is still extant. (It was around this time that a special office for the copying of scriptures in gold and silver inks was established in sutra transcription buildings.) In 1159, for the repose of the spirit of the cloistered emperor Toba (1103–56), Bifuku-mon-in—the mother of Emperor Toba's heir—donated to Kongōbu-ji on Mount Kōya, south of

Osaka, a Tripitaka executed in gold ink on dark blue paper. And in 1164 the imperial minister Taira no Kiyomori (1118–81) and his brother Yorimori (1132–86) presented to Itsukushima Shrine, near modern Hiroshima, a copy of the Lotus Sutra and its opening and closing sutras transcribed in gold ink on dark blue paper, which has survived to the present.

During the eleventh and twelfth centuries a number of printed copies of the Tripitaka were brought to Japan from China or Korea, providing more trustworthy and complete texts than were available as written copies. With printed copies of the Tripitaka at hand for study, the task of copying the scriptures manually became less urgent. The practice of transcribing sutras in gold or silver ink did continue, however, because while those viscous inks could not be used in making printed copies of the sutras, people still wished to leave a legacy of sumptuous scriptures. It is also likely that the practice was continued not as an expression of genuine religious devotion but as a means of displaying the wealth and rank of the people who commissioned such copies.

Following the introduction of printed copies of the scriptures, the practice of copying them by hand in carbon ink may have been continued only as a custom or perhaps even as a novelty. Unusual among the methods of copying scriptures in Japan were the "one-day" or "one-time" transcriptions, in which the entire Tripitaka was copied in a single day by apportioning the work among a great many people. For example, during the reign of Emperor Shirakawa the monk Jiō allotted the work to 10,000 devout Buddhists, who transcribed the Tripitaka in one day. And in 1211 the cloistered emperor Gotoba (1180–1239) visited the Kyoto temple Saishō-shitennō-in, where 13,315 monks transcribed the Tripitaka for him in a single day.

PRINTING THE SUTRAS   Until the T'ang dynasty the Chinese had always transcribed the Tripitaka by hand—a laborious task, since the copies often ran to more than five thousand fascicles. Hence, for more accurate and widespread transmission of Buddhist scripture, printing was a far more practical method of reproduction. As is evident from the various seals and signets that have been excavated from many ancient sites in the Middle East, the principles of printing had long been known, but it was not until around the T'ang dynasty that an efficient means of reproducing long works was developed. Unfortunately, however, because of that country's frequent wars no examples of the earliest printed Chinese texts have survived.

The world's oldest extant examples of printing are *dharani*, or magical incantations, printed in Japan between 764 and 770, during the reign of Empress Shōtoku. A total of over one million copies of four different *dharani* from the Great Dharani Sutra of the Spotless and Pure Light (Rashmivimala-vishuddhiprabhasa-dha-rani-sutra) were printed to be placed in the Hyakuman-tō (One Million Pagodas) built at the command of Shōtoku. In this sutra it is stated that if a person were to build several million small pagodas and place copies of *dharani* in them, that person's life would be lengthened, evil karma would be expunged, and rebels and enemies would be vanquished. Because of that assurance, Empress Shōtoku ordered the construction of just over one million pagodas after the former imperial advisor Fujiwara no Nakamaro (706–64) instigated a revolt against the ambitious, influential monk Dōkyō (d. 772).*

The *dharani* had been printed because of the immensity of the task of transcribing over one million copies of the four *dharani*, each of which ran to about four hundred ideograms. It is said, however, that a few of the copies were transcribed by hand. It is entirely likely that copper plates were used for printing the *dharani*, since the printed characters show little wear, remaining sharp and clear on all copies, even though a quarter of a million copies of one *dharani* must have been struck from a single plate.

These *dharani* were printed almost seven hundred years before

* The wooden pagodas were made in three sizes. Ten of the largest size, thirteen-story pagodas standing seventy centimeters high, were built; one hundred of the next size, seven-story pagodas some sixty centimeters in height, were made; and one million of the smallest size, three-story pagodas twenty-three centimeters tall, were produced. One copy of a printed *dharani* was placed in each pagoda before they were distributed for installation at ten major temples, including Tōdai-ji and Yakushi-ji in Nara, the great Hōryū-ji just outside Nara, and Shitennō-ji in Osaka.

the European development of movable type, with which Gutenberg is traditionally credited. It is believed that printing was known and used in China well before Empress Shōtoku's *dharani* were printed in Japan, possibly even as early as the second century A.D.; but the oldest extant example of Chinese printing is the exquisite wood-block-printed copy of the Diamond Wisdom Sutra made in 868 that was recovered in Tun-huang from the rock-hewn temple complex that includes the famous Cave of the Thousand Buddhas. Although Confucian writings seem to have been printed not long after the Diamond Wisdom Sutra, it was not until the beginning of the Sung dynasty that printing of the massive Tripitaka was undertaken (about one hundred years after the Diamond Wisdom Sutra). Though it would be another seven decades before the Chinese developed practical movable type, the earliest printed Tripitaka appeared nearly five centuries before Gutenberg's Bible.

The first complete Tripitaka printed in China was the Sung Governmental Edition, which is commonly called the Shu-pan, or Shu Edition. The wood blocks from which it was printed were carved at Ch'eng-tu in Szechwan Province at the order of the first Sung-dynasty emperor, T'ai Tsu (r. 960–76). The monumental task of carving and printing the 130,000 wood blocks for that edition, begun in 971, was not completed until 983. The fact that hardwood was used for the blocks to prolong their useful life only increased the difficulty of the carving. The sutras included in the Shu Edition numbered 5,586 fascicles: the 5,048 fascicles listed in the 730 K'ai-yüan shih-chiao-lu (K'ai-yüan Era Buddhist Catalogue), 279 fascicles of new translations completed during the Sung dynasty, and 259 fascicles of pre–Sung-dynasty translations not incorporated in the K'ai-yüan shih-chiao-lu.

On completion of the Shu Edition of the Tripitaka, in 983, copies were installed in major provincial temples. In 984 the Japanese monk Chōnen (d. 1016) from the Nara temple Tōdai-ji, who was then in China on a pilgrimage, was given a complete copy of the Shu Edition, which he took back to Japan on his return, in 987. Highly prized as a rare treasure of the Law, that copy of the Tripitaka was later stored in the sutra repository of the temple Hōjō-ji, built in Kyoto by the powerful regent Fujiwara no Michinaga

(966–1027). Although that copy of the Shu Edition was lost when Hōjō-ji was destroyed by fire in 1058, that edition of the Tripitaka is known through portions of another copy preserved at the Kyoto temple Nanzen-ji and through portions of a third copy recovered from the caves at Tun-huang.

In 990 still another copy of the Shu Edition of the Tripitaka was presented to the Korean king Sŏngjong (r. 981–97), of the Koryŏ dynasty (918–1392). That copy eventually formed the foundation for the famous Koryŏ Edition of the Tripitaka, which has also been known as the Tripitaka Koreana.

The Sung-dynasty government added newly translated sutras to the Shu Edition in 1013 and 1036. By an imperial command in 1071 the wood blocks for the Shu Edition and its supplements were entrusted to the subtemple Shen-shou ch'an-yüan at Hsien-shen Temple, and the printing was transferred to private hands. Copies of the Tripitaka did not immediately become widely available, however, because publication was still supervised by the government.

In northern China the Liao dynasty (947–1125), established by the Khitan Mongols, also embraced Buddhism and aspired to equal the Sung dynasty in cultural development. Under Liao rule, sutras continued to be carved in stone at Yun-chu Temple on Mount Fang in Hopei Province, and a complete set of wood blocks for an edition of the Tripitaka was made. That edition of the Tripitaka, which was based on the Shu Edition and its supplements, seems to have been completed around 1055. Although this edition has not survived, we know that the copy of it presented to the Koryŏ court in 1058 influenced the Koryŏ Edition.

With the Shu and Khitan (Liao) editions as models, at least two editions of the Tripitaka were published in Koryŏ, and both have been called the Koryŏ Edition. It is believed that the first Koryŏ Edition, initiated and completed under King Hyeonjong (r. 1009–31), contained the 5,048 fascicles of the K'ai-yüan shih-chiao-lu and that it followed the format of the Shu Edition.

The second Koryŏ Edition, produced during the reign of King Munjong (r. 1046–82), included translations not incorporated in the K'ai-yüan shih-chiao-lu, in addition to a number of sutras from the Shu and Khitan editions. It is believed that together the two Koryŏ editions contained some 1,524 works. A copy of the original printing of either the first or the second Koryŏ Edition was installed in the temple Kennin-ji in Kyoto, but because almost all of it was lost in a fire in 1837 we cannot be certain which edition the temple received. Additional portions of one of the printings are preserved at other Japanese temples, such as Nanzen-ji in Kyoto and Zōjō-ji in Tokyo.

Well over one hundred years after its first publication, the second Koryŏ Edition was reprinted at Haein Temple in southern Korea. It is the Haein Temple printings that are generally called the Koryŏ Edition of the Tripitaka. (A nearly complete copy of a Haein Temple printing is preserved in the Tokyo temple Zōjō-ji.) The wood blocks used to print the Haein Temple Edition, numbering over eighty thousand, are still maintained at Haein Temple and have been used again in recent times to print additional copies of the Koryŏ Edition of the Tripitaka. One of those copies was presented to Japan and is readily available to scholars.

Under the Chin dynasty (1115–1234), which displaced the Liao dynasty in northern China and established its capital in Shansi Province, a revised version of the Sung Governmental, or Shu, Edition was published. Known as the Chin Edition, it included all the sutras from the Shu Edition (and those sutras were printed in the same format as in the Shu Edition), as well as a number of additional sutras, which were printed in a noticeably different format. (Most of the printing blocks for the Chin Edition were preserved at Kuang-sheng Temple in Shansi Province until World War II.)

Eventually some of the printing blocks for the Chin Edition became badly worn, or were lost, and Kublai Khan (1215–94), founder of the Yüan dynasty (1271–1368), ordered the publication of a revised version of the Chin Edition. That revised Tripitaka, known as the Hung-fa Temple Edition, became widely accepted and was designated a *Ch'in-ting Ta-tsang-ching*, or authorized edition of the complete Chinese canon. From the Chih-yüan fa-pao k'an-t'ung tsung-lu (Chih-yüan Era Complete Buddhist Catalogue), published in 1306, we know all of the sutras that were included in the Hung-fa Temple Edition. The Tibetan school of Buddhism known as

Lamaism, which had been accepted by the Mongols early in the thirteenth century, strongly influenced Kublai and succeeding Mongol emperors of the Yüan dynasty. Thus the Chih-yüan fa-pao k'an-t'ung tsung-lu compared the Chinese and Tibetan translations of the sutras, and the Tibetan translations of certain Sanskrit words were added to the Chinese translations. It is said that when Dr. Nanjio Bunyiu translated the Ta-Ming san-tsang sheng-chiao mu-lu (Ming Dynasty Catalogue of the Tripitaka) into English for publication in 1883, he followed the Chih-yüan fa-pao k'an-t'ung tsung-lu Tibetan transcriptions of names and words that appear in Sanskrit in the English edition.

The editions of the Tripitaka that we have considered so far have all been in the lineage of the Shu Edition, published by the Sung-dynasty government. But at the beginning of the twelfth century an entirely new edition of the Tripitaka, differing in both format and content from all those in the Shu Edition lineage, was published in southern China, in Fu-chou (Foochow), Fukien Province. The Fu-chou Tung-ch'an Temple Edition was the model for editions of the Tripitaka published in southern China during the Southern Sung, Yüan, and Ming dynasties (that is, between 1127 and 1662) and was markedly different from such versions as the Koryŏ Edition, which were based on the Shu Edition. The Tung-ch'an Temple Edition was prepared privately, under the direction of six successive chief priests of the temple during the twenty-three-year period from 1080 to 1103, when it was first printed, but work was not finally completed until 1176. Shortly after its first printing in Fu-chou, the Tung-ch'an Temple Edition was granted the imperial title *Ch'ung-ning Wan-shou Ta-tsang* and came to be regarded as the authorized edition of the complete Chinese canon.

Whereas a format of twenty-three lines of fourteen characters each per printing block was used for the Shu Edition and a format of twenty-five lines of fourteen characters each was used for the Koryŏ Edition, a format of thirty lines of seventeen ideograms each was adopted for the Tung-ch'an Temple Edition. This return to the number of characters per line that had been standard in the earlier, handwritten copies of the Tripitaka made it easier for scholars to compare the printed Tripitaka with old manuscript versions. Although all the old manuscripts had been bound as hand scrolls, and the Shu Edition followed that style, the scroll-length printed sheets of the Tung-ch'an Temple Edition were folded and bound as an accordion-style book. Since each book page was composed of six lines, a single printing block of thirty lines yielded five pages. Interestingly, the Koryŏ Edition, in the Shu Edition lineage, could be bound either as a hand scroll or as an accordion-fold book, its twenty-five-line printing blocks producing five pages of five lines each when bound as a book. Calculations based on the number of wood blocks and the number of characters per block indicate that in content the Tung-ch'an Temple Edition was more than one and a half times the length of the Shu Edition.

Apart from format and binding style, the Tung-ch'an Temple Edition also differed from the Shu Edition of the Tripitaka in its selection and arrangement of sutras. For instance, while the Koryŏ Edition, based on the Shu Edition, included only two fascicles of the sutra Milindapanha (The Questions of [King] Milinda [Menander; the second-century B.C. Indo-Greek king]), the Southern Sung, Yüan, and Ming dynasty editions based on the Tung-ch'an Temple Edition reproduced all three fascicles of this sutra. Because of numerous such differences as this, it is believed that the Tung-ch'an Temple Edition was itself modeled on a Tripitaka in a lineage quite different from that of the Shu Edition.

The wood blocks for the Tung-ch'an Temple Edition were preserved and used for printing until around the end of the Yüan dynasty (1271–1368). A late copy of this early-twelfth-century Tripitaka and a copy of its successor, the Fu-chou K'ai-yüan Temple Edition, appear to have been brought to Japan near the end of the Fujiwara period (897–1185), and portions of those copies were presented to the Imperial Household Library and to various temples, such as Nanzen-ji in Kyoto. A catalogue of the Tung-ch'an Temple Edition, the Kyūzō Tōhon Issaikyō Mokuroku, was compiled in Japan and is still preserved at the Kyoto temple Kōzan-ji.

Like its predecessor, the Tung-ch'an Temple Edition, the K'ai-yüan Temple Edition of the Tripitaka was a private undertaking and was printed in Fu-chou, giving us the name Fu-chou K'ai-yüan

Temple Edition, by which it is most commonly known. The Fu-chou K'ai-yüan Temple Edition, which was prepared and printed between 1112 and 1148, followed the Tung-ch'an Temple Edition so closely that early Japanese scholars were confused when the two were imported together and could distinguish between them only by referring to the dates of publication.

Begun during the Sung dynasty, the Tung-ch'an Temple Edition and the Fu-chou K'ai-yüan Temple Edition were both completed during the Southern Sung dynasty (1127–1279). Further editions of the Tripitaka based on the Tung-ch'an Temple Edition and published during the Southern Sung dynasty include the Ssu-ch'i Fa-pao Temple Edition, the Ssu-ch'i Yüan-chüeh-yüan Edition, and the Chi-sha yen-sheng-yüan Edition. Although the printing blocks for these editions were carved in the same format as those for the Tung-ch'an Temple Edition, these Tripitaka were all bound as hand scrolls rather than books.

A number of copies of the Ssu-ch'i Fa-pao Temple Edition were brought to Japan and are now preserved at such temples as Zōjō-ji in Tokyo, Hase-dera near Nara, and Kita-in in Saitama Prefecture. It is interesting to note that all the copies of this edition brought to Japan had been bound as accordion-fold books. At the beginning of Japan's Edo period (1603–1868), an edition of the Tripitaka was printed with movable type at the Tokyo temple Kan'ei-ji under the supervision of the chief priest, Tenkai. Known as the Tenkai Edition, that Tripitaka was based on the Ssu-ch'i Fa-pao Temple Edition.

Probably reflecting the stimulation of the importation of the Tung-ch'an, Fu-chou K'ai-yüan, and Ssu-ch'i Fa-pao temple editions of the Tripitaka, wood blocks for individual sutras and other works were carved in Nara and Kamakura from the twelfth century into the fourteenth century, and the Nara temple Kōfuku-ji, with the cooperation of a number of other temples, began printing sutras and commentaries. The various publications produced in this way in Nara are known collectively as the Kasuga Edition, after the Shinto deity Kasuga-myōjin enshrined at Kōfuku-ji and because the word "Kasuga" was inscribed on the colophon page of each work. The oldest extant publication from that period is the Commentary on the Treatise on the Establishment of the Doctrine of Consciousness Only (Ch'eng wei-shih-lun shu-chi), printed in 1195, while the second oldest extant work is a ten-fascicle edition of the Treatise on the Establishment of the Doctrine of Consciousness Only (Vijnaptimatratasiddhi-shastra), for which wood blocks were cut in 1201 and 1202. In 1248 and 1249 the Nara temple Hōryū-ji made wood blocks for the Commentaries on Three Sutras (the Lotus Sutra, the Vimalakirti Sutra, and the Shrimala Sutra), written centuries earlier by Prince-Regent Shōtoku. Between 1200 and 1380 several temples in the important town of Kamakura, including Gokuraku-ji, Kenchō-ji, and Engaku-ji, also cut wood blocks for a number of sutras and commentaries.

As I mentioned earlier, during the Yüan dynasty (1279–1368), the Hung-fa Temple Edition of the Tripitaka, in the Shu Edition lineage, was published in Peking, in northern China. In central China, the Ta-p'u-ning Temple Edition was published in Hang-chou around the end of the thirteenth century. The Ta-p'u-ning Temple Edition, which Japanese scholars call the Yüan Edition, followed the content and format of the Ssu-ch'i Fa-pao Temple Edition. Copies of the Ta-p'u-ning Temple Edition are still preserved at a number of Japanese temples, including Zōjō-ji and Sensō-ji in Tokyo. The copy owned by Sensō-ji had at one time been installed in the Shinto shrine Tsurugaoka Hachiman-gū in Kamakura and narrowly escaped destruction when that shrine's Buddhist ritual articles were burned following the 1868 government order officially separating Buddhism from Shinto.

LATER EDITIONS OF THE CHINESE CANON   Between the late tenth century and the late fourteenth century—that is, between the beginning of the Sung dynasty and the end of the Yüan dynasty—about ten editions of the complete Chinese canon, or Tripitaka, were published, in both northern and southern China. Although copies of those editions had been installed in various provincial temples, few of them survived the devastating war that attended the overthrow of the Yüan dynasty. Thus when it was decided to propagate Buddhism during the succeeding Ming dynasty (1368–1662), there were scarcely any extant sutras with which to do so.

To remedy this situation, Emperor Hung-wu (r. 1368–98), the founder of the Ming dynasty, had an edition of the Tripitaka based on the Tung-ch'an Temple Edition published in Nanking not long after he came to the throne. That edition, known as the Southern Ming Edition, contained numerous errors, however, and a revised version, called the Northern Ming Edition, was published some years later in Peking, during the reign of Emperor Yung-lo (r. 1403–24). Both these governmental editions were bound as accordion-fold books, which were awkward to handle.

For the convenience of readers, later privately published editions of the Tripitaka (such as the Leng-yen Temple Edition) adopted a binding style common in Japan until early this century, in which a sheet of paper printed on one side is folded double and a number of sheets are stitched together along the open side opposite the fold to produce a volume much like a present-day book. A single printed sheet of the Leng-yen Temple Edition contained twenty lines of twenty ideograms each, so that each page contained ten lines. The printing of the Leng-yen Temple Edition, which is generally known as the Wan-li Edition, was begun in 1589 and was not completed until several decades later. Made available at a reasonable price, the Wan-li Edition was widely circulated in China, and a large number of copies were brought to Japan, where it was reprinted as the Ōbaku Edition of the Tripitaka.

As I mentioned earlier, the Japanese had begun publishing individual sutras and commentaries during the Kamakura period (1185–1336), but it was not until the Edo period that they began publishing editions of the complete Chinese canon, or Tripitaka.

In 1637 Tenkai (1536–1643), chief priest of Kan'ei-ji in Tokyo, initiated work on the first Japanese publication of a complete edition of the Chinese Tripitaka. The printing of its 1,453 works in 6,323 fascicles was not completed until 1648, five years after Tenkai's death. That edition, known as the Tenkai Edition, was a reprinting of the Southern Sung–dynasty Ssu-ch'i Fa-pao Temple Edition and was printed with movable type, which made the laborious carving of wood blocks for printing unnecessary.

Although the use of movable type (which was made of wood) instead of carved wood blocks made publication easier, and possibly even a bit faster, only a limited number of copies of a work could be printed with movable type. Individual pieces of type, each bearing a single ideogram, were placed in special wooden forms to produce the appropriate lines for a particular page. Once the desired number of copies of that page had been printed, the pieces of type were removed from the form and used in creating another page of text. Thus, without doing the typesetting all over again, it was impossible to print additional copies of a page once the form had been broken up to permit the type to be used elsewhere. For this reason, the more arduous woodblock printing of the Tripitaka may have been more practical in those days, for once a printing block had been carved, it could be used for printing additional copies until it was worn out, in very much the same way that modern printing plates can be used.

Because of the inherent limitations of printing with movable type, the Tenkai Edition, which is also called the Kan'ei-ji Temple Edition, was not widely circulated, and the imported copies of the Wan-li Edition were not sufficient to meet the needs of the Japanese Buddhist world. Thus the Zen master Tetsugen (1630–82), of the Ōbaku sect, who was sorely troubled by the paucity of copies of the Tripitaka, constructed the repository Hōzō-in within the precincts of Mampuku-ji, southeast of Kyoto, in which to store printing blocks for an edition of the Tripitaka. He also established a printing workshop in Kyoto, where he had wood blocks carved. Tetsugen solicited funds for the publication from feudal lords and commoners alike, but when a famine occurred, he promptly gave all the money away in order to alleviate people's suffering. Once again he appealed for donations to pay for publishing an edition of the Tripitaka, and once more he gave away all the funds he had collected. In 1669, however, Tetsugen was at last able to undertake publication of the Tripitaka, which was completed in 1681.

The publication of Tetsugen's Ōbaku Edition of the Tripitaka, a reproduction of the Ming-dynasty Wan-li Edition, contributed greatly to the study of Buddhism in Japan, which experienced a resurgence around the middle of the Edo period. The wood blocks used to print the Ōbaku Edition are still preserved in the Hōzō-in at Mampuku-ji.

While the court noble Iwakura Tomomi (1825–83) was in England—as head of the Japanese mission that visited America and Europe between 1871 and 1873—he was asked to donate a copy of the complete Chinese canon to the British Museum. As a result of that request, a copy of the Ōbaku Edition was presented to the Library of the India Office. Shortly afterward, Samuel Beal (1825–89), an English scholar of Chinese literature, compiled *The Buddhist Tripitaka*, an English-language catalogue of all the sutras in the Ōbaku Edition, which was published in 1876.

In that same year the well-known Japanese Buddhist scholar Dr. Nanjio Bunyiu (1849–1927) went to England to pursue his study of English and to research Buddhist texts in Europe. In the course of his studies Dr. Nanjio discovered that Beal's catalogue was riddled with errors. Nanjio therefore set himself the task of righting Beal's mistakes, and in 1883 he published *A Catalogue of the Chinese Translation of the Buddhist Tripitaka*, a translation that was highly praised by Buddhologists and scholars of Oriental studies throughout the world. That work remains the only reliable English-language record of Chinese translations of Buddhist sutras. Nanjio's catalogue generally follows the Ta-Ming san-tsang sheng-chiao mu-lu (Ming Dynasty Catalogue of the Tripitaka), the compendium of the Northern Ming Edition of the Tripitaka, on which the Wan-li Edition (and hence the Ōbaku Edition) was based.

When Buddhist studies became a recognized discipline in Japan, in the Edo period, scholars began systematic comparison of the Ōbaku Edition (of the Tung-ch'an Temple Edition lineage) and of the Koryŏ Edition (of the Shu Edition lineage). For instance, when the priest Ninchō (d. 1711), founder of the Kyoto temple Hōnen-in, discovered there were numerous errors and omissions in the Ōbaku Edition, he compared it with the Koryŏ Edition stored at the Tokyo temple Zōjō-ji. But that edition, a late printing, was not very helpful. Finally granted special permission by the court noble charged with its protection, Ninchō was able to study the copy of the original printing of the second Koryŏ Edition owned by the Kyoto temple Kennin-ji (almost all of which was lost in a fire over a century after Ninchō's death). With those three versions of the complete Chinese canon at hand, Ninchō undertook an extensive revision of the known Chinese canon in 1706, completing his work more than four years later.

Well over a century later, in 1826, the priest Junkei of the temple Jōshō-ji (in present-day Fukui Prefecture) embarked on a further revision of the Chinese canon, not completed until eleven years later, adding to the Ōbaku Edition some five hundred fascicles that he had found in the Kennin-ji copy of the Koryŏ Edition. Junkei's emendations are preserved at the Tokyo temple Zōjō-ji. Unfortunately for modern scholars, the copy of the Koryŏ Edition consulted by both Ninchō and Junkei was almost totally destroyed by a fire at Kennin-ji in 1837, the year after Junkei completed his revision. Only forty-nine fascicles survive.

At present Zōjō-ji owns three different early editions of the Tripitaka: a Haein Temple printing of the second Koryŏ Edition, a copy of the Southern Sung–dynasty Ssu-ch'i Fa-pao Temple Edition, and a copy of the Ta-p'u-ning Temple Edition (also known as the Yüan Edition)—all donated to Zōjō-ji by the first Tokugawa shogun, Ieyasu (1542–1616). The Koryŏ Edition had been brought to Japan from Korea by the priest Eikō, who installed it in the temple Enjō-ji in Nara between 1469 and 1487; but in 1609 Ieyasu persuaded the temple to part with it in exchange for a plot of land producing 150 *koku* (27,000 liters) of rice annually, and it was presented to Zōjō-ji. The Ssu-ch'i Fa-pao Temple Edition, which belonged to Kanzan-ji in Ōmi (in modern Shiga Prefecture), had been obtained in 1275 by the priest Sengyō. Ieyasu received it in 1613 in exchange for a small mountain forest and land with an annual yield of 150 *koku* of rice. In 1609 Ieyasu acquired the Ta-p'u-ning Temple Edition from Shuzen-ji in Izu (in present-day Shizuoka Prefecture) in exchange for land producing 140 *koku* of rice annually.

The comparative study of northern and southern Chinese editions of the Tripitaka late in the Edo period (1603–1868) influenced Japanese Buddhist studies during the Meiji era (1868–1912) and the Taishō era (1912–26), leading to the publication of three modern editions of the Chinese canon produced by consolidating the Koryŏ and Wan-li editions. The first of these was the *Dai Nip-*

pon Kōtei Daizōkyō, popularly known as the *Shukusatsu-zōkyō,* or Small-Type Canon, which was published between 1880 and 1885. The second was the *Dai Nippon Kōtei Zōkyō,* commonly called the *Manji-zōkyō,* or Fylfot-Letter Tripitaka, published between 1902 and 1905. The third was the *Taishō Shinshū Daizōkyō,* generally called the *Taishō Daizōkyō,* or Taishō Edition of the Tripitaka, which was published between 1924 and 1934.

Each of these editions was an enlargement of its predecessors; thus, the later the edition, the more complete it was, containing sutras and Chinese and Japanese commentaries and treatises not found in earlier compilations of the Chinese canon. The *Manji-zōkyō,* for instance, which even contains a number of Chinese writings not included in the later Taishō Edition, remains a valuable source of material for present-day scholars. Though it is extremely difficult to acquire copies of the original printing of the *Manji-zōkyō,* a measure of its continuing worth is indicated by the fact that an inexpensive reproduction of it was manufactured in Taiwan some years ago.

Publication of the one-hundred-volume *Taishō Daizōkyō,* the most authoritative and complete edition of the Buddhist canon, was undertaken at the request of Professor Takakusu Junjirō, a pioneer Japanese Buddhologist and scholar of Indian philosophy, who supervised its preparation. The Taishō Edition did not follow the traditional system of arranging sutras according to whether they were Hinayana or Mahayana but instead organized the sutras chronologically, according to the historical development of their teachings. Moreover, scholars throughout the world found the Taishō Edition easy to use because, for example, care was taken to point out each Pali or Sanskrit word that corresponded to or was similar to a particular Chinese rendering, and Chinese translations were frequently supplemented with Indic-language notations to increase clarity or to correct errors. Because of its completeness, scholarly thoroughness, and critical examination of all earlier editions of the Chinese canon, the *Taishō Daizōkyō* is still the most widely studied edition of the Tripitaka.

The Taishō Edition, which contains more sutras than any preceding edition, comprises four parts. Part one, containing 2,184 works, consists of fifty-five volumes of the Chinese canon: thirty-two volumes of sutras, texts, and treatises translated from Indic languages and twenty-three volumes of commentaries, catalogues, and other works written in China. The first thirty-two volumes include 1,692 works, well over fifty percent more than the 1,076 listed by Chih-sheng in his 730 catalogue K'ai-yüan shih-chiao-lu. Part two consists of thirty volumes containing a total of 736 works written by Japanese monks and scriptures recovered from the caves at Tun-huang after they were reopened in 1900. Part three consists of twelve volumes containing 363 illustrated works on Buddhist images and art, and part four consists of three volumes containing seventy-seven catalogues. The complete hundred-volume set of the *Taishō Daizōkyō,* comprising some 3,360 works, is incomparably larger and more definitive than any previous edition of the Buddhist canon.

The Japanese scholarship that was responsible for the Taishō Edition of the Buddhist canon also produced a number of other works, including both Japanese-language translations of the Buddhist canon and such collections of commentaries, treatises, and interpretations written in Japan as the 150-volume *Dai Nihon Bukkyō Zensho* (Great Japan Complete Buddhist Works), published between 1911 and 1922, and the 51-volume *Nihon Daizōkyō* (Japan Canon), published between 1919 and 1921. Such publishing activities of course furthered the study of Buddhism in Japan. Then in commemoration of Professor Takakusu Junjirō's contributions to Buddhist studies, a group of Japanese scholars undertook the publication of the *Nanden Daizōkyō* (Southern Route Canon) in 1935, completing their work in 1941. The *Nanden Daizōkyō,* a Japanese-language translation of the Pali Tipitaka and other classical canonical works disseminated in such Southern Buddhist countries as Sri Lanka, Burma, and Thailand, facilitated Japanese research on primitive and fundamental Buddhism.

The world's most complete collection of Buddhist literature, including almost all the works composed in China and Japan, is found in Japan, both in original manuscripts and printed editions and in modern editions. The complete literature of various Chinese sects and schools, the writings of the founders and outstanding priests and monks of various Chinese and Japanese sects, and Japanese-language translations of Pali and Sanskrit scriptures have all been published in Japan in this century. And several versions of the Tibetan Buddhist canon originally published in Tibet and in China have been reprinted in Japan. With copies of all known Buddhist sutras readily available for study, recent Japanese Buddhist scholarship, though little published in Western languages, is making even greater progress than during the pivotal Meiji and Taishō eras. In coming years, as more of their works are translated and become accessible to a wider audience, Japanese scholars can be expected to make greater contributions to present knowledge and understanding not only of the transmission of sutras to China but also of the nature, formation, and historical development of the sutras.

APPENDIX

Scriptures and Catalogues

Works are entered here under their titles in more than one language; complete information, when known, is given in the entry for the title in the language in which the work was originally recorded. When the transliteration of Sanskrit or Pali words appearing in the text differs from the orthodox form, the latter is given in parentheses. In the abbreviations used here, S stands for Sanskrit, P for Pali, and J for Japanese. Ideograms are included for both Chinese and Japanese titles, but only the few Japanese titles are expressly identified.

Abhidharmakosha-shastra (Abhidharmakośa-śāstra, S), A-p'i-ta-mo chü-she-lun (阿毗達磨俱舍論), abbreviated: Chü-she-lun (俱舍論), 30 fascicles, translated between 651 and 654 by Hsüan-tsang; Abhidharma Storehouse Treatise

Abhidharma-mahavibhasha-shastra (Abhidharma-mahāvibhāṣā-śāstra, S), A-p'i-ta-mo ta p'i-p'o-sha-lun (阿毗達磨大毗婆沙論), abbreviated: Mahavibhasha-shastra, Ta p'i-p'o-sha-lun (大毗婆沙論), and P'o-sha-lun (婆沙論), 200 fascicles, translated 656–59 by Hsüan-tsang; Great Commentary

Abhidharma Storehouse Treatise. *See* Abhidharmakosha-shastra

Abridged Flower Garland Sutra. *See* Ch'ao hua-yen-ching

Abridged Great Collection of Sutras. *See* Ch'ao fang-teng ta-chi-ching

Abridged Story of the Bodhisattva Medicine King. *See* Ch'ao fa-hua yao-wang-p'in

Abridged Sutra of a Bodhisattva's Spiritual States. *See* Ch'ao p'u-sa ti-ching

Abridged Sutra of Meditation on the Bodhisattva Universal Virtue. *See* Ch'ao p'u-hsien kuan-ch'an hui-fa

Amitabha Sutra. *See* Sukhavati-vyuha (2)

A-mi-t'o-ching. *See* Sukhavati-vyuha (2)

An-lu, An's Catalogue. *See* Tsung-li chung-ching mu-lu

A-p'i-ta-mo chi-lun. *See* Mahayanabhidharma-samucchaya

A-p'i-ta-mo chü-she-lun. *See* Abhidharmakosha-shastra

A-p'i-ta-mo ta p'i-p'o-sha-lun. *See* Abhidharma-mahavibhasha-shastra

A-p'i-ta-mo tsa-chi-lun. *See* Mahayanabhidharma-samucchaya-vya-khya

Ashtasahasrika-prajnaparamita-sutra (Aṣṭasāhasrikā-prajñāpāramitā-sūtra, S), Pa-ch'ien-sung pan-jo (八千頌般若); (1) Tao-hsing pan-jo-ching (道行般若經), 10 fascicles, translated 179 by Lokakshema; (2) Hsiao-p'in pan-jo-ching (小品般若經), 10 fascicles, translated 408 by Kumarajiva; Perfection of Wisdom Sutra in Eight Thousand Lines

Atthakavagga (P), I-p'in-ching (義品經), 2 fascicles, translated between 223 and 253 by Chih Ch'ien; Meaningful Chapter

Avadana (Avadāna, S), P'i-yü-ching (譬喩經), 1 fascicle, translated 710 by I-ching; Stories

Avatamsaka-sutra (Avataṃsaka-sūtra, S), formally: Buddha-avataṃ-saka-nāma-mahā-vaipulya-sūtra (S), Ta-fang-kuang-fo hua-yen-ching (大方廣佛華嚴經), abbreviated: Hua-yen-ching (華嚴經); (1) 60 fascicles, translated 418–21 by Buddhabhadra; (2) also abbreviated: Ta hua-yen-ching (大華嚴經), 80 fascicles, translated 695–99 by Shik-shananda; Flower Garland Sutra

Biography of the Treasure Forest. *See* Pao-lin-chuan

Bodhisattvabhumi (Bodhisattvabhūmi, S), P'u-sa ti-ch'ih-ching (菩薩地持經), also called P'u-sa ti-ch'ih-lun (菩薩地持論), abbreviated: Ti-ch'ih-lun (地持論), 10 fascicles, translated between 414 and 426 by Dharmakshema; Sutra of a Bodhisattva's Spiritual States, a partial translation of the Yogacharabhumi-shastra, q.v.

Bodhisattva Treasury Sutra. *See* P'u-sa-tsang-ching

Buddha-stage Sutra. *See* Fo-ti-ching

Catalogue of T'ang Dynasty Buddhist Sutras. *See* Ta-T'ang nei-tien-lu

Catalogue of the Sutras. *See* Chung-ching mu-lu

Ch'ang a-han-ching. *See* Dirgha-agama

Ch'ang-fang-lu, Ch'ang-fang's Catalogue. *See* Li-tai san-pao-chi

Ch'ao fa-hua yao-wang-p'in (抄法華藥王品), 1 fascicle, abridged sutra by Southern Ch'i Prince Ching-ling (459–94); Abridged Story of the Bodhisattva Medicine King (chapter 23 of the Lotus Sutra)

Ch'ao fang-teng ta-chi-ching (抄方等大集經), 12 fascicles, compiled by Southern Ch'i Prince Ching-ling (459–94); Abridged Great Collection of Sutras

Ch'ao hua-yen-ching (抄華嚴經), 14 fascicles, compiled by Southern Ch'i

Prince Ching-ling (459–94); Abridged Flower Garland (Avatamsaka) Sutra

Ch'ao p'u-hsien kuan-ch'an hui-fa (抄普賢觀懺悔法), 1 fascicle, compiled by Southern Ch'i Prince Ching-ling (459–94); Abridged Sutra of Meditation on the Bodhisattva Universal Virtue

Ch'ao p'u-sa ti-ching (抄菩薩地經), 12 fascicles, compiled by Southern Ch'i Prince Ching-ling (459–94); Abridged Sutra of a Bodhisattva's Spiritual States

Chapter on the Way to the Other Shore. *See* Parayanavagga

Cheng-fa-hua-ching. *See* Saddharma-pundarika-sutra (1)

Cheng-fa nien-ch'u-chin. *See* Saddharma-smrity-upasthana-sutra

Ch'eng-shih-lun. *See* Satyasiddhi-shastra

Cheng-ting-ching (正頂經), 1 fascicle, spurious sutra by the nun Seng-fa (b. 489); Sutra of the True Summit

Ch'eng wei-shih-lun. *See* Vijnaptimatratasiddhi-shastra

Ch'eng wei-shih-lun shu-chi (成唯識論述記), 10 fascicles, compiled between 659 and 682 by K'uei Chi (632–82); Commentary on the Treatise on the Establishment of the Doctrine of Consciousness Only

Chen-yüan Era Buddhist Catalogue. See following entry

Chen-yüan hsin-ting shih-chiao mu-lu (貞元新定釋教目錄), abbreviated: Chen-yüan shih-chiao-lu (貞元釋教錄), Chen-yüan-lu (貞元錄), or Yüan-chao-lu (圓照錄, Yüan-chao's Catalogue), 30 fascicles, record of 2,417 works in 7,388 fascicles, compiled 800 by Yüan-chao et al.; Chen-yüan Era Buddhist Catalogue

Chieh-shen-mi-ching. *See* Samdhinirmochana-sutra (4)

Chih-sheng-lu, Chih-sheng's Catalogue. *See* K'ai-yüan shih-chiao-lu

Ch'i-hsin-lun. *See* Mahayana-shraddhotpada-shastra

Chih-yüan Era Complete Buddhist Catalogue. See following entry

Chih-yüan fa-pao k'an-t'ung tsung-lu (至元法寶勘同總錄), abbreviated: Chih-yüan-lu (至元錄), 10 fascicles, record of 1,440 works in 5,586 fascicles, completed 1287 by Chi-hsiang et al.; Chih-yüan Era Complete Buddhist Catalogue

Chi-lun. *See* Mahayanabhidharma-samucchaya

Chin Dynasty Edition of the Tripitaka. *See* Chin-pan ta-tsang-ching

Ching-chi. *See* Suttanipata

Ching-mai-lu, Ching-mai's Catalogue. *See* Ku-chin i-ching t'u-chi

Ching-t'ai-lu, Ching-t'ai's Catalogue. *See* Chung-ching mu-lu (3)

Ching-t'u-ching (淨土經), 7 fascicles, spurious sutra by the nun Seng-fa (b. 489); Pure Land Sutra

Ching-t'u-lun. *See* Wu-liang-shou-ching-lun

Chin-kang-ching. *See* Vajracchedika-prajnaparamita-sutra

Chin-kang-hsien-lun (金剛仙論), abbreviated: Hsien-lun (仙論), 10 fascicles, translated early 6th century by Bodhiruchi (fl. ca. 508–35); Diamond Hermit's Treatise

Chin-kang pan-jo-ching, Chin-kang pan-jo po-lo-mi-ching. *See* Vajra-cchedika-prajnaparamita-sutra

Chin-kang san-mei-ching (金剛三昧經), 1 fascicle, a "genuine" sutra; Sutra of Diamond Meditation

Chin-kang-ting-ching. *See* Vajrashekhara-sutra

Chin-kuang-ming-ching. *See* Suvarnaprabhasa-sutra

Chin-kuang-ming tsui-sheng-wang-ching. *See* Suvarnaprabhasottama-raja-sutra

Chin-pan ta-tsang-ching (金版大藏經), the number of works and fascicles recorded is uncertain, prepared and printed ca. 1149–ca. 1173; Chin Dynasty Edition of the Tripitaka

Chi-sha yen-sheng-yüan-pan (磧砂延聖院版), record of 1,532 works in 6,362 fascicles, prepared and printed ca. 1231–ca. 1322; a Southern Sung–dynasty edition of the Tripitaka

Ch'i-shih chung-ching mu-lu. *See* Kao-Ch'i chung-ching mu-lu

Ch'i-tan ta-tsang-ching (契丹大藏經), Khitan (Liao) Dynasty Edition of the Tripitaka

Chou Dynasty Catalogue of the Sutras. *See* Ta-Chou k'an-ting chung-ching mu-lu

Chulavedalla-sutta (Cūḷavedalla-sutta, P), Fa-lo pi-ch'iu-ni-ching (法樂比丘尼經); Lesser Discourse of the Miscellany

Chung a-han-ching. *See* Madhyama-agama

Chung-ching mu-lu (衆經目錄); (1) 2 fascicles, compiled 479–502 by Shih Wang-tsung; (2) also called Fa-ching-lu (法經錄, Fa-ching's Catalogue), 7 fascicles, record of 2,257 works in 5,310 fascicles, compiled 594 by Fa-ching et al.; (3) also called Ching-t'ai-lu (靜泰錄, Ching-t'ai's Catalogue), 5 fascicles, compiled 664 by Ching-t'ai; Catalogue of the Sutras

Chung-ching pieh-lu (衆經別錄), 2 fascicles, thought to have been compiled between 420 and 479; Independent Catalogue of the Sutras

Chung-lun. *See* Madhyamaka-shastra

Ch'u san-tsang chi-chi (出三藏記集), abbreviated: Seng-yu-lu (僧祐錄, Seng-yu's Catalogue), 15 fascicles, record of 1,306 works in 1,570 fascicles, compiled between 510 and 518 by Seng-yu; oldest extant catalogue; Collection of Records Concerning the Tripitaka

Chü-she-lun. *See* Abhidharmakosha-shastra

Collection of Discourses. *See* Suttanipata

Collection of Records Concerning the Tripitaka. *See* Ch'u san-tsang chi-chi

Collection of the Mahayana Abhidharma. *See* Mahayanabhidharma-samucchaya

Commentary on the Lotus Sutra. *See* Miao-fa lien-hua-ching i-chi

Commentary on the Treatise on the Establishment of the Doctrine of Consciousness Only. *See* Ch'eng wei-shih-lun shu-chi

Comprehensive Catalogue of the Sutras. *See* Tsung-li chung-ching mu-lu

Comprehensive Treatise on Mahayana Buddhism. *See* Mahayanasamgraha

Dai Nippon Kōtei Daizōkyō (大日本校訂大藏經, J; Great Japan Revised Canon), abbreviated: *Shukusatsu-zōkyō* (縮刷藏經, Small-Type Canon), 418 vols., record of 1,916 works in 8,534 fascicles, published 1880–85 by Shimada Mitsune and Fukuda Gyōkai et al.; in Europe and America known as Tokyo Edition

Dai Nippon Kōtei Zōkyō (大日本校訂藏經, J; Great Japan Revised Tripitaka), abbreviated: *Manji-zōkyō* (卍字藏經, Fylfot-Letter Tripitaka), 347 vols., record of 1,625 works in 7,082 fascicles, published 1902–5 by Hamada Chikuha and Yoneda Mujō et al.

Dai Nippon Zoku Zōkyō (大日本續藏經, J; Great Japan Supplementary Tripitaka), abbreviated: *Manji-zokuzō* (卍字續藏, Fylfot-Letter Supplementary Tripitaka), 750 vols., record of 1,750 works in 7,140 fascicles, published 1905–12 by Maeda Eun and Nakano Tatsue et al.

Dashabhumika-sutra-shastra (Daśabhūmika-sūtra-śāstra, S); Shih-ti-ching-lun (十地經論), 12 fascicles, translated ca. 508–35 by Bodhiruchi; Treatise on the Sutra of the Ten Stages

Detailed Narration of the Sport of the Buddha. *See* Lalitavistara

Dhammapada (P); Dharmapada (S); Fa-chü-ching (法句經)

Dharmaguptaka-vinaya (S), Ssu-fen-lü (四分律), 60 fascicles, translated 410–12 by Buddhayashas and Chu Fo-nien; Four-Category Vinaya

Dharmatara-dhyana-sutra. *See* Yogacharabhumi-sutra

Diamond Hermit's Treatise. *See* Chin-kang-hsien-lun

Diamond Peak Sutra. *See* Vajrashekhara-sutra

Diamond Sutra. *See* Vajracchedika-prajnaparamita-sutra

Diamond Wisdom Sutra. *See* Vajracchedika-prajnaparamita-sutra

Dirgha-agama (Dirgha-āgama, S), Ch'ang a-han-ching (長阿含經), 22 fascicles, translated 412–13 by Buddhayashas and Chu Fo-nien; Long Sayings

Discourse on the Analysis of the Truths. *See* Sacchavibhanga-sutta

Dvadashamukha-shastra (Dvādaśamukha-śāstra, S), Shih-erh-men-lun (十二門論), 1 fascicle, translated 409 by Kumarajiva; Treatise on the Twelve Gates

Ekottara-agama (Ekottara-āgama, S), Tseng-i a-han-ching (增一阿含經), 51 fascicles, translated by Chia T'i-p'o; Gradual Sayings

Erh-ju ssu-hsing-lun (二入四行論), attributed to Bodhidharma; On the Twofold Entrance to the Way and the Four Types of Practice

Exegesis on the Collection of the Mahayana Abhidharma. *See* Mahayanabhidharma-samucchaya-vyakhya

Fa-ching-lu, Fa-ching's Catalogue. *See* Chung-ching mu-lu (2)

Fa-chü-ching. *See* Dhammapada

Fa-hua-ching. *See* Saddharma-pundarika-sutra

Fa-hua-ching hsüan-lun (法華經玄論), abbreviated: Fa-hua hsüan-lun (法華玄論), 10 fascicles, annotated by Chi-tsang; Profound Treatise on the Lotus Sutra

Fa-hua-ching i-chi. *See* Miao-fa lien-hua-ching i-chi

Fa-hua-ching-lun. *See* Miao-fa lien-hua-ching-lun

Fa-hua hsüan-i. *See* Miao-fa lien-hua-ching hsüan-i

Fa-hua hsüan-lun. *See* Fa-hua-ching hsüan-lun

Fa-hua i-chi. *See* Miao-fa lien-hua-ching i-chi

Fa-hua-lun. *See* Miao-fa lien-hua-ching-lun

Fa-hua wen-chü. *See* Miao-fa lien-hua-ching wen-chü

Fa-lo pi-ch'iu-ni-ching. *See* Chulavedalla-sutta

Fang-kuang pan-jo po-lo-mi-ching. *See* Panchavimshati-sahasrika-prajnaparamita-sutra (2)

Fan-wang-ching (梵網經), 2 fascicles, also called Fan-wang p'u-sa-chieh-ching (梵網菩薩戒經), a "genuine" sutra; Sutra of the Perfect Net

Five-Category Vinaya. *See* Mahishasaka-vinaya

Flower Garland Sutra. *See* Avatamsaka-sutra

Fo-hsing-lun (佛性論), 4 fascicles, translated 557–69 by Paramartha; Treatise on the Buddha-nature

Fo-shuo chieh-chieh-ching. *See* Samdhinirmochana-sutra (3)

Fo-ti-ching (佛地經), 1 fascicle, translated 645 by Hsüan-tsang; Buddha-stage Sutra

Four-Category Vinaya. *See* Dharmaguptaka-vinaya

Fu-chou K'ai-yüan Temple Edition of the Tripitaka. *See* K'ai-yüan-ssu-pan

Fu-chou Tung-ch'an Temple Edition of the Tripitaka. *See* Tung-ch'an-ssu-pan

Fylfot-Letter Tripitaka. See *Dai Nippon Kōtei Zōkyō*

Fylfot-Letter Supplementary Tripitaka. See *Dai Nippon Zoku Zōkyō*

Golden Light Sutra. *See* Suvarnaprabhasa-sutra

Gradual Sayings. *See* Ekottara-agama

Great Collection of Sutras. *See* Maha-samnipata-sutra

Great Commentary. *See* Abhidharma-mahavibhasha-shastra

Great Dharani Sutra of the Spotless and Pure Light. *See* Rashmivimala-vishuddhiprabhasa-dharani-sutra

Great Perfection of Wisdom Sutra. *See* Mahaprajnaparamita-sutra

Great Sun Sutra. *See* Mahavairochana-sutra

Haeinsa-pan (海印寺版, Korean), Haein Temple Edition, usually called the Koryŏ Edition of the Tripitaka, also called Tripitaka Koreana

Heart of Wisdom Sutra, Heart Sutra. *See* Prajnaparamita-hridaya-sutra

Heroic Marching Sutra. *See* Ta-fo-ting ju-lai mi-yin hsiu-ching liao-i chu-p'u-sa wan-hsing shou-leng-yen-ching

History of the Three Treasures in Successive Reigns and Catalogue of the Sutras. *See* Li-tai san-pao-chi

Hsiang-hsü chieh-t'o-ching, Hsiang-hsü chieh-t'o ju-lai so-tso sui-shun-ch'u-liao-i-ching, Hsiang-hsü chieh-t'o ti-po-lo-mi liao-i-ching. *See* Samdhinirmochana-sutra (1)

Hsiao-p'in pan-jo-ching. *See* Ashtasahasrika-prajnaparamita-sutra

Hsien-lun. *See* Chin-kang-hsien-lun

Hsin-ching. *See* Prajnaparamita-hridaya-sutra

Hsiu-hsing tao-ti-ching. *See* Yogacharabhumi-sutra

Hsü Chen-yüan shih-chiao-lu (續貞元釋教錄), abbreviated: Hsü Chen-yüan-lu (續貞元錄), 1 fascicle, record of 277 works in 756 fascicles, compiled 945–46 by Heng-an; Supplementary Chen-yüan Era Buddhist Catalogue

Hua-lin fo-tien chung-ching mu-lu (華林佛殿衆經目錄), abbreviated: Hua-lin fo-tien-lu (華林佛殿錄), 4 fascicles, compiled 515 by Seng-chao; Hua-lin Fo-tien Catalogue of the Sutras

Hua-yen-ching. *See* Avatamsaka-sutra

Hung-fa-ssu-pan (弘法寺版), record of 1,654 works in 7,182 fascicles, prepared and printed 1277–94; Hung-fa Temple Edition of the Tripitaka

Independent Catalogue of the Sutras. *See* Chung-ching pieh-lu

I-p'in-ching. *See* Atthakavagga

Jen-shou-lu. *See* Sui-chung-ching mu-lu

Ju-lai-tsang-ching. *See* Tathagatagarbha-sutra

Ju leng-chia-ching. *See* Lankavatara-sutra (2)

K'ai-yüan Era Buddhist Catalogue. See following entry

K'ai-yüan shih-chiao-lu (開元釋教錄), abbreviated: K'ai-yüan-lu (開元錄) or Chih-sheng-lu (智昇錄, Chih-sheng's Catalogue), 20 fascicles, record of 1,076 works in 5,048 fascicles, compiled 730 by Chih-sheng; K'ai-yüan Era Buddhist Catalogue

K'ai-yüan-ssu-pan (開元寺版), record of 1,429 works in 6,117 fascicles, prepared and printed 1112–48; K'ai-yüan Temple Edition of the Tripitaka, also called the Fu-chou K'ai-yüan Temple Edition (Fu-chou K'ai-yüan-ssu-pan, 福州開元寺版)

Kan'ei-ji-ban (寛永寺版, J), record of 1,453 works in 6,323 fascicles, prepared and printed 1637–48 by Tenkai; Kan'ei-ji Temple Edition of the Tripitaka, also called Tenkai (天海) Edition

Kao-Ch'i chung-ching mu-lu (高齊衆經目錄), also called Ch'i-shih chung-ching mu-lu (齊世衆經目錄), abbreviated: Kao-Ch'i-lu (高齊錄), 1 fas-

cicle, compiled 570–76 by Fa-shang; Northern Ch'i Dynasty Catalogue of the Sutras

Kasuga-ban (春日版, J), collective name of scriptural writings printed in
Nara between the twelfth and fourteenth centuries, all bearing the
word Kasuga in their colophons; Kasuga Edition

Khitan Dynasty Edition of the Tripitaka. *See* Ch'i-tan ta-tsang-ching

Kindred Sayings. *See* Samyukta-agama

Koryǒ Edition of the Tripitaka. *See* Haeinsa-pan

Kuan-ching. *See* Kuan wu-liang-shou-ching

Kuang-tsan pan-jo po-lo-mi-ching. *See* Panchavimshati-sahasrika-prajnaparamita-sutra (1)

Kuan wu-liang-shou-ching (觀無量壽經), abbreviated: Kuan-ching (觀
經), 1 fascicle, a "genuine" sutra; Sutra of Meditation on Amitabha
Buddha

Ku-chin i-ching t'u-chi (古今譯經圖紀), abbreviated: Ching-mai-lu (靖
邁錄, Ching-mai's Catalogue), 4 fascicles, compiled between 627 and
649 by Ching-mai; Record of the Paintings of Ancient and Modern
Sutra Translations

Lalitavistara (S), P'u-yao-ching (普曜經), 8 fascicles, translated 308 by
Dharmaraksha; Detailed Narration of the Sport of the Buddha

Lankavatara-sutra (Laṅkāvatāra-sūtra, S), generic abbreviation: Leng-
chia-ching (楞伽經); (1) Leng-chia a-pa-to-lo pao-ching (楞伽阿跋多羅
寶經), 4 fascicles, translated 443 by Gunabhadra; (2) Ju leng-chia-
ching (入楞伽經), 10 fascicles, translated 513 by Bodhiruchi; (3) Ta-
ch'eng ju-leng-chia-ching (大乘入楞伽經), 7 fascicles, translated 700–
704 by Shikshananda; Sutra of the Appearance of the Good Doctrine
in [Sri] Lanka

Leng-chia a-pa-to-lo pao-ching. *See* Lankavatara-sutra (1)

Leng-chia-ching. *See* Lankavatara-sutra

Leng-yen-ssu-pan (楞嚴寺版), record of 1,655 works, prepared and printed 1586–ca. 1620; Leng-yen Temple Edition of the Tripitaka, generally called the Wan-li Edition (Wan-li-pan ta-tsang-ching, 萬歷版大
藏經), a Ming-dynasty edition

Lesser Discourse of the Miscellany. *See* Chulavedalla-sutta

Liang-tai chung-ching mu-lu (梁代衆經目錄), also called Liang-shih
chung-ching mu-lu (梁世衆經目錄), 4 fascicles, compiled 518 by Pao-
ch'ang et al.; Liang Dynasty Catalogue of the Sutras

Liao Dynasty Edition of the Tripitaka. *See* Ch'i-tan ta-tsang-ching

Li-tai san-pao-chi (歷代三寶紀), abbreviated: Ch'ang-fang-lu (長房錄,
Ch'ang-fang's Catalogue), 15 fascicles, record of 1,076 works in 3,292
fascicles, compiled 597 by Fei Ch'ang-fang; History of the Three
Treasures in Successive Reigns and Catalogue of the Sutras

Liu-men t'o-lo-ni-ching. *See* Shanmukhi-dharani-sutra

Liu-tu-chi-ching. *See* Shatparamita-samgraha-sutra
Long Sayings. *See* Dirgha-agama
Lotus Sutra. *See* Saddharma-pundarika-sutra

Madhyama-agama (Mādhyama-āgama, S), Chung a-han-ching (中阿含
經), 60 fascicles, translated 397–98 by Sanghadeva; Middle-Length
Sayings
Madhyamaka-shastra (Mādhyamaka-śāstra, S), Chung-lun (中論), 4
fascicles, translated 409 by Kumarajiva; Treatise on the Middle
Mahaparinirvana-sutra (Mahāparinirvāṇa-sūtra, S), Ta-ch'eng nieh-
p'an-ching (大乘涅槃經); (1) Ta-pan ni-yüan-ching (大般泥洹經), 6
fascicles, translated between 416 and 418 by Fa-hsien and Buddhabhadra; (2) Ta-pan nieh-p'an-ching (大般涅槃經), also called Pei-pen
nieh-p'an-ching (北本涅槃經, Northern Text of the Sutra of the Great
Decease), 40 fascicles, translated 414–21 by Dharmakshema; (3) Ta-
pan nieh-p'an-ching (大般涅槃經), also called Nan-pen nieh-p'an-
ching (南本涅槃經, Southern Text of the Sutra of the Great Decease),
36 fascicles, revised by Hui-yen, Hui-kuan, and Hsieh Ling-yün; Sutra of the Great Decease
Mahaprajnaparamita-sutra (Mahāprajñāpāramitā-sūtra, S), Ta-pan-
jo po-lo-mi-to-ching (大般若波羅蜜多經), abbreviated: Ta-pan-jo-ching
(大般若經), 600 fascicles, translated 660–63 by Hsüan-tsang; Great Perfection of Wisdom Sutra
Mahaprajnaparamita-upadesha (Mahāprajñāpāramitā-upadeśa, S),
Ta-chih-tu-lun (大智度論), 100 fascicles, translated 402–5 by Kumarajiva; Treatise on the Great Perfection of Wisdom Sutra
Maharatnakuta-sutra (Mahāratnakūṭa-sūtra, S), Ta-pao-chi-ching (大
寶積經), 120 fascicles, translated 713 by Bodhiruchi (672–727) with
addenda; Sutra of the Great Accumulation of Treasures
Maha-samnipata-sutra (Mahā-saṃnipāta-sūtra, S; also called Vaipul-
ya-saṃnipāta-sūtra, S), Ta-fang-teng ta-chi-ching (大方等大集經), abbreviated: Ta-chi-ching (大集經), 60 fascicles, translated between
414 and 426 by Dharmakshema et al.; Great Collection of Sutras
Mahasanghika-vinaya (Mahāsaṅghika-vinaya, S), Mo-ho seng-ch'i-lü
(摩訶僧祇律), 40 fascicles, translated 416–18 by Fa-hsien and Buddhabhadra; Vinaya of the Mahasanghika school
Mahavairochana-sutra (Mahā-vairocanābhisaṃbodhi-vikurvitādhi-
ṣṭhāna-vaipulyasūtrendra-rāja-dharmaparyāya, S), Ta p'i-lu-che-na-
ch'eng-fo shen-pien chia-ch'ih-ching (大毗盧遮那成佛神變加持經), abbreviated: Ta-jih-ching (大日經), 7 fascicles, translated 716–35 by
Shubhakarasimha; Great Sun Sutra
Mahavibhasha-shastra. *See* Abhidharma-mahavibhasha-shastra
Mahayanabhidharma-samuccaya (Mahāyānābhidharma-samuccaya,
S), Ta-ch'eng a-p'i-ta-mo chi-lun (大乘阿毗達磨集論), abbreviated:

A-p'i-ta-mo chi-lun (阿毗達磨集論) or Chi-lun (集論), 7 fascicles, translated 652 by Hsüan-tsang; Collection of the Mahayana Abhidharma

Mahayanabhidharma-samucchaya-vyakhya (Mahāyānābhidharma-samuccaya-vyākhyā, S), Ta-ch'eng a-p'i-ta-mo tsa-chi-lun (大乘阿毗達磨雜集論), abbreviated: A-p'i-ta-mo tsa-chi-lun (阿毗達磨雜集論) or Tsa-chi-lun (雜集論), 16 fascicles, translated 646 by Hsüan-tsang; Exegesis on the Collection of the Mahayana Abhidharma

Mahayanasamgraha (Mahāyānasaṃgraha, S), She ta-ch'eng-lun (攝大乘論); (1) 2 fascicles, translated 531 by Buddhashanta; (2) 3 fascicles, translated 563 by Paramartha; (3) 3 fascicles, translated 648–49 by Hsüan-tsang; Comprehensive Treatise on Mahayana Buddhism

Mahayana-shraddhotpada-shastra (Mahāyāna-śraddhotpāda-śāstra, S), Ta-ch'eng ch'i-hsin-lun (大乘起信論), abbreviated: Ch'i-hsin-lun (起信論); (1) 1 fascicle, translated 553 by Paramartha; (2) 2 fascicles, translated between 695 and 704 by Shikshananda; Treatise on the Awakening of Faith in Mahayana

Mahayana Sutra of the Great Decease. *See* Mahaparinirvana-sutra

Mahishasaka-vinaya (Mahīśāsaka-vinaya, S), Wu-fen-lü (五分律), 30 fascicles, translated by Buddhajiva (fl. ca. 423) et al.; Five-Category Vinaya

Manji-zokuzō. See *Dai Nippon Zoku Zōkyō*

Manji-zōkyō. See *Dai Nippon Kōtei Zōkyō*

Meaningful Chapter. *See* Atthakavagga

Miao-fa lien-hua-ching. *See* Saddharma-pundarika-sutra (2)

Miao-fa lien-hua-ching hsüan-i (妙法蓮華經玄義), abbreviated: Fa-hua hsüan-i (法華玄義), 10 fascicles, annotated 593 by Chih-i; Profound Meaning of the Lotus Sutra

Miao-fa lien-hua-ching i-chi (妙法蓮華經義記), abbreviated: Fa-hua-ching i-chi (法華經義記) or Fa-hua i-chi (法華義記), 8 fascicles, annotated by Fa-yün (467–529); Commentary on the Lotus Sutra

Miao-fa lien-hua-ching-lun (妙法蓮華經論), also called Miao-fa lien-hua-ching yu-po-t'i-she (妙法蓮華經憂波提舍), abbreviated: Fa-hua-ching-lun (法華經論) or Fa-hua-lun (法華論), 2 fascicles, translated by Bodhiruchi (fl. ca. 508–35) and T'an-lin; Treatise on the Lotus Sutra

Miao-fa lien-hua-ching wen-chü (妙法蓮華經文句), abbreviated: Fa-hua wen-chü (法華文句), 10 or 20 fascicles, annotated by Chih-i; Textual Commentary on the Lotus Sutra

Middle-Length Sayings. *See* Madhyama-agama

Milindapanha (Milindapañhā, P), Mi-lan wang-wen-ching (彌蘭王問經), Na-hsien pi-ch'iu-ching (那先比丘經), 2 fascicles and 3 fascicles, translated ca. 200; The Questions of [King] Milinda [Menander]

Ming Dynasty Catalogue of the Tripitaka. *See* Ta-Ming san-tsang sheng-chiao mu-lu

Ming-dynasty editions of the Tripitaka. *See* Leng-yen-ssu-pan; Nan-tsang; Pei-tsang

Mo-ho pan-jo po-lo-mi-ching. *See* Panchavimshati-sahasrika-prajnaparamita-sutra (3)

Mo-ho seng-ch'i-lü. *See* Mahasanghika-vinaya

Na-hsien pi-ch'iu-ching. *See* Milindapanha

Nanjio Catalogue of the Tripitaka. *See* Ta-Ming san-tsang sheng-chiao mu-lu

Nan-pen nieh-p'an-ching. *See* Mahaparinirvana-sutra (3)

Nan-tsang (南藏), record of 1,612 works, published 1372–1403 in Nanking; Southern Ming Dynasty Edition of the Tripitaka

Nei-tien-lu. *See* Ta-T'ang nei-tien-lu

Northern Ch'i Dynasty Catalogue of the Sutras. *See* Kao-Ch'i chung-ching mu-lu

Northern Ming Dynasty Edition of the Tripitaka. *See* Pei-tsang

Northern Text of the Sutra of the Great Decease. *See* Mahaparinirvana-sutra (2)

Northern Wei Dynasty Catalogue of the Sutras. *See* Yüan-Wei chung-ching mu-lu

Ōbaku-ban Daizōkyō (黃檗版大藏經, J), record of 6,771 fascicles, published 1669–81 by Tetsugen; Ōbaku Edition of the Tripitaka, also called Tetsugen Edition (鉄眼版)

On the Twofold Entrance to the Way and the Four Types of Practice. *See* Erh-ju ssu-hsing-lun

Pa-ch'ien-sung pan-jo. *See* Ashtasahasrika-prajnaparamita-sutra

Panchavimshati-sahasrika-prajnaparamita-sutra (Pañcaviṃśati-sāhasrikā-prajñāpāramitā-sūtra, S); (1) Kuang-tsan pan-jo po-lo-mi-ching (光讚般若波羅蜜經), 10 fascicles, translated 286 by Dharmaraksha; (2) Fang-kuang pan-jo po-lo-mi-ching (放光般若波羅蜜經), 20 fascicles, translated 291 by Wu-ch'a-lo; (3) Ta-p'in pan-jo-ching (大品般若經) or Mo-ho pan-jo po-lo-mi-ching (摩訶般若波羅蜜經), 27 fascicles, translated 404 by Kumarajiva; Perfection of Wisdom Sutra in Twenty-five Thousand Lines

Pan-jo hsin-ching, Pan-jo po-lo-mi-to hsin-ching. *See* Prajnaparamita-hridaya-sutra

Pan-jo te-ching (般若得經), 1 fascicle, spurious sutra by the nun Seng-fa (b. 489); Sutra of Attaining Perfect Wisdom

Pao-lin-chuan (寶林傳), also called Ts'ao-ch'i pao-lin-chuan (曹溪寶林傳), 10 fascicles, compiled 801 by Chih-chü; Biography of the Treasure Forest

Pao-ting-ching (寶頂經), 1 fascicle, spurious sutra by the nun Seng-fa (b. 489); Sutra of the Treasure Summit

Parayanavagga (Pārāyanavagga, P), Pi-an tao-p'in (彼岸道品); Chapter on the Way to the Other Shore

Pei-pen nieh-p'an-ching. *See* Mahaparinirvana-sutra (2)

Pei-tsang (北藏), record of 1,615 works, published 1420–40 in Peking; Northern Ming Dynasty Edition of the Tripitaka

Pei-tsang mu-lu. *See* Ta-Ming san-tsang sheng-chiao mu-lu

Perfection of Wisdom Sutra in Eight Thousand Lines. *See* Ashtasahasrika-prajnaparamita-sutra

Perfection of Wisdom Sutra in Twenty-five Thousand Lines. *See* Panchavimshati-sahasrika-prajnaparamita-sutra

Pi-an tao-p'in. *See* Parayanavagga

Ping-p'o-sha-lun. *See* Vibhasha-shastra

P'i-yü-ching. *See* Avadana

Po-lun. *See* Shatika-shastra

P'o-sha-lun. *See* Abhidharma-mahavibhasha-shastra

Prajnaparamita-hridaya-sutra (Prajñāpāramitā-hṛdaya-sūtra, S), Pan-jo po-lo-mi-to hsin-ching (般若波羅蜜多心經), abbreviated: Pan-jo hsin-ching (般若心經) or Hsin-ching (心經), 1 fascicle, translated 649 by Hsüan-tsang; Heart of Wisdom Sutra, also called the Heart Sutra

Profound Meaning of the Lotus Sutra. *See* Miao-fa lien-hua-ching hsüan-i

Profound Treatise on the Lotus Sutra. *See* Fa-hua-ching hsüan-lun

Pure Land Sutra. *See* Ching-t'u-ching

P'u-sa ti-ch'ih-ching, P'u-sa ti-ch'ih-lun. *See* Bodhisattvabhumi

P'u-sa-tsang-ching (菩薩藏經), 20 fascicles, translated 645 by Hsüan-tsang; Bodhisattva Treasury Sutra

P'u-sa ying-luo pen-yeh-ching (菩薩瓔珞本業經), 2 fascicles, a "genuine" sutra; Sutra on a Bodhisattva's Original Action

Pu-tseng pu-chien-ching (不增不減經), 1 fascicle, translated 525 by Bodhiruchi; Sutra on Neither Increasing Nor Decreasing

P'u-yao-ching. *See* Lalitavistara

Queen of Shrimala Sutra. *See* Shrimaladevi-simhanada-sutra

Questions of [King] Milinda [Menander], The. *See* Milindapanha

Rashmivimala-vishuddhiprabhasa-dharani-sutra (Raśmivimālā-viśuddhiprabhāsa-dhāraṇī-sūtra, S), Wu-kou ching-kuang ta-t'o-lo-ni-ching (無垢淨光大陀羅尼經), abbreviated: Wu-kou ching-kuang-ching (無垢淨光經), 1 fascicle, translated 704 by Mitrashanta; Great Dharani Sutra of the Spotless and Pure Light

Record of the Paintings of Ancient and Modern Sutra Translations. *See* Ku-chin i-ching t'u-chi

Sacchavibhanga-sutta (Saccavibhaṅga-sutta, P), Sheng-ti fen-pieh-ching (聖諦分別經); Discourse on the Analysis of the Truths

Saddharma-pundarika-sutra (Saddharma-puṇḍarīka-sūtra, S), generic abbreviation: Fa-hua-ching (法華經); (1) Cheng-fa-hua-ching (正法華經), 10 fascicles, translated 286 by Dharmaraksha; (2) Miao-fa lien-hua-ching (妙法蓮華經), 7 or 8 fascicles, translated 406 by Kumarajiva; (3) T'ien-p'in miao-fa lien-hua-ching (添品妙法蓮華經), 7 or 8 fascicles, translated 601 by Jnanagupta and Dharmagupta; (4) Fa-hua-ching (法華經), 1 fascicle, spurious sutra by the nun Seng-fa (b. 489); the Lotus Sutra

Saddharma-smrity-upasthana-sutra (Saddharma-smṛty-upasthāna-sūtra, S), Cheng-fa nien-ch'u-ching (正法念處經), 70 fascicles, translated between 538 and 543 by Prajnaruchi; Sutra of Stability in Contemplation of the True Law

Samdhinirmochana-sutra (Saṁdhinirmocana-sūtra, S); (1) Hsiang-hsü chieh-t'o ti-po-lo-mi liao-i-ching (相續解脫地波羅蜜了義經), 1 fascicle, and Hsiang-hsü chieh-t'o ju-lai so-tso sui-shen-ch'u liao-i-ching (相續解脫如來所作隨順處了義經), 1 fascicle, both translated between 420 and 479 by Gunabhadra, partial translations of the sutra, generic title: Hsiang-hsü chieh-t'o-ching (相續解脫經), Sutra of the Continuous Stream of Emancipation; (2) Shen-mi chieh-t'o-ching (深密解脫經), abbreviated: Shen-mi-ching (深密經), 5 fascicles, translated between 508 and 535 by Bodhiruchi, Sutra of Profound and Mysterious Emancipation; (3) Fo-shuo chieh-chieh-ching (佛說解節經), 1 fascicle, translated between 557 and 589 by Paramartha, partial translation of the sutra, Sutra on Emancipation; (4) Chieh-shen-mi-ching (解深密經), 5 fascicles, translated 647 by Hsüan-tsang, Sutra of Profound Understanding

Samyukta-agama (Saṁyukta-āgama, S), Tsa a-han-ching (雜阿含經), 50 fascicles, translated 435–43 by Gunabhadra; Kindred Sayings

Saptadasha-bhumika-shastra (Saptadaśa-bhūmika-śāstra, S), Shih-ch'i-ti-lun (十七地論), 5 fascicles, translated by Paramartha; Treatise on the Seventeen Stages of Spiritual Development, a partial translation of the Yogacharabhumi-shastra, q.v.

Sarvastivadin-vinaya (Sarvāstivādin-vinaya, S), Shih-sung-lü (十誦律), 61 fascicles, translated 404–9 by Puṇyatāra and Kumarajiva and revised by Vimalaksha; Ten-Category Vinaya

Satyasiddhi-shastra (Satyasiddhi-śāstra, S), Ch'eng-shih-lun (成實論), 20 fascicles, translated between 402 and 412 by Kumarajiva; Treatise on the Completion of Truth

Seng-yu-lu, Seng-yu's Catalogue. *See* Ch'u san-tsang chi-chi

Shanmukhi-dharani-sutra (Ṣaṇmukhī-dhāraṇī-sūtra, S), Liu-men t'o-lo-ni-ching (六門陀羅尼經), 1 fascicle, translated 645 by Hsüan-tsang; Sutra of the Dharani of the Six Gates

Shatika-shastra (Śatika-śāstra, S), Po-lun (百論), 2 fascicles, translated
  404 by Kumarajiva; Treatise in One Hundred Verses
Shatparamita-samgraha-sutra (Ṣaṭpāramitā-saṁgraha-sūtra, S), Liu-
  tu-chi-ching (六度集經), 8 fascicles, translated between 251 and 280
  by K'ang Seng-hui (康僧會); Sutra of the Collection of the Practices
  of the Six Perfections
Sheng-man-ching, Sheng-man shih-tzu-hou i-ch'eng ta-fang-pien fang-
  kuang-ching. *See* Shrimaladevi-simhanada-sutra
Sheng-ti fen-pieh-ching. *See* Sacchavibhanga-sutta
Shen-mi chieh-t'o-ching, Shen-mi-ching. *See* Samdhinirmochana-sutra
  (2)
She ta-ch'eng-lun. *See* Mahayanasamgraha
Shih-ch'i-ti-lun. *See* Saptadasha-bhumika-shastra
Shih-erh-men-lun. *See* Dvadashamuksha-shastra
Shih-sung-lü. *See* Sarvastivadin-vinaya
Shih-ti-ching-lun. *See* Dashabhumika-sutra-shastra
Shou-leng-yen-ching. *See* Ta-fo-ting ju-lai mi-yin hsiu-ching liao-i chu-
  p'u-sa wan-hsing shou-leng-yen-ching
Shrimaladevi-simhanada-sutra (Śrīmālādevī-siṁhanāda-sūtra, S),
  Sheng-man shih-tzu-hou i-ch'eng ta-fang-pien fang-kuang-ching (勝
  鬘獅子吼一乘大方便方廣經), abbreviated: Sheng-man-ching (勝鬘經), 1
  fascicle, translated 436 by Gunabhadra; Queen of Shrimala Sutra (the
  Lion's Roar of Queen Shrimala), Shrimala Sutra, Shrimaladevi Sutra
Shu Edition of the Tripitaka. *See* Shu-pan ta-tsang-ching
Shukusatsu-zōkyō. See *Dai Nippon Kōtei Daizōkyō*
Shuo wu-kou-ch'eng-ching. *See* Vimalakirti-nirdesha-sutra (3)
Shu-pan ta-tsang-ching (蜀版大藏經), record of 5,586 fascicles, prepared
  and printed 971–83; Shu Edition of the Tripitaka, also called the
  Sung Governmental Edition (Sung-kuan-pan, 宋官版) and the Sze-
  chwan Edition (Ssu-ch'uan-pan, 四川版)
Small-Type Canon. See *Dai Nippon Kōtei Daizōkyō*
Solemn Utterances of the Buddha. *See* Udana; Udana-varga
Southern Ming Dynasty Edition of the Tripitaka. *See* Nan-tsang
Southern Sung–dynasty editions of the Tripitaka. *See* Chi-sha yen-
  sheng-yüan-pan; Ssu-ch'i Fa-pao-ssu-pan; Ssu-ch'i Yüan-chüeh-
  yüan-pan
Southern Text of the Sutra of the Great Decease. *See* Mahaparinirvana-
  sutra (3)
Ssu-ch'i Fa-pao-ssu-pan (思溪法寶寺版), record of 1,459 works in 5,740
  fascicles, prepared and printed 1237–52; Ssu-ch'i Fa-pao Temple
  Edition, a Southern Sung–dynasty edition of the Tripitaka
Ssu-ch'i Yüan-chüeh-yüan-pan (思溪圓覺院版), record of 1,433 works in
  5,824 fascicles, prepared and printed 1132–?; Ssu-ch'i Yüan-chüeh-
  yüan Edition, a Southern Sung–dynasty edition of the Tripitaka

Ssu-ch'uan-pan. *See* Shu-pan ta-tsang-ching

Ssu-fen-lü. *See* Dharmaguptaka-vinaya

Ssu-shih-erh-chang-ching (四十二章經), 1 fascicle, traditionally said to have been translated A.D. 67 by Kashyapamatanga and Mdian Dharmaraksha; Sutra of Forty-two Chapters

Stories. *See* Avadana

Su-hsi-ti chieh-lo-ching, Su-hsi-ti-ching. *See* Susiddhikara-mahatantrasadhanopayika-patala-sutra

Sui-chung-ching mu-lu (隋眾經目錄), abbreviated: Yen Tsung-lu (彥琮錄, Yen Tsung's Catalogue) and Jen-shou-lu (仁壽錄), 5 fascicles, record of 2,109 works in 5,059 fascicles, compiled 602 by Yen Tsung et al.; Sui Dynasty Catalogue of the Sutras

Sukhavati-vyuha (Sukhāvatī-vyūha, S); (1) Larger Sukhavati-vyuha: Wu-liang-shou-ching (無量壽經), 2 fascicles, translated 252 by Saṃghavarman, the Sutra of Infinite Life; (2) Smaller Sukhavati-vyuha: A-mi-t'o-ching (阿彌陀經), 1 fascicle, translated 402 by Kumarajiva, Amitabha Sutra

Sung Governmental Edition of the Tripitaka, Sung-kuan-pan. *See* Shu-pan ta-tsang-ching

Supplementary Chen-yüan Era Buddhist Catalogue. *See* Hsü Chen-yüan shih-chiao-lu

Susiddhikara-mahatantra-sadhanopayika-patala-sutra (-sūtra, S), Su-hsi-ti chieh-lo-ching (蘇悉地羯羅經), abbreviated: Su-hsi-ti-ching (蘇悉地經) and Susiddhikara-sūtra, 3 fascicles, translated 726 by Shubhakarasimha; the Sutra of Good Accomplishment

Sutra of a Bodhisattva's Spiritual States. *See* Bodhisattvabhumi

Sutra of Attaining Perfect Wisdom. *See* Pan-jo te-ching

Sutra of Diamond Meditation. *See* Chin-kang san-mei-ching

Sutra of Forty-two Chapters. *See* Ssu-shih-erh-chang-ching

Sutra of Good Accomplishment. *See* Susiddhikara-mahatantra-sadhanopayika-patala-sutra

Sutra of Infinite Life. *See* Sukhavati-vyuha (1)

Sutra of Innumerable Meanings. *See* Wu-liang-i-ching

Sutra of Meditation on Amitabha Buddha. *See* Kuan wu-liang-shou-ching

Sutra of Perfect Enlightenment. *See* Ta-fang-kuang yüan-chüeh hsiu tolo liao-i-ching

Sutra of Profound and Mysterious Emancipation. *See* Samdhinirmochana-sutra (2)

Sutra of Profound Understanding. *See* Samdhinirmochana-sutra (4)

Sutra of Stability in Contemplation of the True Law. *See* Saddharma-smrity-upasthana-sutra

Sutra of the Appearance of the Good Doctrine in [Sri] Lanka. *See* Lankavatara-sutra

Sutra of the Collection of the Practices of the Six Perfections. *See* Shat-paramita-samgraha-sutra

Sutra of the Continuous Stream of Emanicipation. *See* Samdhinirmo-chana-sutra (1)

Sutra of the Dharani of the Six Gates. *See* Shanmukhi-dharani-sutra

Sutra of the Great Accumulation of Treasures. *See* Maharatnakuta-sutra

Sutra of the Great Decease. *See* Mahaparinirvana-sutra

Sutra of the Herbs. *See* Yao-ts'ao-ching

Sutra of the Most Honored King. *See* Suvarnaprabhasottamaraja-sutra

Sutra of the Perfect Net. *See* Fan-wang-ching

Sutra of the Tathagata Treasury. *See* Tathagatagarbha-sutra

Sutra of the Treasure Summit. *See* Pao-ting-ching

Sutra of the True Summit. *See* Cheng-ting-ching

Sutra on a Bodhisattva's Original Action. *See* P'u-sa ying-luo pen-yeh-ching

Sutra on Emancipation. *See* Samdhinirmochana-sutra (3)

Sutra on Neither Increasing Nor Decreasing. *See* P'u-tseng pu-chien-ching

Sutra on the Stages of Yoga Practice. *See* Yogacharabhumi-sutra

Suttanipata (Suttanipāta, P), Ching-chi (經集); Collection of Discourses

Suvarnaprabhasa-sutra (Suvarṇaprabhāsa-sūtra, S), Chin-kuang-ming-ching (金光明經); (1) 4 fascicles, translated between 414 and 426 by Dharmakshema; (2) 7 fascicles, translated 552 by Paramartha; Golden Light Sutra

Suvarnaprabhasottamaraja-sutra (Suvarnaprabhāsōttamarāja-sūtra, S), Chin-kuang-ming tsui-sheng-wang-ching (金光明最勝王經), abbreviated: Tsui-sheng-wang-ching (最勝王經), 10 fascicles, translated 703 by I-ching; Sutra of the Most Honored King

Szechwan Edition of the Tripitaka. *See* Shu-pan ta-tsang-ching

Ta-ch'eng a-p'i-ta-mo chi-lun. *See* Mahayanabhidharma-samucchaya

Ta-ch'eng a-p'i-ta-mo tsa-chi-lun. *See* Mahayanabhidharma-samucchaya-vyakhya

Ta-ch'eng ch'i-hsin-lun. *See* Mahayana-shraddhotpada-shastra

Ta-ch'eng ju-leng-chia-ching. *See* Lankavatara-sutra (3)

Ta-ch'eng nieh-p'an-ching. *See* Mahaparinirvana-sutra

Ta-chi-ching. *See* Maha-samnipata-sutra

Ta-chih-tu-lun. *See* Mahaprajnaparamita-upadesha

Ta-Chou k'an-ting chung-ching mu-lu (大周刊定衆經目錄), also called Wu-Chou k'an-ting chung-ching mu-lu (武周刊定衆經目錄), abbreviated: Ta-Chou k'an-ting mu-lu (大周刊定目錄), Ta-Chou-lu (大周錄), or Wu-Chou-lu (武周錄), 15 fascicles, compiled 695 by Ming-shuan et al.; Chou Dynasty Catalogue of the Sutras

Ta-fang-kuang-fo hua-yen-ching. *See* Avatamsaka Sutra

Ta-fang-kuang yüan-chüeh hsiu to-lo liao-i-ching (大方廣圓覺修多羅了義經), abbreviated: Yüan-chüeh-ching (圓覺經), 1 fascicle, a "genuine" sutra; Sutra of Perfect Enlightenment

Ta-fang-teng ju-lai-tsang-ching. *See* Tathagatagarbha-sutra

Ta-fang-teng ta-chi-ching. *See* Maha-samnipata-sutra

Ta-fo-ting ju-lai mi-yin hsiu-cheng liao-i chu-p'u-sa wan-hsing shou-leng-yen-ching (大佛頂如來密因修証了義諸菩薩萬行首楞嚴經), abbreviated: Shou-leng-yen-ching (首楞嚴經), 10 fascicles, a "genuine" sutra; Heroic Marching Sutra

Ta hua-yen-ching. *See* Avatamsaka-sutra

Taishō Shinshū Daizōkyō (大正新脩大藏經, J; Taishō Era New Compilation of the Canon), abbreviated: *Taishō Daizōkyō* (大正大藏經), 100 vols., record of 3,053 works in 11,970 fascicles, published 1924–34 by Takakusu Junjirō and Watanabe Kaigyoku et al.

Ta-jih-ching. *See* Mahavairochana-sutra

Ta-Ming san-tsang sheng-chiao mu-lu (大明三藏聖教目錄), abbreviated: Pei-tsang mu-lu (北藏目錄); Ming Dynasty Catalogue of the Tripitaka, translated into English by Nanjio Bunyiu as *A Catalogue of the Chinese Translation of the Buddhist Tripitaka*

Tao-an-lu, Tao-an's Catalogue. *See* Tsung-li chung-ching mu-lu

Tao-hsing pan-jo-ching. *See* Ashtasahasrika-prajnaparamita-sutra

Ta-mo-to-lo ch'an-ching. *See* Yogacharabhumi-sutra

Ta-pan-jo-ching, Ta-pan-jo po-lo-mi-to-ching. *See* Mahaprajnaparamita-sutra

Ta-pan nieh-p'an-ching. *See* Mahaparinirvana-sutra (2), (3)

Ta-pan ni-yüan-ching. *See* Mahaparinirvana-sutra (1)

Ta-pao-chi-ching. *See* Maharatnakuta-sutra

Ta p'i-lu-che-na ch'eng-fo shen-pien chia-ch'ih-ching. *See* Mahavairochana-sutra

Ta-p'in pan-jo-ching. *See* Panchavimshati-sahasrika-prajnaparamita-sutra (3)

Ta p'i-po-sha-lun. *See* Abhidharma-mahavibhasha-shastra

Ta-p'u-ning-ssu-pan (大普寧寺版), 1,422 works in 6,010 fascicles, prepared and printed 1278–94; Ta-p'u-ning Temple Edition of the Tripitaka, also called Yüan Edition (Yüan-pan ta-tsang-ching, 元版大藏經)

Ta-T'ang nei-tien-lu (大唐內典錄), abbreviated: Nei-tien-lu (內典錄), 10 fascicles, compiled 664 by Tao-hsüan; Catalogue of T'ang Dynasty Buddhist Sutras

Tathagatagarbha-sutra (Tathāgatagarbha-sūtra, S), Ta-fang-teng ju-lai-tsang-ching (大方等如來藏經), abbreviated: Ju-lai-tsang-ching (如來藏經), 1 fascicle, translated 420 by Buddhabhadra; Sutra of the Tathagata Treasury

Ten-Category Vinaya. *See* Sarvastivadin-vinaya

Tenkai Edition of the Tripitaka. *See* Kan'ei-ji-ban

Tetsugen Edition of the Tripitaka. *See* Ōbaku-ban Daizōkyō

Textual Commentary on the Lotus Sutra. *See* Miao-fa lien-hua-ching wen-chü

Ti-ch'ih-lun. *See* Bodhisattvabhumi

T'ien-p'in miao-fa lien-hua-ching. *See* Saddharma-pundarika-sutra (3)

Tokyo Edition of the Tripitaka. See *Dai Nippon Kōtei Daizōkyō*

Treatise in One Hundred Verses. *See* Shatika-shastra

Treatise on the Awakening of Faith in Mahayana. *See* Mahayana-shrad-dhotpada-shastra

Treatise on the Buddha-nature. *See* Fo-hsing-lun

Treatise on the Completion of Truth. *See* Satyasiddhi-shastra

Treatise on the Establishment of the Doctrine of Consciousness Only. *See* Vijnaptimatratasiddhi-shastra

Treatise on the Great Perfection of Wisdom Sutra. *See* Mahaprajnapa-ramita-upadesha

Treatise on the Lotus Sutra. *See* Miao-fa lien-hua-ching-lun

Treatise on the Middle. *See* Madhyamaka-shastra

Treatise on the Seventeen Stages of Spiritual Development. *See* Sapta-dasha-bhumika-shastra

Treatise on the Stages of Yoga Practice. *See* Yogacharabhumi-shastra

Treatise on the Sutra of Eternal Life. *See* Wu-liang-shou-ching-lun

Treatise on the Sutra of the Ten Stages. *See* Dashabhumika-sutra-shastra

Treatise on the Twelve Gates. *See* Dvadashamukha-shastra

Tripitaka Koreana. *See* Haeinsa-pan

Tsa a-han-ching. *See* Samyukta-agama

Tsa-chi-lun. *See* Mahayanabhidharma-samucchaya-vyakhya

Ts'ao-ch'i pao-lin-chuan. *See* Pao-lin-chuan

Tseng-i a-han-ching. *See* Ekottara-agama

Tsui-sheng-wang-ching. *See* Suvarnaprabhasottamaraja-sutra

Tsung-li chung-ching mu-lu (綜理衆經目錄), also called Tao-an-lu (道安錄, Tao-an's Catalogue) and An-lu (安錄, An's Catalogue), 1 fascicle, record of 639 works in 886 fascicles, compiled 374 by Tao-an; Comprehensive Catalogue of the Sutras

Tung-ch'an-ssu-pan (東禪寺版), record of 1,450 works in 6,434 fascicles, prepared and printed 1080–1103; first private printing of the canon; Tung-ch'an Temple Edition, also called Fu-chou Tung-ch'an Temple Edition (Fu-chou Tung-ch'an-ssu-pan, 福州東禪寺版)

Tzu-shuo-ching. *See* Udana

Tzu-shuo-p'in. *See* Udana-varga

Udana (Udāna, P), Tzu-shuo-ching (自說經); the Pali sutra Solemn Utterances of the Buddha

Udana-varga (Udāna-varga, S), Tzu-shuo-p'in (自說品); the Sarvasti-vadin sutra Solemn Utterances of the Buddha

Vaipulya-samnipata-sutra. *See* Maha-samnipata-sutra

Vajracchedika-prajnaparamita-sutra (Vajracchedikā-prajñāpāramitā-sūtra, S), Chin-kang pan-jo po-lo-mi-ching (金剛般若波羅蜜經), abbre-viated: Chin-kang pan-jo-ching (金剛般若經) and Chin-kang-ching (金剛經); (1) 1 fascicle, translated between 402 and 412 by Kumarajiva; (2) 1 fascicle, translated 509 by Bodhiruchi; (3) 1 fascicle, translated between 558 and 569 by Paramartha; Diamond Sutra or Diamond Wisdom Sutra

Vajrashekhara-sutra (Vajraśekhara-sūtra, S), formally: Vajraśekhara-sarvatathāgatatattvasaṁgraha-sūtra (S), Chin-kang-ting-ching (金剛頂經), 3 fascicles, translated 753 by Amoghavajra; Diamond Peak Sutra

Vibhasha-shastra (Vibhāṣā-śāstra, S), Ping-p'o-sha-lun (鞞婆沙論), 14 fascicles, translated 383 by Sanghabhuti; partial translation of the Abhidharma-mahavibhasha-shastra (Great Commentary)

Vijnaptimatratasiddhi-shastra (Vijñaptimātratāsiddhi-śāstra, S), Ch'eng wei-shih-lun (成唯識論), abbreviated: Wei-shih-lun (唯識論), 10 fascicles, translated 659 by Hsüan-tsang; Treatise on the Establishment of the Doctrine of Consciousness Only

Vimalakirti-nirdesha-sutra (Vimalakīrti-nirdeśa-sūtra, S), generic ab-breviation: Wei-mo-ching (維摩經); (1) Wei-mo-chieh-ching (維摩詰經), 2 fascicles, translated between 223 and 253 by Chih Ch'ien; (2) Wei-mo-chieh so-shuo-ching (維摩詰所說經), 3 fascicles, translated 406 by Kumarajiva; (3) Shuo wu-kou-ch'eng-ching (說無垢稱經), 6 fasci-cles, translated 650 by Hsüan-tsang; Vimalakirti Sutra

Vinaya of the Mahasanghika school. *See* Mahasanghika-vinaya

Wan-li Edition of the Tripitaka, Wan-li-pan ta-tsang-ching. *See* Leng-yen-ssu-pan

Wei-mo-chieh-ching, Wei-mo-chieh so-shuo-ching, Wei-mo-ching. *See* Vimalakirti-nirdesha-sutra

Wei-shih-lun. *See* Vijnaptimatratasiddhi-shastra

Wei-shih chung-ching mu-lu. *See* Yüan-Wei chung-ching mu-lu

Wu-Chou k'an-ting chung-ching mu-lu, Wu-Chou-lu. *See* Ta-Chou k'an-ting chung-ching mu-lu

Wu-fen-lü. *See* Mahishasaka-vinaya

Wu-kou ching-kuang-ching, Wu-kou ching-kuang ta-t'o-lo-ni-ching. *See* Rashmivimala-vishuddhiprabhasa-dharani-sutra

Wu-liang-i-ching (無量義經), 1 fascicle, a "genuine" sutra; Sutra of In-numerable Meanings

Wu-liang-shou-ching. *See* Sukhavati-vyuha (1)

Wu-liang-shou-ching-lun (無量壽經論), abbreviated: Ching-t'u-lun (淨土論), 1 fascicle, translated 529 by Bodhiruchi; Treatise on the Sutra of Eternal Life

Yao-ts'ao-ching (藥草經), spurious sutra by the nun Seng-fa (b. 489); Sutra of the Herbs

Yen Tsung-lu, Yen Tsung's Catalogue. *See* Sui-chung-ching mu-lu

Yogacharabhumi-shastra (Yogācārabhūmi-śāstra, S), Yü-chia shih-ti-lun (瑜伽師地論), abbreviated: Yü-chia-lun (瑜伽論), 100 fascicles, translated 646–48 by Hsüan-tsang; Treatise on the Stages of Yoga Practice. *See also* Bodhisattvabhumi; Saptadashabhumika-shastra

Yogacharabhumi-sutra (Yogācārabhūmi-sūtra, S), also called Dharmatara-dhyāna-sūtra (S), Ta-mo-to-lo ch'an-ching (達摩多羅禪經), and Hsiu-hsing tao-ti-ching (修行道地經), 2 fascicles, translated between 398 and 421 by Buddhabhadra; Sutra on the Stages of Yoga Practice

Yüan-chao-lu, Yüan-chao's Catalogue. *See* Chen-yüan hsin-ting shih-chiao mu-lu

Yüan-chüeh-ching. *See* Ta-fang-kuang yüan-chüeh hsiu to-lo liao-i-ching

Yüan Edition of the Tripitaka, Yüan-pan ta-tsang-ching. *See* Ta-p'u-ning-ssu-pan

Yüan-Wei chung-ching mu-lu (元魏衆經目錄), also called Wei-shih chung-ching mu-lu (魏世衆經目錄), abbreviated: Yüan-Wei-lu (元魏錄), 1 fascicle, compiled 532–34 by Li K'uo; Northern Wei Dynasty Catalogue of the Sutras

Yü-chia-lun, Yü-chia shih-ti-lun. *See* Yogacharabhumi-shastra

Glossary-Index

Orthodox transliterations and ideograms are not given for items included in the Appendix. Abbreviations used are S for Sanskrit, P for Pali, and J for Japanese. Chinese terms are not expressly identified.

Abhayagiri-vihara (Abhayagiri-vihāra, S; Mount Fearlessness Monastery), Sri Lankan sect, 69, 112–13, 160–61

Abhidhamma-pitaka (Abhidhamma-piṭaka, P; Abhidharma-piṭaka, S; Treatise Basket), 16

Abhidharma Buddhism, 9, 16, 123, 153–54, 158, 162–63; scriptures of, 33, 82–83

Abhidharma Storehouse Treatise (Abhidharmakosha-shastra), 82–83, 99

abridged sutras, 94, 118, 119–20, 146–47

Agama (Āgama, P, S) sutras, 32, 122, 143, 161–62; content of, 16, 20, 114, 132; teachings in, 50, 131, 132–33

Amitabha Sutra. See Sukhavati-vyuha

Amoghavajra (S; 705–74), translator, 57, 108, 109–10

Ananda (Ānanda, P, S), disciple of Shakyamuni, 18, 19–20

"ancient translations," 55

An Shih-kao (安世高; d. ca. A.D. 170), translator, 45, 46, 105

Asanga (Asaṅga, S; 4th or 5th cent.), elder brother of Vasubandhu, 150, 164

Asoka (ca. 274–ca. 236 B.C.), emperor, 28, 29, 30, 41, 43, 112; stone and pillar edicts of, 27, 37, 82, 158

Atthakavagga (Meaningful Chapter), 114–16

Avatamsaka-sutra. See Flower Garland Sutra

Bandhudatta (盤頭達多, S; fl. 4th cent.), Indian priest, 58–59, 60

Biographies of Eminent T'ang Dynasty Monks Who Sought the Dharma in the Western Regions (Ta-T'ang hsi-yü ch'iu-fa kao-seng-chuan, 大唐西域求法高僧傳), 109

Biography of the Treasure Forest (Pao-lin-chuan), 165

Bodhidharma (S; fl. ca. 520), founder of Chinese Zen, 73, 144–45

Japanese Buddhologist, 128, 131–32

Magadhi (Māgadhī, S), language of Shakyamuni, 26, 27, 28

Maha-Kacchayana (Mahā-Kaccā-yana, P), disciple of Shakyamuni, 28, 114–15

Maha-Kashyapa (Mahā-Kāśyapa, S), disciple of Shakyamuni, 18–20

Mahaparinirvana-sutra (Sutra of the Great Decease), 124, 143, 150, 154; trans. by Fa-hsien and Buddha-bhadra, 70, 71, 74, 76; trans. by Dharmakshema, 71, 75–76, 97–98; trans. by Hui-yen, Hui-kuan, and Hsieh Ling-yün, 76

Mahaprajnaparamita-sutra (Great Perfection of Wisdom Sutra), 91–92, 97–98, 170

Mahaprajnaparamita-upadesha (Treatise on the Great Perfection of Wisdom Sutra), 61, 98, 122–23, 139

Maharatnakuta-sutra (Sutra of the Great Accumulation of Treasures), 92, 98, 108, 123

Maha-samnipata-sutra (Great Collection of Sutras), 71

Mahasanghika (Mahāsaṅghika, S), Hinayana school, 87, 152, 153

Mahasanghika-vinaya, 70, 74

Mahavairochana-sutra (Great Sun Sutra), 108

Mahavihara (Mahāvihāra, S; Great Monastery), Sri Lankan Buddhist sect, 112–13, 160–61

Mahayana (Mahāyāna, S; "Great Vehicle") Buddhism, 30, 42, 49, 68, 112, 144; early period, 9–10, 78–79, 154; middle period, 9–10, 78–79, 83, 154; sutras of, 22, 33, 38, 46, 70, 87, 122, 124, 133, 148, 160, 161–62, 164; early-period sutras of, 70–71, 78, 116, 122; middle-period sutras of, 71, 78, 99, 137; teachings of, 32, 123, 130–32, 150

Mahayanabhidharma-samucchaya (Collection of the Mahayana Abhidharma), 98

Mahayanabhidharma-samucchaya-vyakhya (Exegesis on the Collection of the Mahayana Abhidharma), 88

Mahayanasamgraha (Comprehensive Treatise on Mahayana Buddhism), 150

Mahayana-shraddhotpada-shastra (Treatise on the Awakening of Faith in Mahayana), 154

Mahinda (P; fl. 3rd cent. B.C.), priest and son of Asoka, 29, 30, 112

Mahishasaka-vinaya (Five-Category Vinaya), 69, 70

Maitreya (S), bodhisattva and future Buddha, 51, 130, 136

Manji-zokuzō (Fylfot-Letter Supplementary Tripitaka), 128–29

Manji-zōkyō (Fylfot-Letter Tripitaka), 128–29, 184

Mdian Dharmaraksha (Mdian Dharmarakṣa, S; fl. ca. A.D. 67), translator, 44

Miao-fa lien-hua-ching. *See* Lotus Sutra

Miao-fa lien-hua-ching hsüan-i (Profound Meaning of the Lotus Sutra), 143

Miao-fa lien-hua-ching i-chi (Commentary on the Lotus Sutra), 142, 144

Miao-fa lien-hua-ching-lun (Treatise on the Lotus Sutra), 98

Miao-fa lien-hua-ching wen-chü (Textual Commentary on the Lotus Sutra), 155–56

Milindapanha (The Questions of [King] Milinda [Menander]), 177

Ming Dynasty Catalogue of the Tripitaka (Ta-Ming san-tsang sheng-chiao mu-lu), 176, 182

Ming Dynasty editions of the Tripitaka. *See* Leng-yen-ssu-pan; Nan-tsang; Pei-tsang

Ming-shuan (明佺; fl. ca. 695), monk and catalogue compiler, 107

Ming Ti (明帝; r. A.D. 57–75), Later Han emperor, 44, 105